THE NEW NEGRO IN THE OLD SOUTH

The New Negro in the Old South

GABRIEL A. BRIGGS

Rutgers University Press
NEW BRUNSWICK, NEW JERSEY, AND LONDON

LIBRARY OF CONGRESS CATALOGING-IN-PUBLICATION DATA

Briggs, Gabriel A., 1971–

   The New Negro in the Old South / Gabriel A. Briggs.

    pages cm. — (American literaures initiative)

   Includes bibliographical references and index.

   ISBN 978-0-8135-7479-0 (hardcover)

   ISBN 978-0-8135-7478-3 (paperback)

   ISBN 978-0-8135-7480-6 (e-book : ePub)

   ISBN 978-0-8135-7481-3 (e-book : Web PDF)

   1. African Americans—Tennessee—Nashville—History. 2. Nashville (Tenn.)—Race relations. 3. Nashville (Tenn.)—History. I. Title.

F444.N29N42 2015

976.8'5500496073—dc23

2015002735

A British Cataloging-in-Publication record for this book is available from the British Library.

Copyright © 2015 by Gabriel A. Briggs

Visit our website: http://rutgerspress.rutgers.edu

Manufactured in the United States of America

A book in the American Literatures Initiative (ALI), a collaborative publishing project of NYU Press, Fordham University Press, Rutgers University Press, Temple University Press, and the University of Virginia Press. The Initiative is supported by The Andrew W. Mellon Foundation. For more information, please visit www.americanliteratures.org.

For my son, Noah

Contents

Acknowledgments

This project would not have been possible without the interest and encouragement of numerous individuals. I am grateful to Alan Nadel for his enthusiasm and unwavering support of this manuscript from its beginning and for providing me an excellent model of professionalism, collegiality, and intellectual responsibility. I would also like to express my appreciation to others who read and commented on early versions of my work and who inspired me with their knowledge and vibrant scholarship. Andy Doolen always found time for conversation and encouragement. Jeff Clymer consistently directed me to valuable works, old and new. Michael Chaney helped workshop drafts and ideas during my time at the Futures of American Studies Institute at Dartmouth College, and his insightful commentary helped shape revisions along the way. I am especially grateful to Dana Nelson, whose generosity and feedback were invaluable to my completion of this book.

In addition to Dana, I would like to thank Vanderbilt colleagues Mark Schoenfield, Teresa Goddu, Vereen Bell, Jay Clayton, Sam Girgus, Janis May, and Donna Caplan. At Vanderbilt's Jean and Alexander Heard Library I thank Deborah Lilton, Jim Toplon, and Jimmy Webb. I appreciate the generous access granted by LaDonna Boyd and T. B. Boyd III to the R. H. Boyd Company's prodigious archives. I thank Trent Hanner and his many colleagues at the Tennessee State Library and Archives. I am particularly grateful to Leslie Mitchner at Rutgers University Press, not only for guiding me through the process of publication but also for her professionalism and support along the way. I would also like to thank

Tim Roberts and the American Literatures Initiative staff for their assistance with the manuscript.

In a different form, a very small portion of chapter 1 previously appeared in *Callaloo*.

I am grateful to Judy, David, Darren, Joe, John, Idotha, and Noah, who have, in their own unique way, supported me throughout this project. I also acknowledge a tremendous group of friends that includes Jamie, Ken, Mark, Elizabeth, Jennifer, Shawn, Jim King, and Ben Curtis, each of whom enabled me to find a work-life balance that made writing possible.

The New Negro in the Old South

Introduction

O Southland, dear Southland!
Then why do you cling
To an idle age and a musty page,
To a dead and useless thing?

—JAMES WELDON JOHNSON

In 1925 the Howard University professor Alain Locke edited an ambitious anthology entitled *The New Negro*. Building on the March 1925 "Harlem number" of *Survey Graphic*, which emphasized the significance of New York City as an African American cultural center for blacks, Locke's *New Negro* included historical essays, social studies, and various creative representations of black culture written by influential black and white artists, scholars, and intellectuals from the period. According to Locke, countless volumes of literature had been written "about" the Negro but very few were "of him."[1] In light of northern migration by large numbers of blacks seeking improved social and economic opportunities and of the proliferation of black urban communities, Locke believed the "Old Negro" image of blacks—represented by mammies, uncles, and sambos—and the negative internal consequences of those racial stereotypes, had been shed. As a result of these transformational changes, African Americans were in the early stages of a cultural renaissance, and Locke wanted to create a body of work that was capable of representing their spiritual and psychological awakening. Through this cultural recognition, Locke was confident that African Americans would no longer be viewed by whites as a social problem or burden but rather as a race of people who were capable of participating fully in the country's economic, social, and political institutions.

In the 1920s the term *New Negro* thus entered general parlance to denote a modern form of African American racial representation. The emergence of this African American identity is distinctly different from the compliant, rural, and undereducated African American who preceded it and also from the negative racial stereotypes created by whites or drawn from the romantic racialism of white fiction writers. New Negroes self-identified as progressive, urban figures with cultural and intellectual sensibilities generally connected to the period between World War I and World War II.

Twenty years ago Henry Louis Gates Jr. authored a critical essay entitled "The Trope of a New Negro and the Reconstruction of the Image of the Black," which declared 1895–1925 "the crux of the period of Black intellectual reconstruction" and the "era of the myth of the New Negro."[2] In 2007 Gates and Gene Andrew Jarrett edited a New Negro anthology that characterized the New Negro as "one of the most compelling stories of racial uplift that circulated throughout U.S. intellectual society, culture, and politics," and they expanded the dates of their analysis to the years between 1892 and 1938 so as to include "not only essays that explicitly mention the term 'New Negro' but also those involved in a wider critical conversation on race, representation, and African American culture—a conversation of which the trope of a New Negro was, of course, an original, defining feature."[3] Despite Gates and Jarrett's forays into the New Negro's nineteenth-century origins, contemporary scholars, like most of their predecessors, examine the idea of the New Negro as a twentieth-century phenomenon. Most of these critical interpretations locate the New Negro's origins within the first three decades of the twentieth century, in conjunction with historical moments such as the publication of the *Crisis* (1910), the tumultuous "Red Summer" of 1919, or the Harlem Renaissance (1924–29). Scholars of the New Negro phenomenon also see its emergence as a product of northern urban centers, including but not limited to Philadelphia, Washington, D.C., Chicago, and New York City. Conventional wisdom has also suggested that northern migration in the early decades of the twentieth century was responsible for a cultural and intellectual awakening for African Americans who were seeking to escape agricultural disasters and the economic and social inequalities of the New South.

None of the writing on the New Negro, however, recognizes that the characteristics usually attributed to a twentieth-century New Negro—self-help, racial solidarity, urbanization, economic independence, race consciousness, cultural and educational advancement, and agitation for full citizenship rights—were promoted by southern African Americans in the decades following the Civil War. Neither coincidental nor accidental, this fact, I believe, is causally connected to the failure of

Reconstruction signaled by the Hayes-Tilden Compromise of 1877. Although during Reconstruction the majority of African Americans migrated within the South, few went to the North. Even as late as 1900, three-quarters of African Americans still resided in the South. By moving toward larger, more self-sufficient southern communities, African Americans distanced themselves physically and spiritually from the experience of slavery, and their post–Civil War southern migration gave them significant agency. It enabled them to establish a new group identity. Whether they moved to reconnect with family members and loved ones from whom they had become separated by slavery or to find work in a growing southern economy, African Americans were neither passive nor invisible. In fact, whether or not they decided to abandon rural life for an urban existence, many African Americans in the South were busy creating vibrant cultural and intellectual communities and developing profitable economic ventures.

The formation of black communities became even more significant following the Hayes-Tilden Compromise of 1877, which forever redefined the relationship between African Americans and whites in the post–Civil War South, replacing Reconstruction with Restoration, an era in which white southerners reasserted their control of land and institutions previously controlled by the federal government. Free of federal interference, white southerners embraced views that enabled them to stimulate their economy so that it could compete with northern industry and to restore the racial, political, and class hierarchies that existed in the Old South.

Among the consequences of these transformational changes, the segregation of African American and white communities as well as the increasing prejudices that accompanied this physical and psychological distancing caused African Americans to become much more group-oriented. Separation from whites contributed to the rise of an alternate urban social structure and helped African Americans develop greater race consciousness, racial solidarity, and self-reliance. That is why, in this nineteenth-century milieu, we see the "New Negroes."

And to the nineteenth-century South we must turn to understand the origins and full significance of this important figure, for I argue that the New Negro is a southern phenomenon impelled by the failure of Reconstruction and the emergence of the Jim Crow South and crystallized under the unique circumstances that can be traced to the historically specific conditions of urban African American communities during and after the Civil War that produced the economic, social, political, and cultural conditions wherein southern African Americans could flourish. Of particular significance was Nashville, where the postbellum economic, intellectual, social, and political scene became a locus of the concepts and conflicts instrumental in shaping African American cultural and intellectual identity. An exploration of the literary and cultural factors that inform the intricate racial politics surrounding the idea of a modern African American identity, moreover, contributes to the historical and social geography of late nineteenth- and early twentieth-century African American leadership.

By reconsidering the nineteenth-century southern origins of the conditions and sensibility that fostered the New Negro, this study does not seek to invalidate existing scholarly investigations focused on the twentieth-century New Negro. While completing this book, I was cognizant of Kenneth Warren's suggestion that "rather than aim at producing an account of race that attempts to outdo other accounts in telling how black people really are, it might be more effective to situate the scholarly tussle over representational accuracy (and its competing representations of what black people do and think) as a crucial part of the reality of race in U.S. society."[4]

My focus on the centrality of Nashville is not intended as a discourse of primacy, what Robert Reid-Pharr has called a "'Big Bang' conception of Black American life and culture."[5] Many turn-of-the-century southern cities, including Atlanta (education), Durham (economics), and Richmond (media), contained large urban African American communities with structural elements conducive to the growth of the New Negro, but none exemplified, in the way that Nashville did, the diverse conditions productive of the New Negro.

To make this argument, I start by tracing the genealogy of the New Negro from its historical and geographical origins in the post-Reconstruction South. Chapter 1 examines the social, cultural, and political history of the New Negro as it is traditionally configured, showing how contemporary research on New Negro identity, as it intersects with areas that include race, sexuality, and gender studies, continues to place the New Negro in a twentieth-century northern, urban cultural context.

Beginning with a description of Nashville's occupation by Union forces during the early years of the Civil War, my second chapter examines how the city's geography, economics, and political positioning caused it to become an important center of African American life in the South. As a Union Army headquarters for the southern campaign,

Nashville became a central destination for runaway slaves, contraband, and free African Americans who sought to join the army's Colored Infantry units and fight against the Confederacy and the institution of slavery. Because it was one of the few southern cities untouched by the negative consequences of war, Nashville saw its African American population increase exponentially. After amending its constitution to outlaw slavery, moreover, Tennessee became the lone southern state to reenter the Union, in 1866, escaping the harsh period of Reconstruction endured by its former Confederate neighbors. As a result of these sociopolitical changes, Nashville experienced the rise of a unique African American community. Segregated from Nashville's white community, a substantial African American community developed into a "city within a city," an urban model that paralleled that of whites and included educational, religious, financial, intellectual, and social centers that would be the training ground for the growth and development of the New Negro.[6]

The unique environment of Nashville, chapter 3 demonstrates, forever shaped the life and work of W. E. B. Du Bois. Rewriting his time in Nashville (1885–88) reveals a critical period in which Du Bois came of age, developing an appreciation for music, philosophy, and economics and also experiencing his first confrontation with the color line. During these years his summer teaching provided him with his first exposure to rural African American life, an experience that left an indelible impression on him and profoundly shaped his seminal work, *The Souls of Black Folk*. In light of the New Negro sensibility he developed in Nashville, Du Bois came to view differently the social, economic, and political challenges facing African Americans in the New South.

The most significant turn-of-the-century southern African American writer was Sutton E. Griggs. The fourth chapter demonstrates how Nashville enabled Griggs to formulate a perspective on African American subjectivity unavailable to northerners and inexpressible by most southern blacks. As his writing reveals, Nashville, like most southern urban centers, was a site where African Americans encountered an atmosphere of oppression. However, what makes Nashville exemplary when compared to southern cities such as Charleston or Little Rock is an array of conditions that made it a place where an African American man could, in the height of the Jim Crow era, expose and vilify that harassment and oppression. In other words, Nashville was in many ways a typical white southern city and in just as many ways an anomalous black southern city. In consequence it forced the white southerners there to accommodate black attitudes and expressions impossible for them to hold and express elsewhere in America in the late nineteenth and early twentieth centuries. And it is only after those conditions flourish more widely, chiefly after World War I, that we find a prolific enough group of writers, thinkers, and educators to achieve codification under the rubric New Negro.

Chapter 5 examines the 1905 protest of Tennessee's streetcar segregation law by Nashville's African American community. Although the movement was ultimately unsuccessful in its efforts to change the state law, the two-year protest had a number of implications for the development of the New Negro in Nashville. Among them, it showed that Nashville's African American community could establish broad-based support that cut across class lines and that it could initiate effective strategies for resistance. One of these strategies can be seen in the creation of the Union Transportation Company. Owned and operated by African Americans, this local automobile company demonstrated the ability of Nashville's African American community to compete economically with whites without encountering violent reprisal. Perhaps the most significant outcome of the streetcar protests was the creation of the *Globe*, an African American weekly that provided a rhetorical position in which Nashville's African American community debated issues ranging from disenfranchisement to racial violence. Surviving until 1960 and outlasting almost every African American newspaper in the country, the *Globe* identified Nashville's New Negroes as economically as well as socially and politically independent at the dawn of the twentieth century, and it contributed to the attitudes toward African American subjectivity and identity in the decades that followed.

The final chapter revisits the Fisk University student demonstrations of 1924–25, in which Fisk's African American students openly challenged the paternalistic structure of their university's white administration and the autocratic practices of the white university president, Fayette McKenzie. This watershed moment in African American sociopolitical and cultural history was the chrysalis for a movement that questioned the role of whites in the personal and professional development of African Americans at universities across the nation, questioning how these universities could act in the interest of African American students, supporting parents, and invested community members when controlled by white administrators and trustees and staffed by a predominantly white faculty. In other words, it focused an array of issues relating to African American agency and integrity central to the conception of the New Negro.

A return to the nineteenth-century South is vital in redefining our understanding of the New Negro but also in reimagining the discourses that engage the interstices of region, race, and history. While the New Negro of the South did not eliminate white supremacy or reverse its atmosphere of social, political, and economic oppression, its attitudes and responses to such stimuli were responsible for significant fractures in an era many believe to be marked by political inactivity and accommodation. As this study reveals, at the dawn of the twentieth century in Nashville, African Americans were already engaging in the kinds of actions that were emblematic of the New Negro, actions that would not be forthcoming from northern New Negroes for another thirty years. For this reason, in part, Nashville is the initial location for reconsidering the idea of the New Negro as not only a national symbol but also as a southern phenomenon.

1 / The New Negro Genealogy

The generation of negroes which have grown up since the war have lost in large measure the traditional and wholesome awe of the white race which kept the negroes in subjection.

—MEMPHIS COMMERCIAL APPEAL, MAY 17, 1892

As early as 1745 an anonymous eighteenth-century writer contributing to the *London Magazine* noted that the phrase *New Negro* was used by black slaves in America to describe slaves who were newly arrived from Africa.[1] Although this reference is an isolated one, it highlights an early transformation in *African American* identity. Not yet representative of "an entity or group of entities," this New Negro label exists "as a coded system of signs, complete with masks and mythology."[2] Though the label appears to be used only among blacks, its usage has a decidedly somber if not ironic tone. While maintaining their collective identity as Negroes, what the *Oxford English Dictionary* defines as "a dark-skinned group of peoples originally native to Africa south of the Sahara," these relocated persons acknowledge that their arrival in America represents a shift in the direction of their lives and in their identity.[3] This new Negro consciousness acknowledges distance from a previous self and from a former place of residence. The unholy waters of the Atlantic have washed away the old lives of these persons and their familiar points of reference. Within this space of dislocation newly arrived blacks were forced to assume a new identity and a new way of life signified by an absence of self as well as by what Orlando Patterson has called "social death."[4] Although usage of the term *New Negro* will not become popular until the late nineteenth century, this early reference suggests that since their arrival in America in 1619, blacks have been forced consistently to redefine their identity and to establish their place in American society.

In 1988 Henry Louis Gates Jr. published a seminal essay, "The Trope of a New Negro and the Reconstruction of the Image of the Black," identifying African American discourse between 1895 and 1925 as the "crux of the period of Black intellectual reconstruction" and the "era of the myth of the New Negro."[5] This important work was the first to draw attention to the New Negro as a late nineteenth-century rather than solely a twentieth-century figure. Gates expanded his examination of the New Negro to encompass the years 1892–1938 in a 2007 anthology that he coedited with Gene Andrew Jarrett, and the period 1892–95 remains the earliest starting point to date for studies of the New Negro.[6] As a whole, the enormous body of scholarship on the topic over the past twenty years suggests that the first era of New Negro development dates from the 1890s until 1910, with the publication of the *Crisis*.[7] Following the publication of this periodical, a more radical version of the New Negro emerged during the years 1910–24. While this radical figure does not disappear after 1924, a more conservative, cultural interpretation takes center stage and becomes the focal point of intellectual and political conversations well into the 1930s. While the New Negro associated with Harlem and the 1920s has achieved the greatest notoriety, in sociological practice it has exhibited a discernible tension "between strictly political concerns and strictly artistic concerns" since its inception.[8]

A number of works provide a window on the earliest political function of a new racial representation, one that sought to replace white-based notions of black inferiority with a racial consciousness that would help reshape the way African Americans perceived themselves. The activist and reformer Anna Julia Cooper saw the literary marketplace as one of the places where African Americans needed to establish their voices. In her essay "One Phase of American Literature" (1892), Cooper critiqued white renditions of African American characters in literature, noting, "The devil is always painted black—by white painters." Challenging the work of white writers from William Dean Howells to Joel Chandler Harris, Cooper claimed that no white writer had created an "authentic portrait" of African Americans that reflected "a free American citizen . . . divinely struggling and aspiring yet tragically warped and distorted by the adverse winds of circumstance." Cooper urged African Americans to believe in themselves and to use a literary forum to "paint what is true with the calm spirit of those who know their cause is right and who believe there is a God who judgeth nations" rather than leave their image in the hands and imagination of whites.[9]

Many of Cooper's contemporaries shared her belief in blending art and politics to establish positive representations of African

Americans in literature. Among the numerous examples of African American novelists and essayists of the period who followed Cooper's lead were Frances E. W. Harper, whose novel *Iola Leroy* (1892) claimed that "out of the race must come its own defenders. With them the pen must be mightier than the sword," and Victoria Earle Matthews's "The Value of Race Literature" (1895), which encouraged the "race-loving Negro artist to compete with his elder brother in art and succeed where the other has failed."[10]

In the Reverend W. E. C. Wright's "The New Negro" (1894), education becomes a defining feature of post-Reconstruction African American identity, so that formal training makes New Negroes "at once examples and apostles of a new era." Wright argued that, upon graduation from college, educated African Americans should relocate across the country, particularly within the former slave states of the South, where they should quickly take their place "among the foremost leaders of every upward movement" and stand as "New Negro" representatives from an "era of freedom" rather than as remnants of an "Old Negro . . . slave civilization."[11] Wright's foundational perspective reverberates through the writing of numerous African American intellectuals, such as W. E. B. Du Bois, whose own "talented tenth" would become "leaders of thought and missionaries of culture among their people" upon graduation from colleges and universities.[12] Wright hoped, however, to educate all African Americans regardless of class or gender, so that in the near future "the Negro shall be so completely made new as to become wholly an element of strength and hope in the nation's life."[13]

Decades before Alain Locke announced the spiritual and psychological transformation that ushered in the New Negro of the 1920s, J. W. E. Bowen's 1895 "An Appeal to the King" claimed that a renewed "consciousness" or "racial personality under the blaze of a new civilization" would enable the New Negro of the late nineteenth century to achieve his social and political aims. While giving a speech before thousands attending Negro Day at the 1895 Atlanta Cotton States Exposition, Bowen asked the crowd to observe the statue standing at the entrance of the Negro building. What they saw was a large, muscular black man looking carefully at the broken manacles that hung from his wrists. Bowen then exclaimed, "This is the new Negro. . . . He is thinking. And by the power of thought, he will think off those chains and have both hands free to help . . . build this country and make a grand destiny of himself."[14] Building on the significant achievements of African Americans since slavery, the New Negro was also poised to become an integral part of American progress over the next century.

It is no small coincidence that Booker T. Washington's *A New Negro for a New Century* reached American audiences in 1900. Washington deemed the title of his mammoth text, 428 pages long and composed of eighteen chapters, appropriate because "the negro of today is in every phase of life far advanced over the Negro of thirty years ago."[15] To explore the many accomplishments of African Americans since slavery, Washington included historical writings by and about accomplished African Americans, catalogued their valiant participation in America's wars since the Revolution, and included essays that revealed the progressive attitude of African American culture at large. Fannie Barrier Williams's "The Club Movement among Colored Women of America" (1900) is exemplary of the final category of writings included by Washington. Carefully recording the advancements of an organized and sustained women's club movement among African American women, Williams declared that they could no longer be viewed as an "unsocialized, unclassed, and unrecognized" portion of American society. Williams encouraged African American women to join the cause of social reform as a way to escape the confinement of domestic roles and inferiority of second-class citizenship and "to feel that [they] are a unit in the womanhood of a great nation and a great civilization."[16] Williams's coupling of self-respect and respect for one's race, as well as her ability to see the role of African Americans in a national framework, remained defining features of the New Negro and of Washington's thought-provoking work.

Contrary to the effort of so many African American writers who portrayed the inner characteristics of the New Negro, John Henry Adams Jr. provided an alternate perspective for black and white American audiences in his "Rough Sketches: A Study of the Features of the New Negro Woman" (1904) and "Rough Sketches: The New Negro Man" (1904). Adams believed that his work could preserve and honor "race identity and distinction," while also challenging the "Southern social monster which argues the inferiority of the Negro to the white folk." While the superior beauty of white women was, in general, unquestioned in Adams's eyes, few whites were willing to see the merits of the African American woman, whom he claimed must be judged "upon the scales that were employed in the weighing of queens and noble-men's wives and daughters."[17]

Challenging the pseudo-science that declared the physical inferiority of African American men for generations, Adams recast the image as "tall, erect, commanding, with a face as strong and expressive as Angelo's Moses and yet every whit as pleasing and handsome as Reubens's [sic] favorite model. There is that penetrative eye about which Charles Lamb wrote with such deep admiration, that broad forehead and firm chin. . . . Such is the new Negro man." Yet despite the romantic overtones of Adams's portrayals, there is also an undercurrent of more radical New Negro features, of one who seeks "perpetuation of his own social, political, and material advancement" and girds himself to a "fight for manhood—not man. Man dies. Manhood lives forever."[18] With these words Adams revealed the intensified political responses that become the hallmark of the New Negro of the following decade.

Among the notable examples from the second phase of what has been called "New Negro criticism" is a collection of essays from William Pickens.[19] In an effort to challenge a white American majority that has "distorted and buried in contempt" a socially and intellectually relevant African American history, Pickens published *The New Negro* in 1916.[20] Political in its purpose, the text questioned the denial of full citizenship rights for African Americans in the face of constitutional protection and of their own tremendous material and intellectual advancements in previous decades—despite a history of enslavement and subsequent repression at the hands of whites, both northern and southern. Pickens also suggested that whites, not African Americans, were responsible for the evolution of the New Negro.

According to Pickens, a number of decisive factors molded the New Negro out of the Old. Most prominent among these was legal recognition, which altered African Americans' status from chattel to citizen through constitutional amendments thirteen, fourteen, and fifteen. Yet the inability of many whites to accept the transformation from that of "usable article" to man resulted in an atmosphere of intolerance and opposition. When whites no longer recognized the patient, unquestioning, and devoted Old Negro, they began to feel disconnected from him and, according to Pickens, withdrew from acquaintance with African Americans. This distance alienated whites from African Americans, lessening the ability of whites to sympathize with the condition or struggles of African Americans in society. And though it was whites who were responsible for marginalizing African Americans within society, they viewed any evidence of ambition and independence among African Americans or any attempt to express dissatisfaction with their lowered social status as a threat. Within this void the New Negro became an object of distrust and suspicion, one recast by whites as a new racial stereotype synonymous with the thief, the loafer, or the black brute. Pickens challenged the dominant culture and its ideology of supremacy by claiming that the New Negro was "resolved to fight, and live or die, on the side of God and the eternal Verities" in his efforts to obtain equal protection under the laws of the United States. Pickens saw his work as the first in a line of texts over the next fifty years responsible for emphasizing the role of the New Negro in America and for chronicling what he viewed as a cultural "renaissance of the Negro race."[21]

In many ways Pickens's writing was representative of the wartime and postwar New Negro that inserted his voice into intellectual and cultural conversations on a range of issues. This era witnessed the rise of numerous politically charged periodicals, including *Crisis* (1910), *Messenger* (1917), *Negro World* (1918), *Crusader* (1918), *Liberator* (1919), *Opportunity* (1923), and *Worker's Monthly* (1924), that joined established black newspapers to shape and further define the New Negro.[22] It is no accident that many of these publications emerged following the series of explosive race riots that raged in more than twenty locations across the country between April and October 1919.[23] According to Barbara Foley, during what she calls the "revolutionary crucible of 1919," the term *New Negro* "signified a fighter against both racism and capitalism; to be a political moderate did not preclude endorsement of at least some aspects of a class analysis of racism or sympathy with at least some goals of the Bolshevik Revolution."[24] In a letter written one month after Chicago's riot to Victor F. Lawson, editor and publisher of the *Chicago Daily News*, a World War I veteran named Stanley B. Norvell declared that the Old Negro so readily identified with a servile, Uncle Tom plantation caricature was "as extinct as the great auk, the dodo bird, old Dobbin and the chaise, and the man who refused to shave until William Jennings Bryan was elected." Citing the experience and perspective garnered by an estimated 200,000 Negro troops who served overseas during the war, Norvell declared, "Today we have with us a new Negro [who] has become tired of equal rights. He wants the same rights. He is tired of equal accommodations. He wants the same accommodations. He is tired of equal opportunity. He wants the same opportunity."[25] Norvell expressed the dismay of many African American soldiers who fought and saw their comrades die in defense of the civil and political liberties provided by the U.S. Constitution only to be failed by that government and denigrated by the majority of its white citizens upon their return home. According to James Weldon Johnson, who referred to the period of rioting as the "Red Summer," at least one African American soldier was hanged "*because of the fact* that he wore the uniform of a United States soldier."[26] Norvell was not alone when he lamented the country's failure to protect veterans and other African Americans from bodily harm or provide them with legitimate status in their own country or when he claimed that such blatant disregard left America in "grave danger of losing her national integrity."[27]

On the contrary, New Negroes made it clear that they were prepared to challenge the atmosphere of intolerance and oppression at any cost.

In his article "'The New Negro': When He's Hit, He Hits Back!" a white minister and journalist, Rollin Lynde Hartt, claimed, "No mere fanciful bugaboo is the new negro. He exists. More than once I have met him. He differs radically from the timorous, docile negro of the past." During one of these encounters Hartt recalled a New Negro telling him, "The next time white folks pick on colored folks, something's going to drop—dead white folks." In another, Hartt recounted the words of a New Negro soldier who claimed, "We were the first American regiment on the Rhine— Colonel Hayward's, the Fighting Fifteenth; we fought for democracy, and we're going to keep on fighting for democracy till we get our rights here at home. The black worm has turned."[28] Claude McKay claimed that his revolutionary poem, "If We Must Die," "exploded" out of him from reading daily the papers published by African Americans that were filled with "details of clashes between colored and white, murderous shootings and hangings."[29] McKay's words expressed the frustration of African Americans and captured a sense of urgency facing black and white Americans and the country's greatest social "problem": "While round us bark the mad and hungry dogs / . . . Like men we'll face the murderous, cowardly pack, / Pressed to the wall, dying, but fighting back!"[30] The events of the Red Summer also had profound effects on the future of the New Negro, exacerbating rivalries inside and outside the African American community and dividing New Negro factions along political lines in support of nationalist, communist, and even conservative ideologies. In September 1919, one month after Chicago's riot, Du Bois issued a fiery editorial in the *Crisis*:

> For three centuries we have suffered and cowered. No race ever gave Passive Resistance and Submission to Evil longer, more piteous trial. Today we raise the terrible weapon of Self-Defense. When the murderer comes, he shall not longer strike us in the back. When the armed lynchers gather, we too must gather armed. When the mob moves, we propose to meet it with bricks and clubs and guns. . . . If the United States is to be a Land of Law, we would live humbly and peaceably in it—working, singing, learning and dreaming to make it and ourselves nobler and better: if it is to be a Land of Mobs and Lynchers, we might as well die today as tomorrow.[31]

His response to continued violence, however, was not enough to prevent the *Messenger* from publishing images of Du Bois as an "Old Crowd Negro," in strict opposition to the "New Crowd Negro" vision of racial responsibility.[32] (See figure 1.)

FIGURE 1 "Following the Advice of the 'Old Crowd Negro,'" *Messenger* 2 (September 1919): 16.

Messenger editors believed the New Negro of this period must succeed in three vital areas—political, economic, and social—where the Old Negro had failed. Rather than feel secure with "political spoils and patronage," New Negroes demanded "political equality" and stood for "universal suffrage." Their economic philosophy argued that as a working-class majority, African Americans needed labor unions to support higher wages, better conditions, fewer working hours, and protection against racial discrimination. New Negroes distinguished themselves socially from Old Negroes by demanding "absolute and unequivocal 'social equality'" and insisting on "physical action" in defense of such goals rather than pursue a policy of passive resistance.[33] An example of this radical vision is displayed in *Messenger*'s "Riot Issue" of September 1919. Drawing on white Americans' slang for Germans during World War I, the New Negro engages the greatest postwar threat to American democracy: the American "Hun."[34] (See figure 2.)

THE "NEW CROWD NEGRO" MAKING AMERICA SAFE FOR HIMSELF

FIGURE 2 "The 'New Crowd Negro' Making America Safe for Himself,"
Messenger 2 (September 1919): 17.

While the many facets of this second New Negro did not disappear in the second decade of the twentieth century, they were superseded by a more visible, thoroughly reconceptualized version of a racial self.

In many ways the New Negro of Harlem owes its introduction to Charles S. Johnson, a sociologist who served as director of research for the National Urban League of New York and founder and editor of *Opportunity*, a periodical devoted to racial pride and black achievement. Because he saw art as one of the primary ways to bridge cultural differences between African Americans and whites, Johnson used his position with the National Urban League and its literary outlet to organize a now legendary event at Manhattan's Civic Club in March 1924. Ostensibly the forum was held to honor the publication of Jessie Fauset's *There Is Confusion* (1924); however, Johnson sought to bring together Harlem writers such as Langston Hughes, Gwendolyn Brooks, and Countee Cullen with a white intellectual community that included Carl Van Doren, Frederick Allen Lewis, and representatives from mainstream white publishers, who had previously ignored African American intellectual efforts.[35]

This gathering marks an important moment in the evolution of the New Negro of the 1920s, when Paul Kellogg, editor of *Survey Graphic*, America's leading journal of social work, approached the Howard University professor Alain Locke and asked him to edit a special issue devoted to the burgeoning artistic scene in Harlem. This collaboration produced the March 1925 special issue of *Survey Graphic* entitled "Harlem: Mecca of the New Negro," a topic Locke expanded later that year into his cultural and political exploration of African American expression, *The New Negro* (1925).[36] In his 1925 article entitled "Enter the New Negro," Locke proclaimed:

> In the last decade something beyond the watch and guard of statistics has happened in the life of the American Negro and the three norns who have traditionally presided over the Negro problem have a changeling in their laps. The Sociologist, the Philanthropist, the Race-leader are not unaware of the New Negro but they are at a loss to account for him. He simply cannot be swathed in their formulae. For the younger generation is vibrant with a new psychology; the new spirit is awake in the masses, and under the very eyes of the professional observers is transforming what has been a perennial problem into the progressive phases of contemporary Negro life.[37]

Locke's pronouncement of the New Negro's arrival in the early decades of the twentieth century signaled a spiritual and psychological transformation he believed was evident in many African American communities across America. According to Locke, a central component of the transformation from the Old Negro to the New was a change in location. Locke believed that "in the very process of being transplanted, the Negro [was] becoming transformed." This great flux was proof that the New Negro saw America with greater clarity, which granted him a vision of improved social and economic opportunity. Assessing their trek from south to north, and from primarily rural locations to urban centers, Locke asserted that African Americans had finally made the transition from "medieval America to modern."[38]

For Locke, the shedding of the "old chrysalis" not only entailed a physical shift for African Americans but also required a shift in perspective to achieve a spiritual emancipation. According to Locke, the Old

Negro lacked agency, relegating him to the category of myth rather than man. In previous decades the status of African Americans and their future in America was not determined by their community members but by whites, that is, by outsiders who looked upon African Americans as "something to be argued about, condemned or defended, to be 'kept down,' or 'in [their] place,' or 'helped up,' to be worried with or worried over, harassed or patronized, a social bogey or a social burden." Repeated white assertions of African American inferiority and white perpetuation of African American stereotypes reinforced a sense of inadequacy, which Locke believed clouded the ability of Old Negroes to share a positive individual or group identity. Locke argued that in order to shake "off the psychology" of their oppressors, African Americans had to embrace a new form of racial representation and initiate a process of self-discovery.[39]

Locke argued that under the guise of the New Negro, African Americans could achieve a spiritual emancipation through attainment of renewed "inner" and "outer" objectives. Among the inner objectives were many of the hallmarks of racial uplift, including, "race pride," "self-respect," and self-reliance," elements needed to "repair a damaged group psychology and reshape a warped social perspective." Once achieved, these qualities would enable New Negroes to attain their outer goals, "none other than [full participation in and enjoyment of] the ideals of American institutions and democracy." Locke's New Negroes, however, would not violently take to the streets to obtain adequate representation or seek their interests apart from their white counterparts. In a decidedly unradical voice, Locke insisted that African Americans could not advance in a manner that was "wholly separatist . . . even if it were desirable." Instead the New Negro could become both a "collaborator and participant" in American society through the highest forms of artistic expression, where meaningful interaction between the "enlightened minorities of both race groups" might overcome patriarchy and race prejudice.[40] Until cultural recognition was obtained, Locke believed, no genuine reevaluation of African Americans could proceed.

At this point, where Locke's ideology shifts from "radicalism to romantic culturalism," many scholars have criticized him for perpetuating a New Negro ideology apart from its political and activist roots.[41] Foley thinks Locke's formulation of the New Negro as a cultural hero is a "devolution" rather than an evolution, involving "not a dialectic of transmutation but a process of takeover, eradication, and obliteration."[42] Arnold Rampersad notes that although Locke's idea of a New Negro "exudes a

sense of racial pride," it also ignores "the most important mass movement in black America of the 1920s" (Marcus Garvey's Universal Negro
Improvement Association), and "helped Harlem turn its back even more
firmly on radical social movements."[43] Like Rampersad, Wilson Moses
criticizes Locke's New Negro for being composed of cultural elites rather
than a broad (and more representative) spectrum of personalities that
included "bohemian artists . . . staid intellectuals, rugged labor leaders,
tough-minded preachers, and conservative pan-Africanists."[44] For Gates
and Jarrett, Locke was "lubricating" the public with his romanticized
New Negro and pluralistic message in order to "turn from racial antago-
nism to racial amelioration."[45] And while reassessment of Locke and his
New Negro of the Renaissance continues, his work initiated a third New
Negro type, which has endured for generations.

Locke's influence infiltrated critical conversations of the period and
attracted renewed interest in African American culture. An example is
the numerous responses to a 1926 questionnaire "The Negro in Art: How
Shall He Be Portrayed?" distributed by the Crisis.[46] Of central concern
was how artists, white and black, portrayed African Americans in visual
and literary culture. Seeking to move beyond superficial Old Negro
types (plantation uncles, mammies, and sambos), African American
artists questioned the way to enter a viable cultural marketplace without compromising individual expression. In addition to discussing the
context in which African American characters were portrayed and the
complexity of the portrayal, the respondents, including such luminaries
as H. L. Mencken, Walter White, and Alfred A. Knopf, engaged the practical challenges faced by African American writers, whose dependency
on patronage and cooperation from a white-dominated publishing community influenced their artistic endeavors.

Countless artists, writers, and critics joined these conversations
between 1924 and 1934 in order to further delineate the implications
of racial representation for African Americans seeking to negotiate the
boundaries of "culture politics and political culture." Gates and Jarrett define culture politics, or "the politics of culture," as a way "people acquire, understand, and apply power in their relationships to one
another." These power relationships "underwrite the formation of certain
patterns of human values, discourses, attitudes, actions, or artifacts."
The previous definition is contrasted by what they refer to as "political
culture—or the culture of politics," which reveals "how cultural patterns
inform the institutions, organizations, and interest groups of public
policy or governmental activity."[47]

Although Du Bois's "The Younger Literary Movement" (1924) focused chiefly on unraveling the mysteries of Jean Toomer's *Cane* (1923), it expressed as well Du Bois's own gratitude that a number of young African American writers and poets had arisen to "fill the footsteps of the fathers."[48] Locke's essay "Negro Youth Speaks" (1925) also acknowledged the "first fruits of the Renaissance," whose expressions exhibited a race consciousness and a freedom of spirituality that he termed "ultramodern."[49] However, others, such as Benjamin Brawley, condemned younger artists' failure to develop their craft because they too often found praise from outsiders who rewarded their forays into hedonistic subject matter.[50] Agreeing with Brawley, Allison Davis questioned the need to portray bohemian or primitivist aspects of African American life rather than focusing "upon the inner strength" that had defined the African American character for three hundred years.[51]

Lloyd Morris and Martha Gruening, who examined the Negro Renaissance from the vantage point of the 1930s, initiated philosophical debates that continue to occupy scholarly discussions today regarding the success or failure of a movement. Morris viewed the 1920s as a "renaissance of interest on the part of a white audience" rather than a "renaissance of production on the part of Negro artists." Arguing that African American literary accomplishments were "too old to be still considered new," he reminded his audience of the legacy of Jupiter Hammond, Phillis Wheatley, and Benjamin Banneker.[52] Similarly Gruening, who identified few works of merit in "The Negro Renaissance" (1922), regarded Locke's spiritual emancipation as having been "exploited commercially and socially, until it [had] been, to a large extent, degraded into a racket." Gruening decried the inundation of African American art by propaganda but delighted in the work of Renaissance poets (particularly in their novels) because she viewed most poets as members of the proletariat who experienced the "rough and casual menial labor open to American Negroes." Langston Hughes's artistic success especially came from his decision to remain "close to the life of the masses of his race."[53] According to Hughes's essay "The Negro Artist and the Racial Mountain" (1926) the next great African American artist would come from the lowest stratum of African American society, where the "eternal tom-tom" beat steadily among those free within themselves.[54]

Despite his appropriation of the term *New Negro* and his shift in paradigm, Locke's legacy provided current scholars with a welcome glimpse into alternate cultural sources of political import that, until recently, have not been viewed as New Negro texts. Du Bois's germinal essay "The

Sorrow Songs" (1903) and John W. Work's "Negro Folk-Song" (1923) emphasized the melodic beauty and striking depth of meaning that make African American folk songs and spirituals original and defining features of the American musical landscape.[55] Greenville Vernon's "That Mysterious 'Jazz'" (1919) recognized the ability of music to transcend racial and cultural barriers, a belief shared by an anonymous writer whose "Jazzing Away Prejudice" (1919) claimed that "[James] Europe and his band are worth more to our race than a thousand speeches from so-called Race orators and uplifters."[56]

For Rollin Lynde Hartt, theaters such as the Harlem Community House provided a powerful medium that connected with African Americans regardless of class distinctions. Referring to its increasing popularity among African Americans nationwide, Hartt declared, "The negro theatre will become as influential as the Negro press—more influential, possibly."[57] In the realm of fine arts, Locke saw the New Negro artist developing an important "racial school of expression" that moved beyond an imitation of "classic models and Caucasian idols" and brought a much-needed vitality to the American art scene.[58] For Romare Bearden that vitality lay within the artist as "the medium through which humanity expresses itself."[59] Exemplifying what Gates and Jarrett deemed the ever-present tension between concerns artistic and political, Bearden urged the New Negro artist to move beyond his interior conception of art and draw his inspiration from the realities of his own social condition. The New Negro does not disappear from African American discourse in the decades following the 1930s; he remains a viable form of racial representation and a prominent feature of late nineteenth-and early twentieth-century scholarship.

Locating the New Negro

Since the time of Gates's evaluation of the relationship between politics and racial representation, numerous scholars have extended research into the ways in which radicalism, sexuality, aesthetics, race, and gender have intersected with the New Negro identity.[60] These welcome contributions to the field of African American literature and culture nevertheless remain consistent with academic scholarship on the New Negro of the early twentieth century that tends to discuss the New Negro in the context of northern urban culture. As Wilson Moses notes, "We shall never really appreciate the nature of black American language and literature until we have reconstructed the cultural and intellectual life of literate, urban nineteenth-century black America."[61] To Moses's claim I would add that any examination of contemporary African American culture requires a reexamination of the New Negro as a figure who emerged out of the segregation and racial violence of the Reconstruction South.

In fact new critical perspectives seem to indicate the need to start tracing the New Negro from an earlier date. As Erin Chapman notes, New Negroes of the interwar era did not "break radically" from the aspirations of previous generations but rather "built on the inroads made by older volunteer activists, novelists, publishers, and performers" of the nineteenth century such as Ida B. Wells, Pauline Hopkins, and Du Bois "and took up the identity and rhetoric of the New Negroes, using and shaping it as their own."[62] Cherene Sherrard-Johnson similarly notes that since at least 1890 African American artists and writers have waged "a war of images" to reshape and redefine representations of black identity in American culture and have exhibited a "spirit of self-invention and optimism" that fostered the New Negro movement and the Harlem Renaissance.[63] Steven Tracy makes another important point regarding the New Negro's nineteenth-century roots, arguing that the New Negro movement and the popularity of blues music are "a natural historical consequence of what had gone before," during the eras of slavery and Reconstruction. According to Tracy, blues emerged from the South as an "adaptation of older instrumental and vocal techniques (which responded to one kind of oppressive system) to a new kind of music, one that responded to the unique problems posed by the new oppressive system and provided an appropriate way of expressing these problems."[64] It is not surprising, then, that Renaissance-era New Negroes such as Langston Hughes, who referred to the blues as "songs of the black South, particularly the city South," drew on elements of nineteenth-century African American oral and written traditions to create new artistic expressions that embraced themes associated with the New Negro that include race consciousness and race pride.[65] From this perspective, as we shall see, the North is not necessarily the logical place to locate the emergence of the New Negro. Reexamining the southern roots of the New Negro will reconstitute our interpretation of ideas about region, race, and history. As a part of the necessary work in this direction, I redefine our understanding of the idea of the New Negro by following its genealogy back to its historical and geographical origins in the post-Reconstruction nineteenth-century South and examine the literary and cultural factors that influenced the development of a modern African American identity.[66]

The geographic, intellectual, and cultural center that exemplifies that development was Nashville, Tennessee. In *Turning South*, Houston

Baker Jr. argues that the "*framing* of anything suitably called 'modernity' has its primary locus south of Mason Dixon. In Dixieland, black Americans had no choice but to take their stand . . . their performances framed in signifying relation to the mind of the South."[67] For that reason, in part, an understanding of both the modern African American and the New Negro identity needs to begin by returning to the genesis of the New South. The New South created a paradoxical context wherein African Americans shared constitutional freedoms, unknown to previous generations and enforced by an Old South regime under a new name, that sought to limit and fix the position of African Americans in southern society. Unable to shackle African American men and women in irons, white southerners used governmental strictures and local customs to limit their mobility and forestall social, economic, and intellectual advancement.

Conventional wisdom suggests that the nineteenth-century South was a region from which African Americans had to escape—either because of agricultural disasters such as soil depletion and the raging boll weevil or because of uncompromising social and economic segregation—in order to achieve a cultural and intellectual rebirth. Yet even as late as 1900, 90 percent of all African Americans resided in the South. What is to be made of those African Americans? Were they dormant, devoid of political or intellectual activity? Did they don a mask in order to survive? And how should we understand the minority that left the South?

In order to begin to rehistoricize the rise of the New Negro, we must return to the Hayes-Tilden Compromise of 1877.[68] That compromise, a watershed moment that signaled the end of Reconstruction, initiated the Restoration, a period when white southerners reasserted their control and dominance over recently conquered lands and institutions. This moment forever redefined the relationship between African Americans and whites in the post–Civil War South. Following a presidential term fraught with scandal and eroding party support, Republicans, who sought to maintain control of the presidency in the 1876 election, shifted their allegiance from Ulysses S. Grant to the former Union officer and experienced politician Rutherford B. Hayes. His opponent from the Democratic Party was New York's governor Samuel J. Tilden, who had gained notoriety for helping to convict the notorious embezzler William "Boss" Tweed and break up his Tammany Hall ring. After a hotly contested campaign, Tilden won the popular vote by almost 300,000 votes. Disputed returns from a number of states, however, left him one electoral vote shy of victory. With the election unresolved, Congress created a special commission to determine the outcome.

Although the committee was composed of an equal number of Republicans and Democrats, the lone independent responsible for breaking the deadlock was believed to have Republican ties, and the tallied electoral votes were awarded to Hayes. To avoid upsetting Democratic supporters and prevent further challenges to the election, Republican leaders made a number of concessions to Democrats, particularly those in the South, who were eager to begin the reorganization of their state governments. These concessions included control of patronage and federal economic support that would be used to conduct internal improvements and subsidize railroad companies to encourage industrialization. Another significant provision of the compromise was the agreement to remove the remaining federal troops from southern territory. These concessions facilitated the restoration of Democratic Party control and signaled the desire of the federal government to focus on issues other than the enforcement of rights for the majority of its African American citizenry.[69]

With the federal government ostensibly removed from the political interests of southern state governments, white southerners embraced what Paul M. Gaston calls a "New South creed," that is, a combination of philosophies that sought to erase the economic inequalities between North and South while "restoring the racial, political, and class hierarchies that exemplified the ideals of the Old South."[70] According to W. J. Cash, the regeneration of the New South represented "merely a revolution in tactics," a revolution that sought its newness only as a South that would be "so rich and powerful that it might rest serene in its ancient positions, forever impregnable."[71] Rather than dwell on a defeated South or on the sting of federally implemented Reconstruction policies, white southerners embraced the Old South, romanticizing its Lost Cause even as they marched toward modernization.[72] James Cobb argues that the Civil War and Reconstruction "not only provided the white South with its own distinctive experience, but it fast-forwarded the antebellum southern order through its process of aging and historical distancing." For many white southerners the Old South became a pastoral memory, and though this portrayal represented an unrealistic, unattainable state of perfection, it became an essential component of white southern identity. The dynamic between the Old South and the Lost Cause became, in the words of Cobb, "'the dominant historical narrative' among southern whites" and helped the New South achieve numerous objectives, including the restoration of "white supremacy."[73]

One of the ways white southerners sought to reestablish this racial hierarchy was to redefine African American identity and establish the role African Americans were meant to play in the New South. Proponents of the New South philosophy such as Henry Grady believed that the model black citizen would be one who "through determination, thrift, and irreproachable public behavior, and not a little cunning had managed to pull himself 'up from slavery' into a position of influence, prestige, and relative prosperity, all while exhibiting the humility that the New South demanded in equal measure of all its black residents from the lowliest to the most accomplished."[74] It should come as no surprise that African American identity in the New South was idealized by whites along the same lines as those remnants of the Old South to which so many white southerners clung. The ideal African American citizen was meant to replicate the Old Negro, who, most white southerners imagined, understood loyalty, had a sense of duty, and was happy to serve the needs and desires of the white community. The Old Negro was docile and deferential in both manner and speech and led a simple life requiring little knowledge or education outside of those skills needed to fulfill his role as servant or laborer. The Old Negro knew "his place," upheld white expectations of behavior, and didn't question boundaries. Such was the image conjured by the author of an 1893 *Christian Advocate* editorial when he wrote about "the old slaves who watched over their masters' families with so tireless a fidelity in the dark days of 1861–1865."[75] The widespread appeal of this Old Negro was strengthened by his appearance in the popular culture of the day, which embellished his desired characteristics.

According to Gates, who possesses a collection of ten thousand racist images, the post-Reconstruction era was responsible for a remarkable volume of negative visual art that enabled white Americans "to see Sambo images from toaster to teapot cover."[76] Degrading images of African Americans could be found in magazine advertisements for countless products and even on postcards featuring everything from the minstrel figure and mammy to the spectacle of a local lynching. While the literary treatment of African Americans by white southern writers would shift decidedly near the turn of the century in the works of authors such as Thomas Dixon, post-Reconstruction writers embraced more sympathetic stereotypes.

Commenting on the caricature of African Americans by southern writers such as Joel Chandler Harris, John Pendleton Kennedy, and Thomas Nelson Page, C. Vann Woodward notes that it was "no doubt patronizing, sentimentalized, and paternalistic, but there was never anything venomous or bitter about the Negro in their pages."[77] Harris achieved national recognition and entertained generations of white children through his masterful storyteller, Uncle Remus, who epitomized the dutiful slave of the Old South for whom slavery represented a golden age. Within the pages of Harris's books, southern whites reveled in stories of aunties, mammies, and other stereotypical portrayals of slaves who love and laud their masters and their own lives on the plantation. While Sterling Brown credits Harris for creating one of the most enduring figures in American literature, he emphasizes the twofold deception revealed through the dialect of Uncle Remus, whom he considers "a venerable, pampered Negro with a gift for quaint philosophizing and for poetic speech, having (or allowed to have) only pleasant memories" of slavery and its machinations. Although most of Harris's tales are drawn from the folk tales and stories of African American slaves—stories that often originated in Africa—and often celebrate the cunning of characters such as Br'er Rabbit, who eludes and deceives his opponents, Harris supported the mythology of the Old South as well as a revisionist view of racial relationships during the plantation era. Evidence of what Brown terms "orthodox southern attitudes" is revealed through the omnipresent storyteller, who argues against emancipatory goals.[78] In one example the storyteller claims that the attainment of education is the "ruinashun er dis country" because once someone places a "spellin'-book in a nigger's han's, en right den an dar' you loozes a plow-hand."[79] Similar examples endorsing Old Negro characteristics and glorifying Old South culture are prominent features of literary works from the period.

Thomas Nelson Page published a number of influential books and essays that portrayed the Old South as "'the purest sweetest life ever lived,' one that 'made men noble, gentle, and brave and women tender and pure.'"[80] His body of work is considered by many whites to be one of the most enduring portraits of the Old South. In texts such as *In Ole Virginia*, Page illustrates the allure of a plantation-era South through the many adventures of its aristocrats and the advantages of their idyllic community.[81] Rather than provide readers with a defense of slavery, however, Page's apologist rhetoric emphasized the "warm friendship that existed between master and servant." Page argued, "One need not be an advocate of slavery be-cause [sic] he upsets ideas that have no foundation whatever in truth and sets forth facts that can be substantiated by the experience of thousands who knew them [slaves] at first hand." Providing readers with a glimpse into his own plantation experiences, Page recalls "old-time Negroes" such as "Uncle Balla," the "guide, philosopher, and friend" of his boyhood, to illustrate the sympathy and tenderness that existed between white southerners and their slaves, or "retainers," as Page liked to call them. Page believed that, more than anything else, enduring Negro qualities such as responsible behavior, trust, and unquestioned fidelity would enable "future and abiding friendship between the races" that could bridge racial differences of the post-Reconstruction South.[82]

The image of the Old Negro, however, did not simply refer to nostalgia for a bucolic past. It was a form of social control—a way to deal with a large African American population in the South that, if left uncontrolled, represented for many whites a seditious element that threatened the quality of life in the New South. In their creation of the Old South–Lost Cause legend, adherents expected little internal criticism because the challenge to the new order would identify one as an opponent to "progress, tradition, and, for good measure, the status quo."[83] African Americans therefore were expected to play the role whites had developed for them even as they "progressed." When the educator Charles Brantley Aycock discussed plans for the education of the African American population, he assured those in opposition to such plans that educating the African American could be done in a manner "that will enable us to make sure that he acquires no dangerous notions, to control what he is taught, to make sure that he is educated to fit into, and to stay in, his place."[84] Despite Cobb's claim in *Away Down South* that such heavy-handedness by whites in the affairs of the South's African American population left them "largely reduced to invisibility save in the role of happy, loyal, and totally servile retainers who affirmed the wisdom of the New South's racial ethos," it is apparent that a New Negro had appeared to challenge imposed inequalities and that whites living in the New South were taking notice.[85]

Few literary examples characterize the white attitude toward the New Negro in the late nineteenth century better than the 1892 Memphis newspaper article claiming, "The generation of Negroes which have grown up since the war have lost in large measure the traditional and wholesome awe of the white race which kept the Negroes in subjection."[86] This apparent shift in behavior among young African Americans was also recorded by Du Bois in his storied *Souls of Black Folk*, when he described the memorable Josie and others he encountered during his time in Nashville. These African Americans were representative of a generation "to whom War, Hell, and Slavery were but childhood tales, whose young appetites had been whetted to edge by school and story and half-awakened thought.

Ill could they be content, born without and beyond the World. And their weak wings beat against their barriers,—barriers of caste, youth, of life; at last, in dangerous moments, against everything that opposed even a whim."[87] Thus could Page lament the appearance of the "new issue" Negro, who looks with "fine scorn of the relation which once existed all over the South between the old-time South-erner [sic] and the old-time darky" who brings with him "his problem," which will take "all the wis-dom [sic], all the forbearance, and all the resolution of the white race to solve."[88] And so, for many whites living in the post-Reconstruction South, "the critical factor" in evaluating a new generation of African Americans or older generations unwilling to adhere to the Old Negro standard conceived by whites "was the degree of control they could exercise over them."[89] Undisciplined by the guiding hand of slavery and undaunted by the racial inequalities to which they were subjected, New Negroes represented the greatest fears of white southern society and posed an imminent threat to its carefully constructed caste system.

Turning South

If southern African Americans of the period viewed the Old Negro and the New Negro very differently than did whites, we need to understand the conditions that caused the Old Negro to become ineffective as a public form of racial representation and the conditions that engendered a New Negro identity for African Americans of the South. While the New Negro of the South becomes identifiable following the end of Reconstruction, two of his defining characteristics, renaming and mobility, began to develop among African Americans toward the close of the Civil War. The naming ritual has an extensive history in the African American cultural tradition. In order to view its development, Gates suggests we look no further than the literary autobiographies of former slaves.[90]

Upon emancipation Booker T. Washington found two things to be true among African Americans of the South: "that they must change their names, and that they must leave the old plantation for at least a few days or weeks in order that they might really feel sure that they were free." For Washington, dropping the surname of a former owner was emblematic of freedom, and the decision played a role in the physical and psychological distancing from the experience of slavery. Although the selection of his last name was spontaneous, Washington considered the act a "privilege." Rather than resting on the laurels of his ancestry, of his *old* name, Washington viewed the moment of his naming as a chance to begin anew, a way to "leave a record of which my children would be proud, and which might encourage them to still higher effort."[91]

A perusal of Frederick Douglass's *Autobiography* reveals that he used three surnames—Stanley, Bailey, and Johnson—before settling on his better-known appellation.[92] Gates considers the naming ritual to be "emblematic of the anguish in African-American history," an experience exemplified in the words of Sojourner Truth: "My name was Isabella; but when I left the house of bondage, I left everything behind. I wan't goin' to keep nothin' of Egypt on me, an' so I went to the Lord an' asked him to give me a new name. An' the Lord give me Sojourner, because I was to travel up an' down the land, showin' the people their sins, an' bein' a sign unto them. Afterward I told de Lord I wanted another name, 'cause everybody else had two names; an de' Lord give me Truth, because I was to declare the truth to de people."[93] Renaming, in other words, became a strategy for nineteenth-century African Americans consciously seeking a new identity because it signaled a break with a painful past by reasserting agency. According to Mia Bay, this practice continued because, "whether free or slave, educated or unlettered, African-Americans of the nineteenth and early twentieth centuries grew up in a society where both social reality and the relentless influence of racist ideology forced all of its members to define both themselves and others around them in racial terms. These African-Americans confronted their white fellow Americans across a racial divide structured by class, codified by law, and dignified by a white supremacist ideology that deemed the low status of black people to be a reflection of the inferior character and abilities of their race."[94] Is it any wonder, then, that many post-Reconstruction African Americans turned away from the Old Negro label that limited them to intellectual, moral, social, and cultural inferiority? Nevertheless scholars such as Nathan Huggins find the New/Old dichotomy troubling because the creation of a new identity suggests that the previous one was somehow inadequate. Huggins argues that African Americans cannot move forward by negating their past. Once denied, the Old Negro lingers in the consciousness of the New Negro as an element of self-doubt or, worse, self-hate.[95] Should African Americans seek to promote a new racial identity or create a national consciousness, Huggins believes that they share a moral responsibility to acknowledge their own limitations and the obstacles overcome by previous generations. Huggins's words evoke those of Du Bois, who so eloquently defined the generational soul of African Americans "whose dogged strength alone keeps it from being torn asunder."[96]

Each of these examples provides a valid perspective on the evolution of African American identity, especially when one considers that the Old Negro also encompassed Vesey, Gabriel, and Nat Turner. Yet was the sacrifice of these men any greater than that of a slave mother who did not resist because she sought to preserve a semblance of family within the peculiar institution? Douglass, Truth, and Washington show us that past experiences can propel people into action. Like these historical figures, most African Americans living in the post-Reconstruction South, unable to erase the negative connotations associated with the Old Negro image, felt that a New Negro was needed to replace a figure inextricably linked to slavery and perpetuated by the romantic racialism of white fiction writers. That old figure had masqueraded on stages across the nineteenth-century South in the form of plantation uncles and mammies or clownish and imbecilic sambos, pickaninnies, and "happy darkies."

As Cobb points out, "Invented traditions are the key to securing the emotional and political allegiance of the majority of the population at large."[97] Many white southern leaders championed life in the New South and sought a new identity in the wake of Reconstruction and northern involvement. Adherents of the New South philosophy were seeking regeneration, but they were doing so without forgetting their roots, that is, the Lost Cause. Consider a story recounted by W. J. Cash. Walter Hines Page came south in the decade following the 1877 Compromise to begin a series of articles that would prove that any ill will or resentment from the Civil War or Reconstruction was forgotten among the people of the South and that the region, "completely absorbed in new ideas and new goals, was rapidly becoming another yankeedom." After having spent considerable time in the region, Hines abandoned his project, viewing it "incompatible with reality."[98] The experience of life under Reconstruction and what Cash would term an internal colonization of their region by federal agents bonded white southerners together in a way that strengthened their belief in a New South and its guiding principles. In their desire to redefine the racial relationships of the New South, however, white southerners played a crucial role in the development of a collective identity and political platform among southern African Americans during the same period.

Thus if the decision of many African Americans to embrace the New Negro between the years 1895 and 1925 was "a bold and audacious act of language, signifying the will to power, to dare to create a race by renaming it, despite the dubiousness of the venture," the same holds true of African Americans embracing that identity in 1877.[99] Given the New South's restrictions on African Americans and their ever shrinking freedoms, was the assertion of a New Negro identity any less audacious than Douglass's autobiographical publication wrought by "an American slave"? Are New Negroes not also writing and, through their actions, declaring for themselves an existence in the New South?

The legal status of African Americans may have changed following Emancipation, but after the end of Reconstruction this status was reduced to semantics. While the Fourteenth Amendment provided a constitutional definition of citizenship entailing equal protection under state and national laws for those born or naturalized in the United States, it could not prohibit the bias of individuals and institutions that continued to exclude African Americans from social, political, or economic acceptance. The Fifteenth Amendment prohibited state and federal governments from denying citizens the right to vote regardless of race, color, or any previous condition of servitude, and, much like its predecessor, it represented positive changes in public policy toward the treatment of African Americans. Unfortunately these amendments did not ensure African Americans the right to hold office or protect them from cagy rhetoricians or political devices such as poll taxes, literacy tests, or property ownership requirements that prevented them from participating in the democratic process. Despite the unparalleled gains by African Americans of the South during Reconstruction, at its end they were given no legal protections by an absent federal government, their civil rights were impeded by an embittered South, and they enjoyed little material wealth and few economic opportunities. The post-Reconstruction South also made little effort to curb the terror and intimidation of the Ku Klux Klan (formed in Pulaski, Tennessee) and other white supremacist groups.[100]

While the ordeals endured by African American southerners at the hands of whites were not categorically aligned to those of southern whites under the control of northern whites, they were tantamount to that relationship because the experience bonded African American southerners together and was directly responsible for the need for and creation of a new and sustainable group identity. By embracing the concept of the New Negro, nineteenth-century African Americans signaled a desire to redefine their status in the New South's white-dominated society. More than just a label, the New Negro was a political weapon needed to challenge recalcitrant white southern opposition to its legitimate presence as a necessary and equivalent component in the creation of a new southern society.

Although the New Negro emerged out of the South, not out of a migration North, geographical movement was still important to the evolution
of his identity. At the close of the Civil War, long before the Great Migration of the twentieth century, newly freed slaves began migrating around
the South in large numbers. According to Leon Litwack, this movement
was a "way to define and act on their new status," even if their final destination was not clearly identifiable.[101] For many this meant remaining
in the same region, whether it was shifting to an adjacent plot of land or
moving to reconnect with family members who had been torn apart by
slavery and war. Large numbers of African Americans also sought refuge
from the social and political subjugation of the South by migrating to the
sparsely populated Plains states or to locations outside the United States.

In their effort to achieve social and political freedom, approximately
sixty thousand African Americans moved into Kansas and farther west
into the Oklahoma Indian Territories between 1865 and 1881.[102] In
what has been termed the "exoduster movement," thousands of African
Americans migrating from Texas, Louisiana, Mississippi, and Tennessee
were responsible for the creation of "exclusively black towns" in Kansas,
where, it was hoped, a political majority might allow African American
representatives to carry out their challenge to white authority in Congress.[103] The leading migrationists W. A. Sizemore, Benjamin Singleton, and A. W. McConnell even held a "convention of colored people"
in Nashville "for the purpose of looking after the interests of colored
people" who had been swayed in great numbers by rumors that free
transportation, land, and supplies would be available to those persons
willing to make the transition west. While the convention addressed
issues affecting African Americans nationwide, discussions focused on
the particular conditions in the South were accorded "special emphasis."
Although many African Americans did not believe migration from the
South to be the "wisest course" of action for dealing with racial conditions there, migration continued in steady numbers, causing the African
American population to swell in states like Kansas, where it reached over
forty-three thousand by 1890.[104]

Yet despite the loss of approximately 537,000 African American
southerners—and some 1,243,000 white southerners—during the last
two decades of the nineteenth century, the most notable shift in the
African American population took place within the South, where many
African Americans abandoned rural life for urban.[105] According to
Don Doyle, "the number of urban places in the eleven southern states
increased from 51 in 1860 to 103 by 1880," a number that would multiply

eight times, to 396, by 1910.[106] Edward Ayers notes that the "village and town population of the South grew by five million people between 1880 and 1910" and "the average county in the South saw its black population grow by 48 percent between 1880 and 1910."[107] These percentages were even greater in states such as Florida and Alabama, where the increases reached an extraordinary 131 percent and 119 percent, respectively.

One of the primary reasons for this rise in population during the 1880s and 1890s was the increased demand for labor, which drew large numbers of African Americans to find work in a burgeoning southern urban economy. According to Ayers, an array of employment opportunities developed from Virginia to Texas in lumber mills, phosphate and coal mines, iron fields, cotton gin and cotton seed oil businesses, and the rice and sugar fields of the Delta. When compared to other industrializing economies of the nineteenth century, the New South's productivity "actually grew faster . . . than it had in New England during its industrial revolution fifty years earlier."[108] The enormous number of foreign immigrants arriving in the United States at this period, moreover, had little impact on the South. The South's foreign-born population dropped from 10 percent in 1880 to a startlingly low 4.7 by 1910, making African Americans an even more valuable source of labor for southern economies. As Litwack points out, efforts by whites to "utilize immigrants, native whites, even Chinese laborers confirmed a preference for blacks." In the words of one Virginia planter in the years following Emancipation, "I can't do nothin' on my place without 'em. If they send all the niggers to Africa, I'll have to go thar, too."[109] However, an increase in work opportunities is not the only factor motivating African Americans to seek an urban life.

Urban life afforded African Americans opportunities not available in the rural South. Children could enroll in better schools and attend with more regularity, and adults were closer to their neighbors, facilitating the creation of benevolent societies and the churches vital to the creation of African American communities. As African Americans continued to seek changes in the years following the Civil War they shared a popular belief that "freedom was free-er in the towns and cities" than in the isolated countryside.[110] They soon realized, however, that urban life produced a volatile racial dynamic wherein they competed for livelihood amid an unwelcoming white southern element. According to Baker, "Black modernism is not only framed by the American South, but also is inextricable—as cognitive and somatic process of performing *blackness* out of or within tight spaces."[111] Within the contentious racial environment of the urban South a New Negro asserted a southern and, ultimately, modern identity.

The urbanization essential to the creation of a "new group life" among African Americans, August Meier notes, contributed to the growth of race consciousness, racial solidarity, increased self-reliance, and a burgeoning middle class that did not alienate but worked in conjunction with other members of the black community.[112] According to Du Bois, this urban social structure was particularly strong in the South, where segregation often caused African Americans to live, work, worship, and seek education and even entertainment apart from white citizens. And while this separation created "greater differentiation from the white group," it inevitably caused "more harmonious working together" among blacks and opened "a broader field for such cooperation."[113]

These factors created the historical setting in which Nashville, a unique, nontraditional urban center, became a significant site where African Americans exerted sustained and organized resistance to white supremacy and where they experienced a cultural and intellectual development without parallel in any southern African American community—crucial to the genealogy of the New Negro.

2 / Nashville: A Southern Black Metropolis

Every Nashville man ought to at once familiarize himself thoroughly with Nashville's advantages and never lose a chance to exhibit this knowledge to any stranger.

—*NASHVILLE GLOBE*, JULY 21, 1911

If the New Negro is a figure of resistance, it was resistance, as the histories of lynching and Jim Crow have made clear, to very formidable forces. No matter what the inclination of southern African Americans—and until a few decades into the twentieth century most African Americans were southern—only a few sites in the South permitted the possibility of resistance. These included cities such as Richmond and Jacksonville. And even among those places Nashville, because of specific historical circumstances, was preeminent. Unlike most urban centers in the South, Nashville escaped the Civil War relatively unscathed, a circumstance that allowed for a degree of economic prosperity that benefited not only the white community but also the African American community, which had grown very large during and immediately following the war.

Even before the close of the Civil War, Nashville's geography, economics, and political positioning made it an important center for the South's African American population. When Kentucky did not secede from the Union, it left its southern neighbor, Tennessee, a Confederate state, without a buffer against encroaching federal forces.[1] Located a mere thirty-five miles from the Kentucky state line, Nashville, with vital railroad connections to cities throughout the South and essential steamboat waterways, was strategically important to both sides.[2] Yet in February 1862, just months into the war and following swift advances by Union troops across the Ohio River and through Kentucky, overwhelmed Confederate forces withdrew from Nashville, leaving the city in Union hands.[3] The capital city quickly became the headquarters of

Union forces in the South.[4] Escaping the destruction suffered by numerous southern cities during the war, much of Nashville thrived, particularly its merchants and manufacturers, who benefited from the influx of Union soldiers and federal funding for the war effort.

Nashville's wartime circumstances also made it a significant destination for southern African Americans. With a swift influx of runaway slaves, contraband, and free blacks, the African American population grew rapidly.[5] Of the thousands of African Americans who poured into Nashville during the war, many formed Negro military companies such as the 12th and 13th U.S. Colored Infantry units, and many of these soldiers returned to the city after the war.[6] Although, given the dynamic circumstances of the period, census records were somewhat inaccurate, they show that Nashville's African American population nearly tripled between 1860 and 1870, representing almost 40 percent of the city's population of 25,865.[7] Also in 1865 Tennessee amended its constitution to outlaw slavery.[8] In doing so it signaled its desire to reestablish ties with the Union, a political maneuver that enabled Tennessee to become the only Confederate state to rejoin the Union and escape the indignity of a prolonged period of Reconstruction.[9] With "fewer physical and political scars and with advantages gained in the war," as Don Doyle notes, Nashville was well prepared to play "a formidable role in the new order" of a postwar South.[10]

If these circumstances created unique opportunities for Nashville's white citizens, it created the conditions for African Americans for what St. Clair Drake and Horace R. Cayton have called a "black metropolis." As Davarian Baldwin describes it, more than "a simple description of space and place" the black metropolis is an ideology among members of an African American community seeking to promote a collective race consciousness.[11] One cannot forget, however, that those who identified themselves as New Negroes (whether or not they were part of a metropolis model) were neither just men nor solely from an elite class of African Americans. New Negroes in Nashville and elsewhere encompassed a range of occupations, including washerwomen, preachers, day laborers, writers, and entrepreneurs. Regardless of their standing in society, they were challenging proscribed roles of race, class, and identity (American and southern) in an attempt to gain economic, political, and social stability. In many ways Nashville represented for them a black metropolis, a "city within a city."[12]

Education

The sheer number and quality of Nashville's African American schools was unequaled by any other southern city of the period. Despite the fact that only 10 percent of school-age African American children attended school throughout the South between 1865 and 1869, "more than fifty percent of Nashville's school-age children attended the city's public and private schools" during the same period.[13] As a result of migration and exponential growth, the number of African American students in schools and colleges continued to rise. By 1880 the city boasted thirty Negro schools in twenty-five districts and a significant number of higher learning institutions. Serving African Americans of diverse ages and educational backgrounds, these facilities were essential sites of intellectual life, particularly the Negro colleges, which also served as an important contributor to Nashville's reputation as the "Athens of the South."[14]

Nashville Normal and Theological Institute (1864–83) was a product of the American Baptist Home Mission Society that opened as a training ground for African American preachers of the Baptist faith. By 1869 the school included some 265 African American students from across the South in varied stages of preparation, and it ambitiously sought to maintain a college curriculum beginning just two years later. By 1883 the institute, which had relocated and changed its name to Roger Williams University, had become one of the leading African American liberal arts institutions in the country.[15]

Building on the success of Franklin College (1843–62), a white school that coupled agricultural and manual training with Christian education, Tennessee Manual Labor University (1866–74) was formed when a number of artisans, craftsmen, and small businessmen who served as leaders of the Colored Agricultural and Mechanical Institution pushed for another educational outlet for Nashville's freedmen. Among Nashville's notable African American leaders responsible for the formation of this school was Sampson W. Keeble, the first African American elected to Tennessee's General Assembly.[16]

Central Tennessee College (1866–1925), later Walden University, was another freedmen's school formed in association with white northern interests affiliated with the Methodist Episcopal Church. Although the curriculum included only primary education at its 1865 inception, by 1877 it was the only institution in the South with a law department for African Americans. By 1889 it boasted some 545 students engaged not only in industrial training but also in much needed professional fields such as teaching, theology, dentistry, and pharmacology.[17]

Meharry Medical College (1876–present), which also grew out of Central, was the first medical school for African Americans in the South. Meharry began with an enrollment of nine, but that number swelled exponentially, facilitating the need for a School of Dentistry in 1886, a Department of Pharmacy in 1889, and a Nurse Training School in 1902 to meet the demands of almost 250 students. In 1902 Meharry boasted the largest attendance of any African American medical college in the world and enrolled students from Jamaica, Antigua, Liberia, South Africa, Dutch New Guinea, Bermuda, and the Indian Territories. Among the school's 505 graduates that year were teachers, ministers, editors, soldiers, medical missionaries, and approximately 80 percent of the South's African American dentists, nurses, and physicians. These men and women not only provided valuable medical services to Nashville's African American community; a contingent of doctors, nurses, and dentists created their own businesses throughout the South and offered African American communities an alternative to white health care professionals.[18] (See figure 3.)

The Fisk Free Colored School (1865–67), founded at the close of the Civil War, provided primary and secondary education to a portion of the South's four million freedmen. Its goal was to educate African American teachers with a "broad Christian foundation" in a college environment that would provide a liberal arts education equivalent to that of any white university in the country.[19] Under the direction of the American Missionary Association and the optimistic leadership of numerous white northern supporters, including John Ogden, Erastus M. Cravath, and Edward P. Smith, the Fisk School (1867–present) was realized just two years later and was authorized to train men and women of all races and to confer all honors and degrees obtainable by similar institutions across the nation. Fisk quickly established a reputation as the premier African American training facility in the South, and its reputation soon extended into the northern states and overseas following the successful touring of Fisk's Jubilee Singers, which showcased the value of African American spirituals as an important element of America's cultural heritage.[20] The success of the Fisk singers not only bolstered the reputation of their university and its southern setting but also helped fill the university's library with books and expand its campus to include Jubilee Hall, a magnificent architectural accomplishment resting at the university center. (See figure 4.)

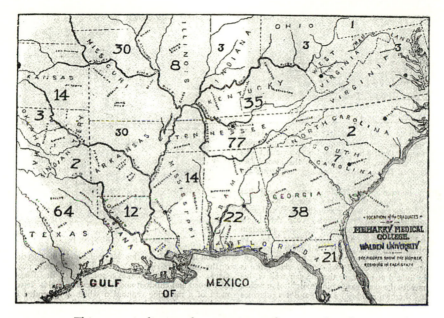

FIGURE 3 This map indicates the growing influence of Meharry Medical College graduates across the South and neighboring states. (Source: *National Baptist Union*, March 1902.)

Despite the financial challenges and growing pains common to all universities, Fisk continued to expand through the final decades of the nineteenth century. By 1900 the combined theology, normal, and music departments could claim over one thousand former students engaged in occupations ranging from law and government to ministry and teaching, in various locations around the country. The university's list of alumni and faculty, a who's who of African American culture, includes W. E. B. Du Bois, Charles Johnson, James Weldon Johnson, Arna Bontemps, and John Hope Franklin. Institutions such as Fisk also sowed the seeds for the creation of other educational institutions for African Americans, such as the Tennessee Agricultural and Industrial State College (1912), which later became Tennessee State University, and the American Baptist Theological Seminary, later renamed American Baptist College (1924).[21] The marked effects from the development of an educated class of African Americans during the postwar years became omnipresent in the years following Reconstruction.

FIGURE 4 Jubilee Hall was dedicated January 1, 1876. (Courtesy of Fisk University, John Hope and Aurelia E. Franklin Library, Special Collections.)

Religion

Religious institutions also figured significantly in Nashville's black metropolis throughout the late nineteenth and early twentieth centuries. Before the Civil War Nashville's African American community used quasi-independent churches such as Capers Colored Methodist (1832), First Colored Baptist Mission (1848), First Colored Christian (Disciples of Christ) Church (1855), and Central Baptist Church's African Mission (1861) as centers for religious life.[22] As in many other African American communities, these churches were also utilized as schools, meeting halls, and places for social interaction. While these functions continued after Emancipation, they also grew to include meetings and conventions that informed congregations on issues that affected their civil and moral rights. According to the historian Bobby Lovett, "Meetings involving black politics and movements for civil rights and suffrage always took place in the churches."[23] Additional evidence that points to the role of the church as a center of African American community life following Emancipation could be seen in the streets of Nashville's "Black Belt," where the number of independent black churches grew almost eightfold, from eight to sixty in just fifteen years. As an important venue free from white control, the churches became a place where African Americans could assemble freely, vote for officers, and experience other social and political freedoms unavailable to them in Nashville's mainstream community.

These religious institutions also contributed to Nashville's prominence as a home to numerous African American religious publishing houses, placing its members at the heart of cultural and intellectual production within the post-Reconstruction South and also the nation. Established in Bloomington, Illinois, in 1884, the American Methodist Episcopal Sunday School Union and Publishing House relocated to Nashville in 1886. The first in America to publish Sunday school literature by African Americans, the A.M.E. Sunday School Union and Publishing House produced *Teacher's Quarterly Magazine, Scholar's Quarterly, Juvenile Lesson Paper,* and the *Gem Lesson Paper,* periodicals with a combined circulation of nearly 150,000.[24] Unlike the American Methodist Episcopal Zion Publishing House and the Colored Methodist Episcopal Publishing House, two other influential nineteenth-century African American–owned religious publishers, the A.M.E. Sunday School Union and Publishing House extended its focus beyond religious subject matter to include secular works.[25] Among the numerous texts that exemplified the size and scope of issues relevant to black history and culture were Lucretia H. Coleman's *Poor Ben: A Story of Real Life* (1890) and Charles S. Smith's *Glimpses of Africa, West and Southwest Coast* (1895).[26] According to Donald Joyce, the diverse offerings of this publisher exhibited the willingness of its executives to address "the spiritual and the intellectual needs" of its members.[27]

When R. H. Boyd established the National Baptist Publishing Board in 1896, he could not possibly have imagined that it would grow to become the largest and most successful African American publishing company in the world. The question of whether to create an African American Baptist Publication Society was posed in September 1891, when members representing three Baptist organizations from across the country—the Baptist Foreign Mission Convention, the American Baptist Convention, and the National Baptist Educational Convention—met in Louisville to discuss the decision by the American Baptist Publication Society (Philadelphia) to withhold articles written by African American authors. Because the African American groups were splintered, consensus on the creation of a distinct African American publishing venture, and its organization, could not be agreed on. Increasingly at odds with the white-dominated Philadelphia Society and the American Baptist Home Mission Society in New York, organizations that dismissed the idea of a "Negro Baptist book concern" in the following years, the National Baptist Convention, the National Baptist Educational Convention, and the Baptist Foreign Mission Convention united in 1895 to form the National Baptist Convention of the United States of America.[28]

Following its creation, many National Baptist Convention members acknowledged that the white-run American Baptist Publication Society had performed admirably in "Christianizing and Evangelizing the Negro Baptists of the South" and were hesitant to engage in a "mercenary, commercial or manufacturing object." Engaging such opposition within the recently united organization, the Reverend Richard Henry Boyd, a former slave who, influenced by Booker T. Washington and his ideals of individualism, would become one of the country's leading businessmen, argued that to be viewed as a "distinct and separate denomination," African American Baptists needed religious literature suited to their "peculiar needs," meaning literature written, published, and printed by African Americans.[29] Though some internal resistance remained among African American members of the National Baptist Convention between those with connections to white Baptists, their institutions, and their work, and those supporting independent representation for African American Baptists, Boyd secured constitutional revisions that sanctioned a Printing Committee and enabled the National Baptist Publishing Board of the National Baptist Convention to begin operations in 1896. (See figure 5.)

Boyd believed that Nashville, well established as the South's premier religious publishing center, provided a central location from which his operation could access large, urban, African American populations across the South. Despite the reticence of white Nashville lenders, who doubted that an African American could effectively organize such an enterprise or maintain the scholarship needed to sustain such a venture, Boyd secured financing with various letters of credit that identified his holdings in Texas and his wife's estate as collateral.

Due to the time involved in creating a series of African American literature by African American authors and editors, Boyd initially reprinted Sunday School literature from white Baptists and relied on white printers

FIGURE 5 Reverend Dr. R. H. Boyd, founder and head of the National Baptist Publishing Board. (Courtesy of the R. H. Boyd Company.)

to create his first series. This decision exacerbated tensions between the National Baptist Publishing Board, the American Baptist Home Mission Society of New York, and the American Baptist Publication Society of Philadelphia because it created competition that rendered their southern publication houses, located in Atlanta and Dallas, unnecessary. However, Boyd's early relationship with white printers was largely dictated by economics. Following the failure of two white-owned businesses, the Enterprise Printing Company and the Southern News, Boyd obtained two presses, one paper cutter, binding boards, and considerable printing resources needed to bolster his business. These economic advantages also enabled Boyd to establish the ideological position behind his organization, one that enabled African Americans to determine the subject matter of their publications and to control the extent of their distribution, maneuvers that Boyd believed would free African American religious institutions from white influence and control.

When the National Baptist Publishing Board established their modern facility in downtown Nashville at the corner of Second Avenue North and Locust Street in 1898, it was widely acknowledged as the publishing and book concern for the entire population of African American Baptists of the United States.[30] (See figure 6.)

In a matter of years Du Bois noted that the board's millions of periodicals had moved beyond the "length and breadth of the American continent" to reach "the islands, and across the great waters, in the dark continent of Africa, Asia and Europe."[31] Among dozens of periodicals published was the *National Baptist Union* and the *National Baptist Hymnal*. As a means of increasing profits and as a way of attracting a broader readership, the National Baptist Publishing Board also began book printing and binding in 1899. In addition to religious subject matter that included biographies, church histories, collected sermons, essays, and papers, secular offerings were as varied as John H. Holman's *Methods of Histology and Bacteriology* (1903), R. H. Boyd's *The Separate or "Jim Crow" Car Laws* (1909), J. W. Grant's *Out of the Darkness; or, Diabolism and Destiny* (1909), and James H. Thomas's *Sentimental and Comical Poems* (1913). Boyd even helped finance the novelist Sutton Griggs's first work, *Imperium in Imperio* (1899).[32]

The unparalleled success of the National Baptist Publishing Board contributed to Boyd's reputation as a visionary and a race man. James M. Frost, pastor, founder, and first secretary for the Sunday School Board of the Southern Baptist Convention, called Boyd's efforts to separate from northern white Baptists "a distinct movement of Negroes, by Negroes and for Negroes—a great vision born of a vision for the future, and a commendable effort at self-help and self-improvement." He considered Boyd's creation of the National Baptist Publishing Board to be "unsurpassed by any institution or enterprise among [African American] people . . . in its influence and power for the uplift of the Negro race."[33] This success allowed Boyd affiliate himself with numerous civic and professional organizations in Nashville and to expand creative and business interests in the city to include founding the One-Cent Savings Bank and Trust Company,

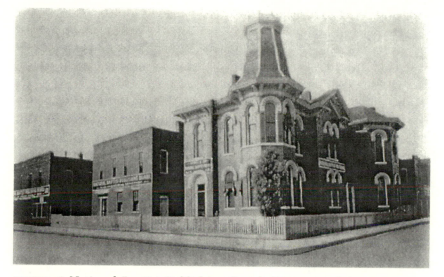

FIGURE 6 National Baptist Publishing Board. (Courtesy of the R. H. Boyd Company.)

the *Nashville Globe*, the National Baptist Church Supply Company, and the Union Transportation Company. Boyd, like so many of Nashville's New Negroes, played an important leadership role within his community and was an ardent agitator for social and economic independence among African Americans nationwide.

Following a rift among members of the National Baptist Convention over ownership of the National Baptist Publishing Board, the Sunday School Publishing Board of the National Baptist Convention, USA was established in 1915 as a separate publishing entity in Nashville. To house their organization, members selected a plot at the intersection of Fourth Avenue and Cedar Street. The location, and the new venture, were significant for a number of historical reasons. The new six-story facility was erected on a site where the Old Commercial Hotel once stood. The antebellum hotel was built by slave hands and was a popular gathering point for slave owners and traders, who enjoyed ready access to the city's primary slave auction block. The irony of past and present was not lost on McKissack & McKissack, the African American architectural firm that designed the new building, the African American contractor responsible for overseeing the construction, or the African American laborers working on the project, many of whom incorporated bricks from the previous structure into the new one. When it was completed, the new Baptist organization began operation in an $800,000 facility widely recognized as one of the "most modern and best-equipped publishing houses" in America.[34] While its primary focus was publishing Sunday School literature, the board also produced a number of books to support Baptist clergy and to record the history of African American Baptists. A true race venture from beginning to end, the establishment of the Sunday School Publishing Board of the National Baptist Convention, USA, was another African American business venture that provided professional opportunities for its community and stood as a symbol of progress and possibilities in a new century.

Economics

Resourcefulness was not an uncommon trait among Nashville's New Negroes, who understood the need for economic independence that could sustain racial progress independent of white assistance or interference. Because northerners occupied Nashville during most of the Civil War, African Americans were able to work in a range of skilled positions formerly closed to them. By 1868 signs of economic emancipation among the city's African Americans was notable enough to garner an article in the white *Nashville Press and Times* newspaper, which featured twenty-nine African American men whose "industry, economy, and acquisitiveness" symbolized the success of their community following slavery.[35] Twenty-five of the twenty-nine men were former slaves who, just years removed from bondage, had accumulated an aggregate wealth of nearly $300,000. Many of them, such as William Sumner, who paid taxes on $80,000, were property owners. Among their numbers were pastors, barbers, blacksmiths, wheelwrights, carpenters, grocers, saloon operators, a florist, and a man named Randall Brown, who was an assistant overseer of the Street Department and a candidate for county commissioner. During Reconstruction, when Republicans enjoyed political control, other articles reported on similar economic advances among Nashville's African Americans who excelled in freight, transport, and real estate industries.[36] However, as Democrats regained state and local governmental control, they forced the city's African American population into marginal spaces, causing them to lose broad political support and a white business base that had spurred African American economic growth in previous years.

In response Nashville's African Americans turned to "secret societies" that enabled their community members to "discuss progressive issues in detail, set and maintain codes of ethics, and develop strategies for black uplift."[37] Among the early organizations were the Negro Masonic Lodge (1865), the Sons of Relief (1869), the Colored Benevolent Society (1865), and more visible business organizations such as the Nashville Barbers Association (1865) and the Nashville Colored Mechanics Association (1866). Such groups provided forms of power through which Nashville's New Negroes defined themselves, and they paved the way for later and more public organizations like the National Negro Business League (1903), Nashville Urban League (1912), Nashville Board of Trade (1912), the NAACP (1919), and the Commission of Interracial Cooperation (1920).[38] These organizations helped Nashville's African American community pool intellectual and financial resources to establish many of the city's first African American–owned and –operated businesses.

Signs of steady economic progress following Reconstruction are evident in the pages of Nashville's 1878 City Directory, the first to include African Americans in its business pages. While many of these men and women perform unskilled labor common to the period, a significant amount work in skilled positions as tailors, blacksmiths, and railway men. There is also a growing professional class of doctors, lawyers, saddle and harness makers, ice dealers, undertakers, and owners of hostelries, restaurants, feed stores, grocery stores, and saloons.[39]

By 1900 the presence of African American professionals and artisans had risen significantly. Among the classified ads that year are sixteen doctors, fifteen attorneys, twenty nurses, two building contractors, three undertakers, and a host of shoemakers, machinists, florists, and boardinghouse operators. More than half of the city's restaurants and barbershops are owned and operated by African Americans. The number of African Americans working in skilled positions had also escalated dramatically and ranges from stone and brick masons to plumbers, carpenters, and electrical contractors. Notable among these artisans is the firm of McKissack & McKissack, founded by brothers Moses and Calvin in 1905 and to date the oldest minority-owned architectural and engineering company in the United States.[40] As these figures indicate, Nashville's African American community benefited from access to industrial and traditional education, generated economic growth despite inequalities, and created business opportunities indicative of the city's burgeoning middle class.

While there were a number of service-oriented businesses in operation and a growing professional class to meet the community's needs, the banking industry became a prominent feature of the business landscape. Opening in 1865, the Freedmen's Bank of Nashville was one of thirty-three established by Congress in former slave states and was the most successful of Tennessee's four branches.[41] Although the bank president was white, its manager and one of its cashiers were black, and a number of Nashville's

African American citizens served as trustees. After the collapse of the Freedmen's Banks in 1874, Nashville's New Negroes saw the need for more sustainable "capital-producing institutions" within their community and began discussing plans for a suitable replacement.[42]

In 1904 the One-Cent Savings Bank, now Citizens Savings Bank and Trust Company, became the first minority-owned bank in Tennessee and the first in the South to qualify as a trust company capable of managing and administering estates as a guardian.[43] In the poorly regulated and volatile economic climate of the late nineteenth and early twentieth centuries, banking often proved an unstable venture. The prospect of success for African American banking institutions was compounded, however, by a number of factors: limited financial capital, a dearth of management experience, the lack of a strong and expanding business base, competition with white banks for African American business, community confidence, and discrimination. Facing such obstacles, African American entrepreneurs found banking a particularly difficult path toward established financial independence.

Despite these challenges, R. H. Boyd, Preston Taylor, and James C. Napier served as organizers and officers of the venture, which sought to restore faith in deposits and savings among Nashville's African American community members while also encouraging them to invest their money in black businesses. "It will be impossible for the colored people of this country, or their sons or daughters, ever to receive proper recognition or respect that an intelligent people desire until we convince the world that we have the means, ability, and confidence in each other to launch and command large and laudable financial enterprises among ourselves."[44] Nashville's African American community answered the call to support local African American institutions; in the first five months deposits soared from $5,325.27 on opening day to an impressive $175,670.85.[45] While they intended to teach their customers the value of frugality, organizers also wanted to instill confidence of the race in itself.

The bank's directors used race pride as a means to attract additional business from African Americans in the city who still banked with white-owned institutions. They argued that "a number of large white banks, if the truth were known, would prefer not to be bothered with the small deposits of these Negro patrons," and warned that "polite treatment" by white clerks did not translate into respect beyond the institution walls. Concerned One-Cent executives argued that the decision of African Americans to continue banking with white institutions would in fact have a detrimental effect on the community as a whole: "The business white men of this and other Southern cities have far more respect for a Negro that will give his patronage to his own institutions than they have for the Negro who both by words and actions show[s] that he prefers not to deal with his own people." At the stockholder meetings bank executives celebrated the bank's unparalleled success as evidence of the community's economic viability and emphasized community over profit: "Our officials are paid no lucrative salaries—in fact, [the venture] is a labor of love."[46] The One-Cent Savings Bank enjoyed continued prosperity, even surviving the economic collapse of 1929 that claimed so many banking institutions (black and white), through its conservative lending policies and by encouraging systematic savings. Today it is the oldest continuously operating minority-owned bank in the United States.

The One-Cent Savings Bank was one of many significant African American businesses nestled between City Hall and the state capitol, in an area commonly referred to as "Black Wall Street." This cluster of economic activity was located just blocks from the white banking, insurance, and securities firms that established turn-of-the-century Nashville's reputation as the "Wall Street of the South." For several decades this district came to symbolize the pride and progress of the city's African American community. Included among its many businesses were the Colored YMCA; Lincoln and Star theaters; Citizens Saving and Trust Company Bank; Sunday School Publishing Board of the National Baptist Convention; the R. H. Boyd Building, which housed the *Nashville Globe* offices; two Masonic halls; a life insurance company; the Young People's Economic League office; a pharmacy; several boardinghouses, pool halls, barber shops, dry cleaners, groceries, and restaurants; and a number of professional offices that housed real estate agents, attorneys, undertakers, dentists, nurses, and medical doctors.[47] While such a concentration of establishments could be found outside of Nashville, those located along Fourth Avenue constitute a demographic with enough entrepreneurship and capital to rival better known urban African American economic centers such as Parrish Street in Durham, North Carolina, and the Greenwood community in Tulsa, Oklahoma.

The importance of Nashville as a symbol of social and economic uplift for African Americans was highlighted in a *Crisis* article from the period. Among its points of emphasis were the city's eighty-seven African American churches, multiple publishing houses, educational facilities, banks, a hospital, and the "considerable portion of the skilled labor [conducted] by colored men."[48] These outlets provided the leadership and financial resources that enabled the city's African American community to achieve a number of national firsts, including the National Negro Doll Company (1904); the establishment of Fisk's Negro Carnegie Library (1905); the creation of Hadley Park, the nation's first city-owned park for African Americans (1912); and the nation's first African American Girl Scout troop (1924).[49]

Politics

As early as 1865 African African delegates (many of whom had participated in the first national convention one year earlier) from Nashville participated in the first State Colored Men's Convention to discuss their role in Reconstruction. When their right to vote was not secured a year later, Nashville's African American leaders were among those responsible for the formation of Tennessee's National Equal Rights League chapter. This organization staged daily demonstrations before the General Assembly chamber until the governor signed a bill granting Tennessee's African American citizens the right to vote. When Nashville's African American community cast its votes in the 1868 election, it overwhelmingly supported Ulysses S. Grant, establishing a base of Republican support that endured for decades. Unfortunately, despite brief representation in the General Assembly by Republicans Sampson W. Keeble (1873–75) and Thomas A Sykes (1881–83), the influence of Nashville's African Americans in political affairs was severely limited because, just months after the presidential election, conservatives regained control of the state government and began repealing legislation enacted by the Radical Republicans.[50] In addition to repealing laws that challenged the segregation of railroads and limited Klan activity, Democrats levied a poll tax and passed laws preventing interracial mixing in schools and in marriage.

Despite such setbacks Nashville was not without its New Negro leadership in politics, and constant efforts to improve the political status of its African American citizenry were carried out by leaders such as James C. Napier, a Nashville native who attended Oberlin College before receiving his law degree from Howard University in 1872.[51] Even before he obtained his law degree, Napier led a delegation from Tennessee's State Convention of Colored Men to Washington in 1870 to petition Congress and President Grant for the removal of Tennessee's conservative government. One year later they petitioned to "establish a national school system and to pass special legislation to enforce southern compliance with the Fifteenth Amendment."[52] Following the completion of his law degree, Napier married Nettie Langston, daughter of a future Republican congressman, John Mercer Langston, which strengthened his political ties and assured his prominence in the highest African American social circles. Their wedding was considered the "biggest social event in nineteenth-century black Washington."[53] Despite the opportunities available to him through his familial ties, Napier remained in Nashville, where he was an active political figure.

Napier served five terms on the Nashville City Council, from 1878 to 1886, during which time he became the first African American to preside over the council. He helped African Americans find work as teachers in Nashville's black public schools and played a role in the organization of Nashville's first African American fire engine company. Napier's effectiveness eventually led him to the White House, where he served as register of the U.S. Treasury under President William Taft. Among his many business ventures, he cofounded the One-Cent Savings Bank, served as the head of the National Negro Business League and Negro Board of Trade, and was a board member of both Fisk and Howard universities. A longtime friend of Booker T. Washington, Napier worked tirelessly to include African Americans in the political process and battled for equal treatment under the law through active protest and resistance.

The Arts

Despite the fact that research into Nashville's intellectual life, particularly its African American literary community, has largely been ignored by local and national scholars, the city served as a vital training ground for African American artists and intellectuals during the late nineteenth and early twentieth centuries. Although Nashville served as his home only from 1885 to 1888, it was a location that forever shaped the life and work of W. E. B. Du Bois. It is during his years as a student at Fisk University that Du Bois truly comes of age—developing an appreciation for music, philosophy, and economics but also experiencing his first sexual encounter and his first confrontation with the color line. [54]

Another prominent New Negro working in Nashville was Sutton Elbert Griggs. Griggs moved to Nashville in 1893, soon after graduating from Richmond Theological Seminary in Virginia, to assume the position of corresponding secretary of the National Baptist Convention (a merger between the American Baptists and the Southern Baptist Convention) and pastor of the First Baptist Church of East Nashville. Griggs's work as a minister remained his primary focus during his early years in Nashville, and in that capacity he was exposed to a number of influential African American professionals, such as fellow Texan Dr. R. H. Boyd, who encouraged

Griggs to expand his creative and political interests. Among the ventures Griggs pursued was the creation of the Orion Publishing Company, one of the few African American–owned publishing outlets in the country, from which he published, promoted, and distributed pamphlets, essays, and books that addressed a range of African American concerns, ranging from economic and social oppression to immigration and nationalism. Orion became a vehicle from which Griggs debated the race question with African American community members throughout the South and even in national arenas, where his work challenged the stereotypes and plantation literature of white writers such as Thomas Dixon Jr. and Thomas Nelson Page. A member of the Niagara movement and one of the few African American novelists publishing during the period, Griggs established a national reputation as a race leader and intellectual dedicated to serving the African American community at all socioeconomic levels.[55]

Media

Among the signs of a burgeoning literate community of African Americans in Nashville was its proliferation of news and literary outlets. Nashville's African American community exchanged information through a wide range of secular and religious publications that blended cultural and political issues of the day. Most prominent among these were the *Weekly Pilot* (1878–79), *Educator and Reformer* (1879–81), *Herald and Pilot* (1873–80), *Colored Cumberland Presbyterian* (1890s–1920s), *National Baptist Union Review* (1899–), and a number of lodge and fraternal papers, including the *Phythian News* and the *Royal Banner*; university publications such as the *Fisk Herald* (1883–) and Roger Williams University's *Rogerana* (1893–1906); and several mainstream newspapers with heavy circulation, such as the *Colored Tennessean* (1865–67), the *Palladium* (1883–1909), the *Tennessee Star* (1887–91), the *Citizen* (1893–1905), and the *Clarion* (1896–1935). As I examine in chapter 5, Nashville's most enduring African American daily, the *Globe* (1905–60) emerged as a platform to protest the city's streetcar segregation law yet endured to succeed most of the country's African American newspapers in duration, including Indianapolis's *Freeman*.[56]

THE GLOBE

Born out of protest, the *Globe* provided a vital forum for Nashville's New Negroes to engage prominent local and federal issues. Within three years of its creation, the *Globe* expanded its circulation to become the most widely read African American newspaper in the state. Soon after, it was recognized as an important voice of progressivism throughout the South, one that boasted readers from well beyond the region, to include Washington, California, Massachusetts, and Rhode Island. The *National Baptist Union* was among many outlets that recognized the *Globe's* increasing popularity, calling it "no doubt one of the greatest, most wide-awake, and best circulated, secular papers in the United States."[57]

Like many African American newspapers, the *Globe* included prominent national and international news reports from the Associated Negro Press and exchanged stories with other African American papers from around the country. In addition to news and editorial commentary, the paper contained sections reporting births, deaths, weddings, sports, and the latest society events. In contrast to most African American newspapers, however, the *Globe* remained fiercely independent in tone and content, a quality it enjoyed thanks in no small part to the independent financial resources of its publisher, the prominent entrepreneur Dr. Richard Henry Boyd. The credible talents of its leading editor, Henry Allen Boyd, the publisher's son, further shaped the paper.

The *Globe* proved invaluable to the development of Nashville's New Negro for a number of reasons. In its pages African Americans acquired a voice that challenged the judgmental renderings of African Americans so prevalent in Nashville's white media. News reports highlighted African American achievements locally and abroad, providing a sense of racial solidarity. Other articles and opinion pieces offered Nashville's New Negroes an opportunity for self-reflection and enabled them to find a renewed sense of racial pride. Advertising space allowed access to black-owned goods and services, ads that were buried in or absent from white publications, promoting self-improvement and championing economic independence. The survival of the *Globe* despite the economic pitfalls that accompanied such business ventures reveals the dedication of Nashville's New Negroes to media as a necessary component in their struggle for civil rights and of a defiant presence that refused to be silenced by an established and resourceful white community.

As these examples illustrate, Nashville created conditions for African Americans unlike any in the South, even if in part it replicated aspects of several urban centers. The following chapters examine more closely the literary and cultural factors that influenced the development of black modernity in Nashville. They reveal how the New Negro established precedents for black militancy and enabled southern African Americans to maintain resistance to white supremacy at critical junctures during an era Rayford Logan notably termed "the nadir of the Negro's status in American society."[58]

3 / Soul Searching: W. E. B. Du Bois in the "South of Slavery"

The white south is the most reactionary modern social organization which exists today in the civilized areas of the world.

—W. E. B. DU BOIS, "HO! EVERYONE THAT THIRSTETH," MAY 26, 1958,
W. E. B. DU BOIS PAPERS, MS 312, SPECIAL COLLECTIONS AND
UNIVERSITY ARCHIVES, UNIVERSITY OF MASSACHUSETTS
AMHERST LIBRARIES

William Edward Burghardt Du Bois epitomized the qualities that would come to be called the New Negro, and the fact that some of his major work antedates the consolidation of that concept is evidence that his work was as influential as it was prescient. He was born in Great Barrington, Massachusetts, on February 23, 1868. At just fifteen Du Bois began an intellectual career that spanned nearly a century. After graduating as valedictorian from Great Barrington High School, he attended Fisk University in Nashville, where he completed his Bachelor of Arts degree in 1888. Du Bois then returned to Massachusetts, where he earned another bachelor's (1890) and a master's degree (1891) from Harvard. Following two years in which he studied at the University of Berlin (1892–94), he became the first African American to earn a PhD at Harvard (1895), with his dissertation, "The Suppression of the African Slave Trade to the United States of America, 1638–1870."[1]

Du Bois held a number of teaching appointments during his lifetime. His first experience was at Wilberforce University in Ohio, where he taught for two years while completing his doctoral dissertation. His second appointment was at the University of Pennsylvania (1896–97), where his proximity to African American urban residents facilitated his much-lauded sociological study *The Philadelphia Negro* (1899).[2] Du Bois again traveled south in 1897 to accept a position at Atlanta University, where he taught history and economics for thirteen years, during which time he published numerous articles and book manuscripts on African American life, including his best-known work, *The Souls of Black Folk*, published in 1903.[3] After many years in New York he returned to Atlanta University in 1934, where he spent a decade as the department chair of sociology. Among the highlights from these years were his publication of *Black Reconstruction in America, 1860–1880* and his creation of the academic journal *Phylon* (1940).[4]

During the early years of the twentieth century Du Bois's pursuits were not confined to academia. In 1905 he helped found the Niagara Movement, an important civil rights organization that doggedly protested inequalities based on race. Though the Niagara Movement's activities were short-lived, its work paved the way for the creation of the NAACP in 1909, where Du Bois served as the lone African American member on the board of directors. In addition to his board duties, he served as the director of research and publicity and, perhaps most notably, as the editor of *Crisis*, the organ of the NAACP and an important vehicle for agitation of the nation's "race question." Though Du Bois left the NAACP in 1934, he remained in contact with the organization, even returning in 1944 for a four-year stint as its director of special research.

In 1961 Du Bois abandoned his American citizenship and moved to Ghana, where he died just two years later, on August 27, 1963. His was a life of unparalleled success. He sought many platforms as an activist and scholar, from his years as an adversary of Booker T. Washington to his commitment to socialism and, ultimately, to communism. He used these ideological positions to focus international attention on issues of race. Herbert Aptheker's bibliography of Du Bois's published works contains 1,975 citations.[5] This compendium of books, essays, novels, and poetry is a daunting representation of Du Bois's unyielding commitment to his people and to the improvement of racial relationships across the globe.

That scholars have written extensively on Du Bois's life and his voluminous writings goes without saying. While numerous publications have examined his experiences in Berlin, his years at Harvard, and his prolific achievements in Atlanta and New York, critical attention to his years in Nashville has been limited to brief mentions or footnotes or has been sketched out in the pages of biographies and historical surveys. This scholarship, however, neglects a formative period of time in Du Bois's life to which his later work is indebted. Despite what Houston Baker calls the "restless turnings and abrupt shifts" that mark a life spanning nearly one hundred years, Du Bois's writing reveals a consistent and deep admiration for his time at Fisk and for his work among the South's rural black population.[6] A close look at his Nashville years suggests how strongly the kind of African American community that developed there during the Jim Crow era helped forge and foster in Du Bois the perspective and sensibility that would be codified as New Negro.

Modeling Artistry

To examine how America's most influential New Negro develops in the South, we first should understand how Du Bois's northern upbringing caused him to experience physical and spiritual isolation. Du Bois recalled as a child little that set him apart from others his age. Despite being the sole African American student attending the local school, he claimed to have felt "no sense of difference or separation from the main mass of townspeople." African Americans numbered a slight "25, certainly no more than 50" in a community of five thousand, and according to Du Bois, they shared a similar system of values and mores that connected African Americans to their white neighbors. Among his friends Du Bois counted a number of white students from established families, such as Jim Parker, whose father was a watchmaker; Boardman Tobet, a jeweler's son; and Ned Hollister, whose father owned a local grocery store.[7]

While Du Bois recognized social distinctions between African Americans and whites based on longevity or economic standing in the community, he felt that little or no significance was placed on skin color. He even shared the prejudices of the white majority, castigating Great Barrington's Irish population, a community that found itself distanced from other townspeople by virtue of its religion and "monopoly of house service." So seamless did his ties to Great Barrington's whites appear to be that Du Bois confidently asserted, "[The Irish] did not belong to my traditional community," which believed that the "dirty, stinking Irish slums were something that the Irish themselves preferred and made."[8]

Only when he reached high school age did the "veil of color" descend upon Du Bois and begin to alter his perception of the larger world around him.[9] His recognition of race came at an age when any physical difference could be construed as an abnormality or become grounds for social ostracizing. While exchanging visiting cards with his New England elementary school classmates, Du Bois's realization of color "bursts" upon him in an instant, when "a tall, newcomer" refused to exchange visiting cards with him "peremptorily, with a glance," during a classroom gathering. This stinging rejection prompted a range of emotions in Du Bois, whose inward responses vacillated among anger, shame, and resentment. Despite his youth and striking similarity to his white classmates with regard to "heart and life and longing," he recognized a separation that had always existed but remained undefined until that moment. In an effort to quantify the unspoken impediment between his own racial consciousness and that of white students, Du Bois drew on the meta-phorical qualities of a "vast veil" to illustrate the distinction.[10] Because he was unwilling to challenge this racial barrier as a teen, he withdrew emotionally, choosing to live with his thoughts "in a region of blue sky and great wandering shadows," an isolated and imaginative space unsul-lied by inequalities and obstacles.[11]

The sudden exclusion provided an epiphany for Du Bois, who disen-gaged from the northern community he had considered a haven. The incident became a catalyst for his burgeoning expression of double con-sciousness: "This sense of always looking at one's self through the eyes of others, of measuring one's soul by the tape of a world that looks on in amused contempt and pity. One ever feels his two-ness,—an American, a Negro; two souls, two thoughts, two unreconciled strivings; two warring ideals in one dark body, whose dogged strength alone keeps it from being torn asunder." While he later drew on this "second-sight" as a means of inspiration, Du Bois's immediate reaction was to view the rejection of his white community members as a negative, divisive moment. The "shadow" of that veil not only swept "across" his face, but it also dark-ened the picturesque portrait of his New England home, "where the dark Housatonic winds between Hoosac and Taghkanic to the sea."[12] The lyri-cal, rhythmic prose that once connoted an idyllic, free North romanti-cized for its beauty and remembered for its abolitionism was suddenly marred by the influence of color prejudice.

Du Bois began to feel "lonesome in New England" and realized, at the age of seventeen, that the "close cordial intermingling" he had previ-ously enjoyed with white students would "grow more restricted" with age. Acknowledging that the interminable lines of color had become more visible beyond the grounds of his public school, he wished to avoid the notoriety that accompanied black skin, a stigma that he believed would inevitably become "a matter of explanation or even embarrass-ment to [his] schoolmates" should their associations continue.[13] Rather than seeking "to tear down that veil, to creep through," he withdrew and viewed the "pale world" with contempt.[14]

Aware of the spiritual isolation in which he was living, Du Bois eagerly headed south. Ever since his school principal and early mentor Frank Hosmer encouraged him to take college preparatory courses, he had planned to continue his education beyond the secondary level. He had "blithely picked Harvard because it was oldest, and largest and most widely known" university, but he was aware that "even the mill owners' sons had aimed lower."[15] Even if his dream of Harvard materialized, Du Bois wondered what opportunities would be available to him in the North upon graduation. Sympathetic and probably aware of the social and economic realities facing African Americans in their community, Edward Van Lennep and the Reverend C. C. Painter, white men involved with the Congregational Church, concurred with Hosmer that Du Bois's interests were best served by choosing the post-Reconstruction South for his place of education and "field of work."[16] Through their efforts and the generous donation of four churches, each contributing twenty-five dollars a year for a scholarship, Du Bois was able to attend Fisk University.

Rather than celebrating the good fortune that enabled Du Bois to attend Fisk, his family members and other African American friends "resented the idea." According to Du Bois, their "Northern free Negro prejudice" caused them to view the episode as a regressive maneuver, and they "naturally revolted" against the possibility of his moving South "for education or for living." As one "Northern born and bred," he was expected to use his education to obtain employment equivalent to other educated youths in Great Barrington, who found work as bookkeepers, teachers, or other worthwhile professions. Du Bois, however, sensed something about his future that others had either failed to realize or were unwilling to admit. While the superficial cordiality of Great Barrington insulated him from overt racial prejudice, the veil he recognized from his youth still stood between himself, his white classmates, and a predominantly white community that "was not able to conceive" of an African American citizen occupying a position equivalent to that of recent white graduates eager to begin the task of earning a viable wage. For Du Bois conditions in Great Barrington had become untenable. He claimed that he had outgrown his home and that, like the "New England schoolmarm," he believed he was answering the "call of the black South."[17] Seemingly unaware of his conflicting desire to be connected to "his people" while distinguishing himself from African American southerners in a manner that revealed the prejudices of his northern upbringing, he eagerly began his journey to "the South of slavery, rebellion and black folk."[18]

It took little time for Du Bois to discover that this period in his life would change him immeasurably. In his first memoir, *Darkwater*, he separates his life into "four distinct parts"; the first of these begins with his arrival at Fisk, a period he terms "The Age of Miracles."[19] Prior to his arrival at Fisk, his interaction with African Americans had been limited. He recalled only "glimpses of the colored world" beyond his community, at places like Rocky Point on Narragansett Bay, where, during an annual picnic, he stared wide-eyed at "the whole gorgeous color gamut of the American Negro world." At Fisk, however, Du Bois found himself among some 450 African American students of a similar age and ambition in a central location. He was awestruck. It was not simply that he was exposed to "so many people of [his] own color" but that they represented "such various and extraordinary colors."[20]

Among the visual reflections recorded in his autobiographical accounts are those of Ortho Porter, "a brown boy from Bowling Green"; Ransom Edmondson, "olive-skinned with a mass of brown hair"; and Frank Smith, "a yellow dandy," whom he had just met but felt bound to "by new and exciting and eternal ties."[21] And while he recalled "pretty girls" from his days in Great Barrington, he was immediately taken by Fisk women such as Little Sissie Dorsey, "a golden fairy"; Mattie Nichol, who was a "dark cream"; and Lena Calhoun (the great-aunt of Lena Horne), whom, Du Bois believed, "no human being" could surpass in beauty.[22] They came from places like Shelbyville, Tennessee, Fort Smith, Arkansas, and Georgetown, Texas, and shared with him their stories about life in the postwar South. Almost immediately Du Bois recognized "a microcosm of a world and a civilization in potentiality" at Fisk. Invigorated by a new racial consciousness, he declared, "A new loyalty and allegiance replaced my Americanism: henceforward I was a Negro."[23]

Du Bois reveled in his academic studies at Fisk, and his work there became an essential building block for future endeavors. Fisk's resources were limited, but its environment suited Du Bois, who appreciated "the excellent and earnest teaching, the small college classes, the absence of distractions, either in athletics or society." He was particularly "impressed" by William Morris, the first African American faculty member at Fisk, whom he considered "as good as any of the whites"; Thomas Chase, who, despite his "ridiculously small laboratory," managed to teach Du Bois "something of science and life"; and Adam Spence, who was "a great Greek scholar by any comparison."[24] Du Bois would later benefit from his German studies with Professor Bennett while studying in Berlin and from his instruction in philosophy and ethics with Paul Cravath, who provided him excellent foundational support for his work with William James and George Palmer of Harvard. (See figure 7.)

The close-knit community at Fisk instilled a sense of solidarity in Du Bois, who "became a member of a closed racial group with rites and

FIGURE 7 W. E. B. Du Bois seated with classmates from Fisk University, ca. 1888. Source: W. E. B. Du Bois Papers (MS 312), Special Collections and University Archives, University of Massachusetts Amherst Libraries.

loyalties, with a history and a corporate future, with an art and philosophy."[25] Within this secure space he began to "arrange and build [his] program for freedom and progress among Negroes." He realized that formal training was vital to his generation's success and that educated African Americans had a responsibility to share their knowledge with the uneducated masses. Together they would work to eliminate segregation and separateness in American society. A new and invigorating racial pride enveloped Du Bois, eclipsing the spiritual and physical isolation he had once felt: "I replaced my hitherto egocentric world by a world centering and whirling about my race in America."[26]

Du Bois found an excellent forum for the expression of new ideas when he joined the editorial staff of the *Fisk Herald*. He had published a number of newspaper articles in his early teens, but his career as a writer and as an "impassioned orator" began at Fisk.[27] During his sophomore year he wrote a column entitled "Exchanges" for the *Fisk Herald*, where he reported on items of interest from student publications across the country. During his junior year he served as literary editor, contributing to the "Sharps and Flats" column, and from November 1887 until his graduation he assumed the duties of editor in chief. His work at the *Herald* allowed him to develop his craft and to represent an authentic voice for a generation of New Negroes.

During Du Bois's tenure the pages of the *Herald* openly addressed a number of critical issues, such as the formation of the Negro League: "Let the Negro be divided politically, but come together as brothers and right their wrongs when their rights have been unduly infringed upon. Let us have this league, but with some modifications"; the political organization of African American women: "The age of Woman is surely dawning, and we hope the ladies will take the tide at the flood"; professional responsibility: "Such a noble calling as teaching should not be taken hold of as an experiment. It is a profession"; and personal accomplishment: "Unbridled ambition is a great evil, yet the lack of sufficient ambition is just as great an evil."[28] He showed no favoritism or fear of rebuff. When Fisk faced financial hardship, he challenged African American leadership and the courting of white philanthropists by university administrators, clamoring, "The Negro is no longer a baby, he is a man and as such must provide for himself. If the leaders of the race cannot endow one Negro University in the South, then they cannot despise the ignorant masses who do not provide themselves with homes."[29] Under his supervision the *Herald* was not simply a forum that related gossip or followed social gatherings. It was a medium through which Du Bois engaged relevant social and political issues for African Americans and where he discovered the ability to inform, to challenge, and to inspire readers.

However, writing and speaking were not the only talents he honed during his time at Fisk. According to Du Bois, "No student ever left Fisk without a deep and abiding appreciation of real music."[30] He first heard African American folk songs sung by Hampton Institute singers at his Congregational church in Great Barrington; used to English hymns, often set to German music, he "seemed to recognize something inherently and deeply [his] own."[31] At Fisk, however, Du Bois not only heard the university's renowned Jubilee Singers in person but also had the opportunity to meet and sing with some of them. Encouraged by Professor Spence, he joined the Mozart Society, a singing group composed of the university's best singers. There he was exposed to a broad spectrum of musical genres, including traditional religious oratorios such as the *Messiah*, *Elijah*, and *Twelfth Mass*, works he believed "did great things for my education."[32] He fondly recalled singing the "Hallelujah Chorus" each year at commencement, a moment that often moved him to tears.

Even walking across campus, Du Bois was cognizant of the musical legacy that sustained the university during periods of financial hardship. He often admired "the great temple (Jubilee Hall) builded of these songs towering over the pale city," one that seemed to him "ever made of the songs themselves, and its bricks were red with the blood and dust of toil. Out of them rose for me morning, noon, and night, bursts of wonderful melody, full of the voices of my brothers and sisters, full of the voices of the past."[33] In the summertime, when Du Bois taught in the rural countryside beyond Nashville, he heard the sorrow songs sung "by those who made them and in the land of their American birth." He was deeply moved by the "rhythmic cadence of song—soft, thrilling, powerful, that swelled and died in our ears." Afterward he claimed that renditions by Hampton or Atlanta singers were but "second-hand, sung by youth who never knew slavery."[34] For Du Bois the music of Fisk was sacred and was embedded within his soul. When he traveled to Africa for the first time in 1923, he heard at a village on the outskirts of Monrovia, Liberia, music "liquid and sonorous"; it was "tricked out and expounded with cadence and turn."[35] He immediately sensed a familiar rhythm, "raised and carried by men's strong voices, while floating above in obbligato, come the high mellow voices of women," and connected the experience to his time in Tennessee, where the "soft melody and mighty cadences of Negro song fluttered and thundered."[36] After graduating from Fisk, Du Bois worked diligently to enhance the reputation of African American folk music, a medium he believed to be "mistaken and misunderstood" despite its place as "the singular spiritual heritage of the nation and the greatest gift of the Negro people."[37]

The protected vantage ground of Fisk could not, however, safeguard him from exposure to the realities of southern racism. He later wrote, "No one but a Negro going into the South without previous experience of color caste can have any conception of its barbarism." He learned much about life in the New South from his interactions with Fisk's student population, men and women who came from locations across the South where they had "faced mobs and seen lynchings; who knew every phase of insult and repression." Grandison Field was one of several Fisk students with whom Du Bois associated who "hated the white South" and carried a pistol wherever he traveled. When Du Bois asked about his weapon, Field quipped, "You don't need it often, but when you do, it comes in handy!"[38] Thoroughly segregated, and marred by racial violence, Nashville introduced him to "discrimination in ways of which [he] had never dreamed."[39]

Du Bois did not have to experience physical violence to feel the sting of southern racism. He once bumped into a white woman on a Nashville street. Though he tipped his hat in apology, the indignant woman was furious, causing a puzzled Du Bois to wonder if he had "transgressed the interracial mores of the South." Reeling with emotions, he tried to understand this purported offense: "Was it because I showed no submissiveness? Did I fail to debase myself utterly and eat spiritual dirt? Did I act as equal among equals? I do not know. I only sensed scorn and hate; the kind of despising which a dog might incur." This pivotal moment caused him to develop "a belligerent attitude toward the color bar." He realized that most southern whites did not distinguish between African Americans in terms of education or accomplishment. When the woman on the street looked at him she did not recognize an individual, only a representative of a despised race. Adopting a similar attitude toward whites for almost half a century, Du Bois imagined whites as invisible and "contrived to act as if totally unaware that [he] saw them or had them in mind."[40] If such encounters broadened his understanding of the New South's racial boundaries, they also made him eager to learn more about the color line beyond Nashville's urban landscape.

A Small World

The two summers Du Bois spent teaching in Tennessee's rural school system forever shaped his understanding of the race problem in America and profoundly influenced his seminal work, *The Souls of Black Folk*. The chapters that reveal the significance of his time in Nashville play a critical role in *Souls*. The fourth chapter, "Of the Meaning of Progress," begins Du Bois's journey into the Black Belt of the South, and "Sorrow Songs," the final chapter, exemplifies his efforts to craft a narrative capable of expressing the African American soul. A number of scholars have noted that the fourth chapter, like so many other pieces collected to form the body of Du Bois's 1903 manuscript, was published previously. The essay so often cited as the precedent for the chapter in *Souls*, "A Negro Schoolmaster in the New South," published in an 1899 issue of *Atlantic Monthly*, was, however, adapted from earlier narrative pieces written and published by Du Bois while he was still a Fisk student.[41] The first of these, "The Hills of Tennessee," appeared in an October 1886 edition of the *Fisk*

Herald, and the second, "How I Taught School," appeared one month later.[42] Together these pieces provide a window on Du Bois's initial foray into "the real South," where he lived and worked among Tennessee's rural "folk."[43] That he revised these earlier accounts and combined their narratives under a new heading for use in the fourth chapter of *Souls* does not obscure the profundity of his earlier works or the experiences of his youth. Rather these revisions reflect his overarching goal for a comprehensive text rather than a collection of essays that dealt individually with matters of race.

Peter Conn has noted that Du Bois's title "Of the Meaning of Progress" is meant to be ironic because "for America's black people, especially in the South, progress is a delusion."[44] Conn emphasizes the significance of the phrase "Once upon a time," which begins the fourth chapter, suggesting that Du Bois deliberately draws on the "narrative predictability and ideological tidiness" of the fairy tale in order to dismantle effectively that narrative form with his own, one that tells a tale of "disillusionment and death."[45] Such a decidedly bleak reading, however, not only misreads the importance of Du Bois's journey south but also misinterprets his observations regarding the current and future status of African American folk. In fact the phrasing for the chapter title was probably drawn from a passage in the first chapter of *Souls*, where Du Bois attempts to balance the negative consequences of living in an atmosphere of obdurate racial prejudice. Rather than succumbing to the effects of "self-questioning, self-disparagement, and lowering of ideals," he challenges African Americans to find "something of good,—the more careful adjustment of education to real life, the clearer perception of the Negroes' social responsibilities, and the sobering realization of the meaning of progress."[46]

To better understand how Du Bois prepares readers for his ensuing narrative, we must read carefully the epigraph at the beginning of chapter 4. From this informed vantage point he intends readers to view the Black Belt and its African American inhabitants. Although the two unique compositions that preface the fourth chapter come from different cultures, they share fundamental artistic elements that coalesce to form the foundation of his exploration into the souls of black folk. The first of these compositions is a passage from Friedrich Schiller's dramatic play *Die Jungfrau von Orleans* (1801):

Wilst Du Deine Macht verkunden,
Wahle sie, die frei von Sunden

Steh'n in Deinem ew'gen Haus!
Deine Geister sender aus!
Die Unsterblichen, die Reinen,
Die nicht fuhlen, die nicht weinen!
Nicht die zarte Jungfrau wahle
Nicht der Hirtin weiche Seele![47]

An astute historian, Schiller consciously crafted an ahistorical interpretation of Joan of Arc's life to challenge what he perceived to be a
denigrating treatment of her in Voltaire's *La Pucelle d'Orleans*. Schiller's
Jungfrau exalts Joan in a play that emphasizes "the dramatically effective
aspects of her struggle with her conscience." Perhaps no scene in the play
better represents Joan's inner struggle than the lines chosen by Du Bois
for his epigraph. Having bested her English rival Lionel on the field of
battle, Johanna is unable to kill him but unwilling to hold him captive.
Realizing that she has fallen in love with Lionel, Johanna allows him
to escape, but, tormented by the decision to let her enemy go, she hears
voices that "wind around [her] heart! Every force burning within [her]
bosom / They dissolve in tender yearning / Melt to tears with sadness
burning." During this moment in the play, where Johanna struggles to
find an explanation for her actions, we find the lines Du Bois selected for
use in his epigraph. Turning toward the sky Johanna pleads:

Wilt thou have thy might proclaimed,
Choose but those by sin unblamed,
Standing in thy long-lived home.
Thine own spirits send to roam,
Those most pure, those undying,
Those who know not feeling, crying!
Do not choose the tender maiden,
Shepherdess with soft heart laden.[48]

These powerful words capture a dramatic moment of human frailty and
emphasize mankind's never-ending search for purpose and meaning in
a life filled with complexities. It is likely that Du Bois believed Schiller's
words provided an appropriate and symbolic representation of the status
of southern African Americans struggling for their rights as citizens in
the post-Reconstruction era.

The second composition in Du Bois's epigraph comprises four bars of
music from an African American spiritual. (See figure 8.) While neither
the title of the song nor its lyrics are included with the four bars of music,

FIGURE 8 Musical excerpt from "My Way's Cloudy," in the fourth chapter of W. E. B. Du Bois, *The Souls of Black Folk* (Chicago: A. C. McClurg, 1903).

the song is identified in the final chapter of *Souls* as the composition "My Way's Cloudy."[49] One of the many standard works made famous by the Jubilee Singers, it is almost certainly a song Du Bois became familiar with as a Fisk student. The Jubilee Singers lead sheets indicate that the following lyrics accompany the melody included by Du Bois in his epigraph and were meant to be sung after each verse of the song without breaking time: "Oh breth-er-en, my way, my way's cloud-y, my way, Go / send them an-gels down, Oh! Breth-er-en, my way." Much like the lines from Schiller's play, these words depict human suffering. They too portray an individual at an impasse who openly acknowledges that culminating forces have caused his path (purpose) to become "cloudy." The weight of this individual's burden is emphasized by the melodic composition selected by Du Bois. Although it is not known which sheet music he copied these bars from, when compared to popular reproductions of the Jubilee Singers' music in pieces such as Marsh's *Story*, the bars he includes exhibit a more soulful approach to composition. Each version is written in the key of D in a slow four (four beats to a measure). However, insertions such as the use of a noted B for the second note in the first bar rather than the A found in Marsh's version causes the emphasis on "breth-er-en" to be more recognizable, and the accents make the notes more melodic. Subtle variations such as this highlight the weariness of those in a material world who look to spiritual guidance for relief. The speaker calls to "send them angels down," believing that there is justice in a world beyond his grasp—and so "to the promised land" he is "bound to go."[50]

Du Bois offers little explanation for his decision to include these two works as a preface for "Of the Meaning of Progress." Only a brief statement in the final chapter of *Souls* identifies "My Way's Cloudy" as a "song of groping." To understand why he selected these particular works as an epigraph for his fourth chapter and to see how they prepare readers for the story he is about to tell, we must reread the final chapter of *Souls* and examine another instance in which Du Bois pairs African American slave music with words from German folk culture. In this instance there is a brief piece of music accompanied by lyrics that identify the selection as the work song "Poor Rosy, Poor Gal":

> Poor Rosy, poor gal; Poor Rosy,
> poor gal; Rosy break my poor heart.
> heav'n shall a be my home.

Beyond the veneer of what he terms "evident dross" and "conventional theology" in the lines, Du Bois insists that there is a more poetic connection between those who sing "Poor Rosy" and the voices that utter the German folk phrase "Jetz geh i' an's brunele, trink' aber net" (Now I go to the little well but I don't drink). The underlying connection between the two becomes evident, according to Du Bois, when considering the words of an old woman who sang "Poor Rosy" during her days as a slave. Referring to the song, she claimed, "It can't be sung without a full heart and a troubled sperritt."[51] In this instance Du Bois pairs elements of German and African American folk culture to express fundamental human emotions that transcend cultural differences. While he conveys a similar message in the epigraph that precedes "Of the Meaning of Progress," he also pairs lines from German and African American culture to suggest that people with differences between them can use cultural elements to create a new space where transformational dialogue can take place between them.

To see how *Die Jungfrau* exemplifies this concept, we must reexamine the reason for Johanna's internal conflict. In the scene prior to the one in which she speaks the lines included in the epigraph, she insists that she is bound by heavenly oath "to slaughter with the sword each living thing, whate'er the God of battle faithfully doth send [her] way." The reason Johanna cannot conquer her enemy and fulfill her destiny when the opportunity arises is found in the duel between her and Lionel—the event responsible for her inner struggle—in which she "seizes him from behind by the plume of his helmet and tears the helmet down violently *so that his visage is laid bare.*"[52] Unseen, unrecognized, Lionel is just another enemy or obstacle. Once Johanna *sees* her perceived enemy, however, without the veil that stands between them, she recognizes a connection between herself and Lionel that transcends reason and historical relevance. It is through this deeper connection between Johanna and Lionel that one is able to identify Du Bois's larger purpose for pairing these works in his epigraph.

It is no coincidence that the veil is Du Bois's dominant metaphor in *Souls*. In "Forethought," he purposely "stepped within the Veil, raising it that [readers] might view faintly its deeper recesses . . . the passion of its human sorrow, and the struggle of its greater souls."[53] By raising the veil Du Bois asks those who live beyond it (whites) to set aside their prejudices and to see the depth and vitality of African Americans and their struggles within America's racist culture. In other words, individuals must be stripped of their prejudices and of their signifiers—as Johanna stripped Lionel of the helmet that identified him as an Englishman and an enemy—in order to create a spiritual bond between them. Du Bois asks white readers to no longer see individuals in terms of black or white, superior or inferior, or to view one race as a problem for which the other race must find a solution. He asks whites, as the dominant majority in turn-of-the-century America and as members of a race that overwhelmingly perceived themselves as moral and genetic superiors to African Americans, to join African Americans, an "invisible" people, on a journey to witness "progress," and to see the "soul" of another.

Robert B. Stepto argues that "prior to *The Souls*, the seminal journey in Afro-American narrative literature is unquestionably the journey North," culminating in a "quest for literacy as well as for freedom." In *Souls*, however, Du Bois inverts this paradigm by turning south on a journey that becomes a "narrative manifestation of Du Bois's cultural immersion ritual," one that reconfigures our understanding of African American life in the South.[54] No longer is a trip downriver emblematic of a slave's journey into hell. A descent into the South becomes a journey of enlightenment that reveals the true racial spirit of African Americans. Readers enter this narrative space through a Tennessee ritual ground that appears much like Du Bois encountered it when he arrived some twenty years earlier, only recently removed from New England and from Nashville's bustling urban environment. As Du Bois set foot in the Tennessee backcountry, the distance between the New South and the Old South collapsed: "I travelled not only in space but in time. I touched the very shadow of slavery. I lived and taught school in log cabins built before the Civil War. My first school was the second held in the district since Emancipation. I touched intimately the lives of the commonest of mankind—people who ranged from bare-footed dwellers on dirt floors, with patched rags for clothes, to rough, hard-working farmers, with plain, clean plenty."[55]

Du Bois's experiences take place in Wilson and DeKalb counties, two of sixteen middle Tennessee counties that make up the state's Central Basin. Often referred to as the "Garden of Tennessee" for its fertile soil and the variety of crops grown there, the Central Basin consistently provided the region's highest yields during the late nineteenth century.[56] The majority of landowners in Tennessee's Central Basin were white, and the relatively small number of whites who were engaged in tenancy (one-quarter) tended to be younger farmers who expected to own land in the future and enjoy the security such ownership provided. The prospects for Tennessee's African American farmers, however, were not as bright. While data for the period in which Du Bois writes are incomplete, agricultural studies show that as late as 1900, 76.5 percent of African American farmers in middle Tennessee engaged in tenancy to make a living. Louis Kyriakoudes notes that while the rate of white farm laborers declined statistically as they aged, indicating that these farmers achieved ownership, the number of African American farmers who achieve ownership "was extremely small." As a result African American tenant farmers worked much smaller plots than their white counterparts because landowners subdivided the land in a manner that "promote[d] intensive land use."[57] Often these small plots were located on the least suitable areas of white-owned farms. Though it was perhaps an unlikely setting for a narrative of discovery, this rural Tennessee community represented a way of life for many African American southerners, and it provided a unique perspective for outsiders who were unaware of or unconcerned with the realities of African American life in the South. (See figure 9.)

Among the most poignant moments in Du Bois's narrative are those focused on the travails of Tennessee's rural African American youth, whose education came in spurts, if ever, and materialized around a grueling agricultural cycle. When he arrived at Fisk, Du Bois commented on the limited yet adequate facilities. Nothing in his previous experience, however, could have prepared him for the conditions of his rural schoolhouse. Rather than the "neat little desks and chairs" of his New England classrooms or even the minimal resources he found at Fisk, Du Bois encountered a rural schoolhouse with no door, backless plank benches for students, a desk created from three boards, and a secondhand chair that "had to be returned every night" to the landlord's wife.[58] These additions to the log building were only, perhaps, a slight improvement over its previous state as a location for storing the white property-owners' corn. It was not the façade, however, that drew Du Bois's attention. It was the bright and eager students who filled the dilapidated space.

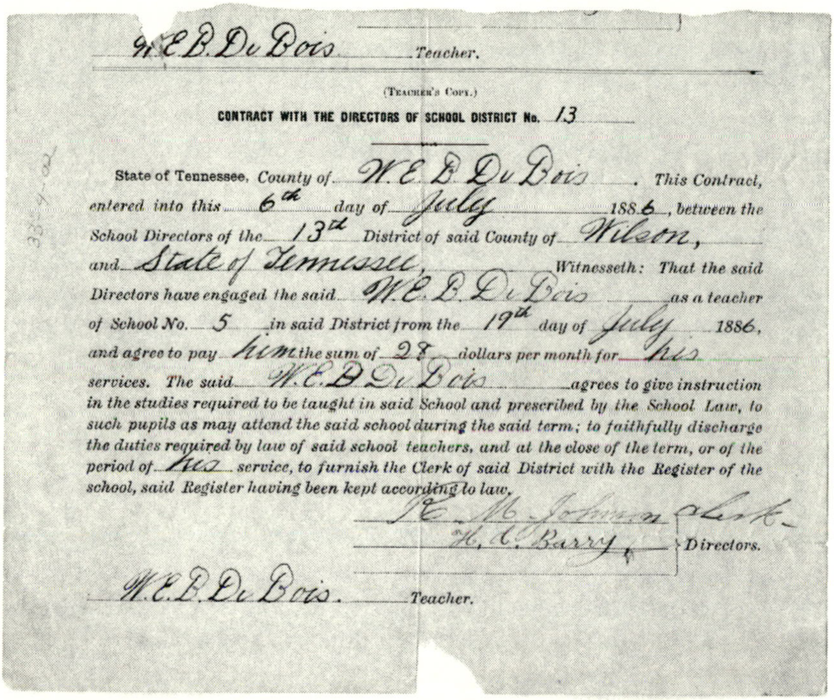

W. E. B. Du Bois Teacher.

(Teacher's Copy.)

CONTRACT WITH THE DIRECTORS OF SCHOOL DISTRICT No. 13

State of Tennessee, County of W. E. B. Du Bois. This Contract, entered into this 6th day of July 1886, between the School Directors of the 13th District of said County of Wilson, and State of Tennessee, Witnesseth: That the said Directors have engaged the said W. E. B. Du Bois as a teacher of School No. 5 in said District from the 19th day of July 1886, and agree to pay him the sum of 28 dollars per month for his services. The said W. E. B. Du Bois agrees to give instruction in the studies required to be taught in said School and prescribed by the School Law, to such pupils as may attend the said school during the said term; to faithfully discharge the duties required by law of said school teachers, and at the close of the term, or of the period of his service, to furnish the Clerk of said District with the Register of the school, said Register having been kept according to law.

R. M. Johnson Clerk
H. C. Barry } Directors.

W. E. B. Du Bois. Teacher.

FIGURE 9 Du Bois was eighteen when he signed this contract to teach in a rural Tennessee school for twenty-eight dollars a month. Source: W. E. B. Du Bois contract with the directors of school district no. 13, Wilson County (Tenn.), July 6, 1886, W. E. B. Du Bois Papers (MS 312), Special Collections and University Archives, University of Massachusetts Amherst Libraries.

Du Bois reveled in his opportunity to interact with a new racial group. Nervous as he awaited the arrival of his students, his anxiety increased when he heard "the patter of tiny feet down the dusty road." In vivid detail he recalls the "smooth black face and wondering eyes" of Fanny; the "jolly" 'Thenie and her bow-legged brother, Tildy, "a midnight beauty"; the "brown and yellow" Burke lads; the "hulking" Lawrences; and numerous others who crowded into the tiny classroom to assume their studies.[59] Though challenging, the work greatly interested Du Bois, who applied all the "additional zest and vigor which personal experience is apt to arouse." Many of the students' advances were elementary, such as when they "discovered" that they resided in the state of Tennessee or when they were "surprised" to learn that their hearts were located on the opposite side of their chest than they believed. Yet in more academic areas such as reading and arithmetic, Du Bois's students showed "rapid advancement."[60] Surprisingly not all of his instruction was well received by African American community members.

What might be termed a decidedly Old Negro element of the community began an "active campaign" against Du Bois for attempting to remove the vaunted "blue back" Webster's spelling book, circa 1857, from students' hands. Webster's book was viewed by many elder African Americans as not only the "'white folks'" book but also as the text responsible for teaching generations of African Americans "to read, write and ciphah" prior to Emancipation. Many older community members such as "Uncle" Moses believed that any alternative learning strategies employed by Du Bois "would be suicide." Du Bois, however, circumvented further controversy by announcing that students were being "promoted" out of the beloved reader.[61]

Du Bois knew that his students were capable of much greater intellectual accomplishments and that there was no reason to shield them from exposure to current methods. Having "broken down their stronghold" on the dated spelling book, he quickly introduced his students to the "word-method" and applied other contemporary learning techniques to their instruction.[62] The walls of the humble log cabin echoed with Cicero's *pro Archia Poeta* and other complex lessons he brought with him from Fisk.[63] The students showed an aptitude for higher learning and proved that they had the intellectual capacity to perform tasks beyond the menial and agricultural labor that constituted their daily lives. As the months of summer instruction passed, Du Bois noticed that he too had changed and that "whatever the pupils may have gained, it was little to what [he] acquired."[64]

In New England Du Bois envisioned himself not unlike the white northern schoolmarm whose talent and education was needed to uplift an African American majority from the depths of intellectual depravity. He viewed southern African Americans as a separate and distinct people with whom he shared no connection. This rift is evident in conversations he had before leaving Massachusetts in which he suggested that "they" (southern blacks) needed trained leadership and assistance obtaining privileges.[65] However, following months living in Tennessee's backcountry, Du Bois's writing exudes a very different tone: "We read and spelled together, wrote a little, picked flowers, sang, and listened to stories of the world beyond the hill."[66] As examples such as this reveal, there is no longer a distinction between Du Bois and these rural folk; neither he nor the children represent a peculiar "other." Du Bois is no longer an educator or an outsider; he is part of a community.

Du Bois's characterization of Tennessee's rural folk plays an important role in his effort to redefine African American identity within his narrative. He provides a lens through which to view a side of African American life that is normally seen only by those inside their community. Among these memorable portraits are those of Uncle Bird, a man who was "full of tales" and who, "with his children, berries, horses, and wheat," was "happy and prosperous," and Josie, who exudes " a certain fineness, the shadow of an unconscious moral heroism that would willingly give all of life to make life broader, deeper, and fuller for her and hers." Du Bois was particularly fond of Doc Burke, a "great, loud, thin Black" who forever worked the seventy-five acres he hoped to buy despite the mutterings of those who claimed he would certainly fail and that the "white folks would get it all." Du Bois also admired Doc's wife, "a magnificent Amazon, with saffron face and shining hair, uncorseted and barefoot," and their children, who were "strong and beautiful." The Burkes' home, like so many others in the community, reflects the dignified if simple bearing of its inhabitants. Though only a "one-and-a-half-room cabin," the home boasts "great fat white beds, scrupulously neat," and a kitchen that overflows with southern fare such as "fried chicken and wheat biscuit, 'meat' and corn pone, string beans and berries."[67]

In contrast to the racist stereotypes and caricatures so often drawn from rural African American life, Du Bois presents men and women with virtue, imagination, spirit, and purpose. Much like the work of the documentary artist Walker Evans, whose powerful black-and-white images of Hale County, Alabama, residents Bud Fields and Allie Mae Burroughs captured rural southern life during the Great Depression, Du Bois's narrative snapshots record the inner strength of ordinary African Americans enduring the extraordinary challenges of racism and peonage in the New South.

Yet despite his powerful narrative images, many critics have challenged Du Bois's experiential knowledge of rural African Americans and characterized him as incapable of portraying a side of African American life of which he was never a part. Among them is E. Franklin Frazier, who considers Du Bois a "finished product of the aristocratic intellectual culture of the last decade of the Nineteenth-Century," at home only within the "congenial environment" of New England and the "genteel intellectual tradition of Harvard."[68] Frazier claimed that despite his "short sojourn in the South" Du Bois "never was thoroughly assimilated into Negro life" and that "in spite of the way in which Du Bois has written concerning the masses, he has no real sympathetic understanding of them."[69]

Du Bois does not, however, belittle "folk," nor does he measure their success by white standards. As Bernard Bell has shown, Du Bois, like the Prussian philosopher Johann Gottfried von Herder, saw a distinction between "the folk and rabble on one hand and the folk and intellectuals on the other."[70] If he is an elitist, by education or access, there is certainly nothing elitist about his focus on the more rural elements of African American society. Nor is Du Bois's suggestion that, through the folk, described by Baker as those who create "beauty from wretchedness, intellectuals from victims of slavery, and viable institutions from rigidly proscribed patterns of action," Americans (white and black) have much to gain an elitist perspective.[71] We must remember that even when Du Bois speaks of a "talented tenth" he is speaking of "an aristocracy of talent and virtue who have themselves risen from the lower class instead of an aristocracy of birth and wealth."[72] His interaction with members of this rural Tennessee community supports his narrative strategy and frames his text in a manner that emphasizes the folk elements of African American society rather than focusing on an elite African American community. In doing so Du Bois lessens the distance between himself (as exemplary of the elite) and rural folk such as Josie, who are seeking "the great school in Nashville" but have yet to locate their path.[73] For African American readers the crux of his message is recognizing one's potential for greatness or success. Du Bois does not exclude someone based on circumstance, and he refuses to place limitations on a mind that has just begun to awaken.

Unfortunately the burgeoning consciousness that Du Bois discovered among rural Tennessee community members has been neglected or glossed over by scholars eager to examine ritual grounds in *Souls* that are located farther south. Foremost among the passages that must be reconsidered is one in which he reveals a generational divide among African American community members in their response to pressing social, economic, and political forces: "I have called my tiny community a world, and so its isolation made it; and yet there was among us but a half-awakened common consciousness, sprung from common joy and grief, at burial, birth, or wedding; from a common hardship in poverty, poor land, and low wages; and, above all, from the sight of the Veil that hung between us and Opportunity. All this caused us to think some thoughts together; but these, when ripe for speech, were spoken in various languages."[74] Traditional wisdom suggests that this passage speaks to an impaired community that is unable to overcome its current challenges because its members cannot communicate with a common tongue. Viewed as such, this Tennessee community becomes one of countless rural southern communities explored by Du Bois where a "history can be read but a future can barely be expressed."[75] Yet his quotation expresses a reality faced by rural towns (and townspeople) across the South, if not the country, that, regardless of their racial composition, will either succumb to dire circumstances or will rise to meet the challenges of each new day. Du Bois's words therefore do not refer to an impasse but to an awakening.

Among those standing in the way of community progress are those Old Negroes previously encountered by Du Bois. These men and women represent a generation of African Americans who, twenty-five years earlier, witnessed "the glory of the coming of the Lord," only to find themselves decades later seated like a "swarthy spectre sits in its accustomed seat at the Nation's feast." They are unable to speak about the future with a collective voice because their past and their present represent a history of seemingly insurmountable obstacles that has left most of them dispirited. According to Du Bois, defeatism infiltrated their consciousness, and they either "sank into listless indifference, or shiftlessness, or reckless bravado"[76]

The future of rural African American communities resides within the hearts and minds of New Negroes. Represented by Du Bois in his characterizations of Josie, Jim, and Ben, this generation views slavery, Reconstruction, and second-class citizenship as obstacles from the past that will not impede their future progress: "Ill could they be content, born without and beyond the World. And their weak wings beat against their barriers,—barriers of caste, of youth, of life; at last, in dangerous moments, against everything that opposed even a whim."[77] Even at a young age they desire economic independence and hunger for educational advancement. While many believe that these goals can be accomplished without abandoning rural life, others see the possibilities afforded by urbanization. They embrace their cultural identity and will agitate to attain a status equal to whites. His interpretations clearly indicate a degree of naïveté associated with youth, but through them Du Bois revels in the possibilities for these children and in their potential for future success.

Home Again

Ten years passed before Du Bois returned to the rural Tennessee community he once called home. While delivering a commencement address at Fisk, something "swept" over him, and he longed "to pass again beyond the blue hill, and to see the homes and the school of other days, and to learn how life had gone with my school-children."[78] He records these observations at the end of chapter 4 of *Souls*, where he draws heavily on the power of symbolism to emphasize the changes he witnessed. What he reveals through his reexamination of this community is that for all of the challenges standing in the way of African American progress, their advancements far outweigh their setbacks.

Among the first places Du Bois visits is his former schoolhouse. Instead of the dilapidated cabin he left behind, he finds a "jaunty board house" with windows and a door that locks.[79] As he peers inside, he recognizes some pieces from the past, backless wooden benches, and a blackboard that has grown by a couple of feet. Though incremental, the changes show that African American education in Alexandria is no longer an experiment but an integral part of community life. The county has purchased the lot and implemented regular school sessions each year. Du Bois acknowledges these signs of progress and is pleased by them, but he is also nostalgic and misses the rustic simplicity of earlier days.

However, Du Bois recognizes that progress is "necessarily ugly," and he prepares himself for the inevitable changes that come to places and people with the passing of time. Many of those whom he once educated and with whom he interacted have died or moved since his last visit, but he finds "babies a-plenty" among those who remain. One of these babies belongs to his former student, a daughter of Uncle Bird, who "bristled with pride" while speaking about the home she shared with her new husband and about their future plans. At another location Du Bois encounters a log home and recalls the "broken, blighted family that used to live there."[80] He is eager to learn the fate of two family members in particular, Ben and Tildy, former students who he is certain have not fared well. Yet he learns from several local families that Ben is a successful farmer and Tildy is happy and recently married. Because there is not enough time to rekindle every relationship, Du Bois hurries past the cottage of the Neill boys and bypasses the Hickmans' home, but he stops and lingers at the entrance to the Burkes' property.

For Du Bois, Doc Burke's farm is an important location that expresses both literal and figurative qualities. At first glance the property appears to be unchanged: "The inclosure looked rough and untrimmed. . . . there were the same fences around the old farm." The property's appearance seems to represent an exercise in futility, an ongoing attempt by the owners to eke out an existence on land that is not their own. Du Bois writes about the scene before him as if depicting a point of conflict, and he eagerly seeks to discover "who won in the battle, Doc or the seventy-five acres."[81]

The Burke family property, however, serves as an important example of regeneration. Once a "one-and-a-half-room cabin in the hollow," their home has "climbed the hill and swollen to a half-finished six room cottage" resting on a one-hundred-acre farm. Rising out of the dale and up the hill, the Burke farm is a symbol of progress. Though he maintains a mortgage, Doc Burke has succeeded; he has created a home and a living out of nothing. The farm's growth speaks to his determination and, perhaps, his defiance to African Americans and whites convinced he would fail. Doc's "massive frame is showing decline," and his wife has lost her "lion-like physique," but their son Rob is now "the image of his father . . . loud and rough with laughter," their daughter Birdie has "grown to a picture of maiden beauty, tall and tawny," and their son Edgar has "gone to work in Nashville."[82] Doc Burke and his wife have not simply survived; they have thrived, and when they choose to cease working, they have capable and willing hands to continue their legacy.

Summum Bonum

Prior to the conclusion of this chapter, Du Bois queries, "How shall man measure Progress there where the dark-faced Josie lies? How many heartfuls of sorrow shall balance a bushel of wheat? How hard a thing is life to the lowly, and yet how human and real! And all this life and love and strife and failure,—is it the twilight of nightfall or the flush of some faint-dawning day?" These rhetorical questions ponder the meaning of life and death, profit and loss, identity and purpose in the post-Reconstruction South and provide a fitting end to a narrative that examines the lives (and fate) of rural African Americans who lived and died within the "shadow of one blue hill." However, these reflections are not the final words in the chapter. Du Bois follows these questions with a critical and profound statement: "Thus sadly musing, I rode to Nashville in the Jim Crow car."[83]

With these words Du Bois eliminates the intellectual distance that separates him from the practical concerns he seeks to resolve and draws important connections between his own life and the experiences of rural African Americans. The decade that has passed since he set foot in this Tennessee hamlet represents "the ten years that follow youth, the years when first the realization comes that life is leading somewhere."[84] During that time Du Bois earned a Harvard PhD, studied extensively in Berlin, held three university teaching appointments, and published widely on America's race problem. His accomplishments identify him as a New Negro and place him among the most talented members of his race. Yet he seeks answers to questions about racial progress while sitting idly in the defined and confining section of a segregated railway car—a space symbolic of the limitations of Negroes (New and Old) in turn-of-the-century America.

Thus Du Bois's final words reflect the sad musings from his epigraph and echo their own sorrow song. Outside the windows of that railway car lie southern communities that differ from Lebanon, Alexandria, and Watertown by name only. They are battlegrounds where African Americans contest daily the effects of racism, poverty, and peonage behind the rural hills and dales that hide them from sight. Their lives are hard and their circumstances interminable, but they fight their battles and win their victories. Like the lives of those described in the sorrow songs, the lives of post-Reconstruction African Americans are both solemn and inspiring. Their experiences provide Du Bois with a powerful moment of self-reflection. Though his battlefield is different from theirs, both face a similar foe. Du Bois has education and opportunities unknown to rural African Americans, but does he have their strength and their grit? At the beginning of the chapter Du Bois notes that rural community members knew "it was a hard thing to dig a living out of a rocky side-hill," yet they persevered.[85] Their example helps him conceptualize the test of manhood that lies before him and the racial mountain he must climb. His closing words also force readers to ponder the American dream that has been so long deferred for the nation's African American citizenry and to resolve the problem of the color line that stands between twentieth-century Americans.[86]

4 /   "Mightier than the Sword": The New Negro Novels of Sutton E. Griggs

The Negro is cherishing the dream that the South may one day prove to be an ideal home for the race.
—SUTTON E. GRIGGS, *NASHVILLE AMERICAN*, SEPTEMBER 5, 1905

In Sutton Elbert Griggs's novel *The Hindered Hand* (1905), a young African American boy named Henry Crump stands before a judge in an Almaville, Tennessee, courtroom.[1] He has been tried and found guilty of assault for throwing rocks at a group of white boys who had also thrown rocks but had the presence of mind to appear empty-handed when approached by a white city policeman responding to the disturbance. As punishment for his crime, the young boy is sentenced to ten months on the Almaville County Farm. Well aware of the conditions there and of the treatment of its African American prisoners, the boy, now panicked by the verdict, leaps from an open courthouse window and runs southward across the town square and onto a street with a bridge that intersects the city. Though startled by the turn of events, several city policemen pursue the boy, some on foot and others by streetcar and buggy. When Henry reaches the far end of the bridge, he finds his path blocked by a policeman with his revolver drawn. In desperation the boy leaps over the railing and drops two dozen feet to the embankment below. Drawn to the scene by the flurry of excitement, hundreds of townspeople flock to the bridge and stand witness to the unfolding events. Policemen, many of whom shout obscenities and threats at him, surround the boy on all sides. Uncertain whether there is greater danger in wading farther into the depths of the river or toward the policemen on the shore, the boy hesitates. In that moment of hesitation, a shot rings out from the bridge above, and the boy sinks beneath the water. By the time his body is pulled from the river, the crowd has dispersed.

At the beginning of the novel, Almaville, a Queen City of the South, is described as a heaven on earth:

> In the long ago when the earth was in process of formation, it must have been that those forces of nature most expert in the fashioning of the beautiful were ordered to come together as collaborators and give to the world Almaville. . . . On an eminence crowning the center of the area whereupon the city is planted, the State has builded its capitol, and from the tower thereof one can see the engaging network of streets, contemplate the splendid architecture of the buildings, and gaze upon the noble trees that boldly line the sidewalks, and thus testify that [Almaville's citizens] are not afraid of civilization.[2]

Yet for all its scenic beauty, and its many testaments to civilization, Almaville hides a hideous heart, one whose blackness Griggs symbolizes in part through the river that swallows Henry Crump and whose "dark stream flows through the lives of all . . . who dwell upon [Almaville's] banks."[3] In *The One Great Question* (1907), a book-length treatise on the race question published two years after *The Hindered Hand*, Griggs reveals that he was among the crowd of people who watched from a bridge while white policemen murdered a young African American boy, in water up to his neck, for the crime of being afraid.[4] The location where the crime took place was not the fictional city of Almaville but Nashville, through which the Cumberland River flows.

Griggs's use of Nashville as a site of significance in his fiction is not incidental. References to the city, whether thinly veiled or overt, permeate his writing and illustrate a critical connection between Griggs, his fiction, and a city that provided him a window into southern race relations in turn-of-the-century America. Griggs was born in Texas and formally educated in Virginia, but he lived more than half of his life in Tennessee.[5] Between 1913 and 1930 he lived in Memphis, where he worked as a minister, publisher, and writer.[6] However, his formative and most productive years as a novelist and publisher were spent in Nashville. Not only did Griggs write his first novel, *Imperium in Imperio* (1899), while living in Nashville, but he also established the Orion Publishing Company (1901), one of the country's first secular African American publishing companies, in Nashville, and he used Orion as an outlet to publish his four subsequent novels—*Overshadowed* (1901), *Unfettered* (1902), *The Hindered Hand; or, Reign of the Repressionist* (1905), and *Pointing the Way* (1908)—and two additional book-length works, *The One Great Question*

(1907) and *Wisdom's Call* (1911).[7] Even without his nonfiction works, Griggs's publication and distribution of five novels over a span of nine years makes him the South's most prolific African American writer and places him among the best known and widely read African American writers of his era. The body of work he created in Nashville provides the world with a unique exploration of the New Negro and a valuable time capsule of early twentieth-century southern African American life.

Writing the South

According to Griggs, Nashville at the turn of the century was "an exponent of Southern civilization at its best." Surrounded by lush green hills and visited by temperate climates throughout the year, Nashville provided an ideal, bucolic location for settlement. While it had long been an important city situated strategically between North and South, Nashville thrived in the wake of the Civil War and the period of Reconstruction. Its progress was highlighted on an international stage when the city hosted the 1897 World's Fair, an exposition showcasing Nashville as an important center for trade and manufacture and a strategic educational center for African Americans and whites, characteristics that contributed to the city's reputation as "the Athens of the South." According to Griggs, many people, in both North and South, viewed Nashville as progressive with regard to matters of race. Even Booker T. Washington, following a 1906 visit, called Nashville a hospitable city, one that "threw open its doors to me to address the white people." And while one might expect to hear such reassuring public sentiment from southerners, whether African American or white, Griggs notes that even those who lived outside of the South were taken by Nashville's charms. Among them he cites an endorsement from the longtime U.S. congressman Charles H. Grosvenor of Ohio, who declared famously, "Taken all in all, Nashville is about the best city in the South."[8]

Because Nashville enjoyed widespread appeal among northerners and southerners, Griggs believed it an ideal city through which to examine the country's racial divide: "If, then, in Nashville we are to behold the South's highest mountain peak, the imagination of the reader is at liberty to conceive its deepest valley."[9]

Having carefully surveyed the city's cultural terrain as an African American resident, Griggs knew that Nashville (and therefore the South) must be judged by its treatment of those least visible within its political jurisdiction. While it was the pinnacle of southern society for others,

Nashville remained for Griggs a "repressionist" city located within in a "repressionist region": "Choose whatever spot you will where repression reigns, thrust in the lance and you will find oozing there from helplessness on the part of the Negro in the face of aggression, unrestrained maltreatment on the part of the mean at heart, cruel indifference, paralyzing self-interest and sometimes wanton oppression on the part of the chosen governing agencies—chosen with the distinct understanding that the Negroes, having no voice in their making, are to be utterly ignored as a factor in determining their policies."[10] Beyond its scenic landscape, modern infrastructure, and the unique characteristics that distinguish it from the South's many urban centers, Nashville is revealed to be a site of political oppression, enforced labor, harassment, false imprisonment, vigilantism, mob rule, and murder. However, it is also a southern location where an African American writer, at the height of the Jim Crow era, is able to expose and vilify the city's racist atmosphere, where an array of conditions have created an African American community poised to overturn the debilitating conditions they face.

In Griggs's first novel, *Imperium in Imperio*, a group of well-dressed African American students stand before their teachers on the campus of Stowe University in Nashville.[11] The president who is late for the assembly, arrives to find an envelope on his desk, placed there by one of the students now gathered before him. After reading the contents of the letter, the headmaster is flustered. He botches lines from his devotional scripture and forgets to select someone to deliver the morning prayer. In his frustration he chastises the students for communicating with him on a matter that is not their concern. He then strikes a gong repeatedly, indicating that it is time for the students to disperse. Unwilling to retire, the students maintain their places, and each raises a white board on which is written the words "Equality or Death." While the president and teachers stand aghast, the student leader, Belton Piedmont, steps forward and reiterates the students' demands cited in the letter. The students will disband only after white members of the administration and faculty agree to allow the university's lone African American teacher to eat with them. After a brief consultation, the president and faculty relent. Upon obtaining their desired result, the students raise a black flag decorated with the word "Victory," and they march from the room singing, "John Brown's body lies mouldering in the grave, and we go marching on." The white teachers stare in disbelief, "like hens who had lost their broods," and the implications of the protest become clear: "The cringing, fawning, sniffling, cowardly Negro which slavery had left, had disappeared, and a new Negro, self-respecting, fearless, and determined in the assertion of his rights was at hand."[12] The successful student protest of conditions at Stowe University represents a significant turning point in the novel. In its wake similar rebellions take place at African American universities across the country. These interventions not only upset the precarious balance of power between African American students and white administrators and faculty at schools established for their education but also signal further challenges to the boundaries of caste within southern society. However, the most significant aspect of the protest is the unveiling of the New Negro in Nashville. This is the first literary representation of the New Negro in an African American novel, and it focuses on an array of issues relating to agency and integrity central to the conception of the New Negro. Nashville's racial climate highlights for Griggs the injustices and indignities perpetrated against African Americans by whites in cities across the South, but it also provides him critical insight into the possibilities for African American responses to white injustice and a pathway to reconciliation between the two sides.

Griggs is one of many African American writers confronting the realities of racial life in turn-of-the-century America, but he offers a perspective that is distinct from his contemporaries. W. E. B. Du Bois (Great Barrington, Massachusetts), Pauline Hopkins (Cambridge, Massachusetts), Charles Chesnutt (Cleveland, Ohio), and Frances Harper Watkins (Baltimore, Maryland) all wrote about southern experiences, yet each was born and spent the majority of his or her life outside of the South. Griggs writes about the South because it is where he was born and reared, where he attended school, married, worked, wrote, preached, and lived. He writes about the South because it is a world he loves and protects yet struggles to understand. Yet Griggs's South is no monolith; its landscapes are as diverse as they are beautiful, and its inhabitants are as sapient as they are perverse.

His oeuvre delivers lasting images of Tennessee, its countryside dotted by fields and woodlands along the length of the Cumberland River. He captures the rugged simplicity of West Virginia, its sloping mountains and the stillness to be found atop its peaks. His characters amble the beaches of Galveston, Texas, where they watch the waves tumble in from the Gulf, and along a Mississippi hamlet, where they admire stark white stars floating across the night sky. Griggs's characters also venture beyond rural backwaters like Cadeville, Louisiana, and Tuskegee, Alabama, often aboard southern railways, to modern cityscapes like Richmond, Virginia, and Nashville. Upon arrival, by hack or on foot they traverse busy thoroughfares, seek comfortable accommodations, attend church services, and peruse the wares of local merchants. At times his characters ramble among the alleyways of Hell's half-acre in search of saloons, brothels, and gambling dens. These southern settings are not merely backdrops for Griggs's novels; they are integral to his message. They reveal his investment in distinct southern environments and his connection to the speech, dress, and customs of the people who inhabit them.

However, as previous examples have shown, his canvas is no pastoral; it reproduces the complex portraits that make up southern and, ultimately, American life. Alongside its marvels are to be found its misfortunes: poverty, insults, violence, jealousy, bitterness, doubt, and ignominy. Griggs was well aware that race prejudice was not a southern virus and that white northern attitudes also contributed to limited social, political, and economic advancement for African Americans. However, his failure to render more precisely the experience of northern African Americans should be seen less as an oversight or shortcoming of his than an important statement regarding race and place. For Griggs the distinction between the South and other regions of the country was one of geography. Migration from the South did not ensure African Americans freedom from discrimination or an opportunity for rebirth. Living in a country where race prejudice is embedded within the national consciousness, Griggs understood that theirs was not an identity so easily shed.

In his autobiography, *Along This Way* (1933), James Weldon Johnson wrote, "It is *in the South* that the race problem must be solved; because it will not be completely solved in any other section of the country until it is solved there; because essentially the status of the Negro in all other sections will depend upon what it is in the South."[13] Johnson penned these words while living and working in Nashville, where he was the Adam K. Spence Chair of Creative Literature at Fisk University from 1931 until his death in 1938.[14] A well-known African American writer, activist, and educator, Johnson too was a southern-born New Negro and was well acquainted with the implications of color in American life. However, I cite Johnson not as another example of Nashville's significance as a center of New Negro activity but to emphasize an idea shared between the two men, one that influenced Griggs's body of work. Griggs, like Johnson, believed that America's success or failure depended on a solution to the race problem, and the only way to achieve a solution was by bridging the chasm created by whites that separated the two races in the South. At the center of this contest was an ideological struggle, one that required a shift in whites' attitude in order for African Americans to be viewed as equal participants in the democratic process.

Although he agitates forcefully for African American equality and consistently employs a radical problem-solving methodology in his fiction, Griggs's novels have been maligned and his message misinterpreted as conciliatory, causing the South's most prolific turn-of-the-century African American writer to be relegated to the margins of critical discourse for decades.[15] The basis for much of this neglect comes from critics of Griggs's fiction who saw a fierce radicalism in *Imperium in Imperio* that was not repeated in the novels published afterward. Even today a thorough evaluation of source material reveals that more than two-thirds of the scholarship on Griggs is fixated on his first novel, a trend suggesting dominant readings of his radical viability and, moreover, his success as an important voice from his era were short-lived. Even Finnie Coleman, who is among the first to write a book-length work on Griggs, suggests that Griggs's repeated literary appeals for decency and fair play from whites deprecates African American autonomy. Coleman claims that along with Paul Laurence Dunbar, Harper, and Johnson, Griggs is one of several turn-of-the-century authors who "developed characters and narrators who struggled with the possibility that innate White supremacy may have been more than myth—that at some level Blacks were inferior to Whites."[16]

However, Griggs's fiction consistently challenges the popular assumption of African American inferiority among members of America's dominant race. In his preface to *Overshadowed*, for instance, he acknowledges the difficult task faced by African Americans who must be "fitted to the civilization" in order to compete with whites, considered to be the "most cultured" and "most virile" race on earth.[17] Taken at face value, it is possible to see where one could misinterpret these lines as a conciliatory admission of inferiority on the part of African Americans or as an alignment with a Washingtonian perspective wherein faced with white domination, it is at the bottom of American society that African Americans must begin rather than at the top.[18] Griggs does not, however, concede African American inferiority; he merely acknowledges the popularity of the concept in American society. He then challenges the notion by suggesting that *if* African Americans are inferior to whites in any measure, it is not due to any deficiency in their character, intellect, or nature but rather their condition.

In many ways Griggs perpetuates an argument divisive among African Americans and whites since the country's inception, but for early twentieth-century readers he highlights the problem of caste that delimits the country's "Negro problem." In doing so Griggs effectively turns the tables on whites by raising a different question: Just how civilized are the members of America's dominant majority? Rather than offering an assessment of African American inferiority, his novels place whites under a microscope in order to determine how well they are able to live up to their own vaunted standard of civilization. Focusing on the most significant southern African American writer at the turn of the twentieth century, this chapter explores the connections between race and region and, more specifically, discusses how the appearance of a southern New Negro is connected to the emergence of segregation and racial violence in the post-Emancipation South.

A Sight Unseen

One of the ways Griggs challenges notions of whites' moral superiority is by examining their propensity for violence. The initial setting for *Unfettered* is an idyllic Tennessee town on the banks of the Cumberland. The tranquility of this place quickly evaporates following fisticuffs between Lemuel Dalton, a white plantation owner, and Harry Dalton, the African American son of a former plantation slave. Lemuel is bested in the altercation but emerges victorious after shooting and seriously wounding Harry. As a result of the dispute the town is divided along racial lines. According to town whites, they are "not opposed to negroes *per se*, but to 'sassy' Negroes that tried to put on airs and represent themselves to be as good as white people."[19] By besting Lemuel, Harry transgressed an invisible social color line that whites believed to be understood. In response to Lemuel's dishonorable use of force in a contest of men, African American townspeople decide to abandon the town completely.

Upon hearing of the exodus, whites become incensed. Not only do they view the decision to leave town as a sign of disrespect, but they lament the loss of a labor force that enables them to maintain their comfortable existence. Angered by these circumstances, a number of whites seek out the remaining African Americans on whom they can perpetrate violence. Among the last to depart the town is Beulah Dalton, Harry's sister. Whites particularly dislike Beulah because she refuses to speak with them unless they address her as "Miss Beulah." Thrilled at the opportunity for revenge for what they perceive to be multiple insults against the white community, the men surround her house, blanket the ground with kerosene, and ignite the structure. A terrified Beulah races out the back door in hope of making it to the safety of the woods, but she is prevented by a young white man who strikes her in the back of the head with a piece of stove wood taken from her kitchen. The chapter closes with the smoldering ashes of the Dalton family home and, beside it, the silent body of Beulah, "her face in a puddle of blood."[20]

The incident is senseless and cold. The men involved were not wronged; they were not assaulted or wounded; they were not seeking an eye for an eye or justice for an unpunished transgression. Their violent response is not about crime; it is about color. They are not seeking a particular Negro; they are seeking any Negro. The gender or the defenselessness of that individual is of no consequence. What is at stake for these men is racial dominance, a principle they uphold through harassment and terror. Though brief, Beulah's death is a poignant reminder from Griggs of whites' "aggressive" nature and the unbridled excess of their behavior.[21]

Perhaps none of Griggs's episodes of violence better depicts the bloodlust among America's whites than the instances of lynching that he describes so adeptly. Among the most powerful of these scenes occurs in *The Hindered Hand*. Falsely accused of murder and trying to stay one step ahead of a lynch mob, Bud Harper leaves Almaville with his wife, Foresta, to begin life anew in a small Mississippi town. The couple choose the location based on its reputation for cruelty to African Americans, believing it to be the last place any whites searching for them would look. Bud and Foresta purchase a farm, make friends with their African American neighbors, and try to enjoy the solitude of country life. Despite their efforts not to draw attention, they are quickly identified as troublemakers by local whites for their decision to purchase land rather than lease it and their efforts to better the lives of their African American neighbors.

In response to the Harpers' behavior, whites appoint Sidney Fletcher, a local man with a reputation for eliminating "every biggity nigger" who has attempted to settle in their comfortable hamlet. Fletcher accosts Foresta at her home, causing her to run in search of Bud, who is out hunting. When Fletcher senses Bud in range of his weapon, he fires three quick shots, each to no avail. Seeing that Fletcher is determined to continue his harangue, Bud fires in defense, killing Fletcher immediately. In what is so often in Griggs's novels an unstoppable cycle of persecution at the hands of malicious whites, the African American characters again find themselves in peril through no fault of their own. When the mob arrives they ask if it is true that Bud killed Fletcher, to which he replies, "I shot him. And if he died I suppose I must have caused it. But it was in self-defense." Uninterested in mitigating circumstances, the mob leader cries out, "You hear that, do you. He has confessed," a reply that causes his associates to prepare for recompense.[22]

However, it is not only Bud who must suffer for this perceived offense but also Foresta. The mob selects a location beside a Negro church, a site where they hope to make a lasting impression on members of the African American community. After tying the two to trees so that they face one another, they douse Bud and Foresta with oil and pile wood at their feet. The angry mob leers and shouts in exultation at the unfolding spectacle. To satisfy their hunger, pieces of Foresta's hair is cut off and tossed to onlookers as souvenirs, followed by her fingers, which are cut from her hand one by one. Although Bud closes his eyes and turns his head from the awful sight, members of the crowd pry open his eyes and force him to watch his wife's mutilation. Before a crowd that includes a number of small children, a corkscrew is used on one of Foresta's breasts to "pull forth the live quivering flesh." When it is determined that the innocent woman has been "tortured sufficiently," the mob's focus is directed toward Bud.[23]

Bud's fingers too are cut off one at a time, and he too feels the corkscrew bored into his body. He is also struck in the head with a bat, a blow delivered with such force that one eyeball is made to dangle from its socket. This unexpected outcome thrills the crowd and prompts one white observer to snatch the eyeball "as a souvenir." After three hours of taunting and torture, the mob commences its final act, and the couple is set aflame. Once the flames subside, there is a "mad rush" for pieces of the bodies to bring home as trophies. Amid the melee one white child, afraid to be outdone by his peers, grabs a portion of charred flesh and also their hanging rope as a special prize. Later that afternoon an out-of-town visitor questions why Foresta was killed if it was Bud who was responsible for the crime. A local man responds succinctly, "We lynch niggers down here for anything. We lynch them for being sassy and sometimes lynch them on general principles. The truth of the matter is the real 'one crime' that paves the way for a lynching whenever we have the notion, is the crime of being black."[24] Textual moments such as the one detailing the murder of Bud and Foresta are meant to unsettle readers and to emphasize the grotesque nature of white violence against African Americans.

Though a work of fiction, Griggs's novel depicts vivid scenes that feel as if they were torn from the headlines. According to NAACP records, there were eighty-six documented lynchings in the United States in 1904, the year prior to Griggs's publication of *The Hindered Hand*.[25] Seventy-nine of those victims were African Americans, and seven were whites.

As was so often the case, African Americans found themselves victims of vigilante "justice" seekers in numbers significantly disproportionate to their population. While Griggs, like many other Americans, had certainly read reports of lynchings in newspaper accounts, it is also likely that he was familiar with violent acts recorded by African American activists such as Ida B. Wells, whose *A Red Record* (1895) catalogued the lynching of numerous African Americans at the hands of white mobs a decade earlier.

In fact Griggs's lynching episodes share a number of similarities to instances rendered by Wells. In the chapter entitled "Lynched for Anything and Nothing," Wells describes the murder of Lee Walker, an African American man who is murdered for allegedly assaulting two white women in Memphis. In the following passage Wells details the mob's actions following Walker's death:

> The rope that was used to hang the Negro, and also that which was used to lead him from the jail, were eagerly sought by relic hunters. They almost fought for a chance to cut off a piece of rope, and in an incredibly short time both ropes had disappeared and were scattered in the pockets of the crowd in sections of from an inch to six inches long. Other relic hunters remained until the ashes cooled to obtain such ghastly relics as the teeth, nails, and bits of charred skin from the immolated victim of his own lust.[26]

While such behavior among lynch mobs was not limited to the examples described by Wells, the indiscriminate attitude of such vigilantism and the insatiable bloodlust exhibited in such circumstances are elements implemented effectively by Griggs in his fictional rendering. Too often journalistic accounts of white-on-black violence were just another news story, cast alongside reports of local streetcar strikes, unrest among union workers, or the latest demonstrations over the Russo-Japanese War. The identity of the victims and the fervor among the crowd became blurred and diluted and vanished from the reader's mind with the turn of a page. In order to restore such moments to the minds of readers and to tap into America's historical memory, Griggs recasts them within the pages of his fiction. In doing so he fulfills a promise he made at the beginning of his novel: "that in no part of the book has the author consciously done violence to conditions as he has permitted to view them, amid conditions he has spent his whole life, up to the present hour, as an intensely absorbed observer."[27]

Griggs's depiction of Bud and Foresta's murder is vivid and precise. His prose neither sensationalizes nor vilifies through language or lens;

rather it carefully organizes an account of the unfolding chaos: "The mob decided to torture their victims before killing them and began on Foresta first. A man with a pair of scissors stepped up and cut off her hair and threw it into the crowd. There was a great scramble for bits of hair for souvenirs of the occasion. One by one her fingers were cut off and tossed into the crowd to be scrambled for. A man with a cork screw came forward, ripped her clothing to the waist, bored into her breast with the corkscrew."[28] Until the two are finally dead there is hardly time for readers to exhale. A number of critics argue that Griggs's work lacks artistry and depth. Yet, as the excerpt shows, he is capable of producing powerful prose fraught with intensity and emotion. His is a unique style that will be celebrated in the work of Ernest Hemingway decades later, epitomized by potent passages such as the following from *In Our Time* (1925), which describes the execution of six Greek cabinet ministers:

> They shot the six cabinet ministers at half-past six in the morning against the wall of a hospital. There were pools of water in the court-yard. There were wet dead leaves on the paving in the courtyard. It rained hard. All the shutters of the hospital were nailed shut. One of the ministers was sick with typhoid. Two soldiers carried him down-stairs and out into the rain. They tried to hold him up against the wall but he sat down in a puddle of water. The other five stood very quietly against the wall. Finally an officer told the soldiers it was no good trying to make him stand up. When they fired the first volley he was sitting down in the water with his head on his knees.[29]

Like this example, which Hemingway adapted from journalistic accounts of genuine events for the purpose of fiction, Griggs's violent depic-tion becomes more than words on a page. His language highlights the deliberate, macabre proceedings and emphasizes that the point of such gatherings is not only to kill or to eradicate victims. If it was, the blows would be quick and decisive. The simplicity of Griggs's delivery unveils a harsh if silent admonition of whites. Griggs shows that whites are not only violent but also cruel, sadistic, and unrelenting. Their bloodlust continues even after the death of their victims. White-on-black violence is portrayed as celebratory and commonplace. Such acts are also carried out in the presence of children, violating their innocence and encour-aging future race-based crimes. With such vignettes Griggs challenges any notion of southern honor or of any code of conduct among whites that suggests their natural or moral superiority over African Ameri-cans. In addition to whites who participate in mob activities, he indicts those who are passive as well; whether they turn a blind eye to injustices against African Americans or grant immunity to those participating in mob violence, they have lessened the value of human life.

Even though most of Griggs's violent white characters escape civil prosecution, few remain free from punishment for their crimes. *Overshadowed* features Horace Christian, a white southern politician who believes that he can upset his Republican rival for office if he is able to establish an antilynching record that will garner attention and political support from African American voters. In order to establish this record, he facilitates trumped-up charges of improper contact between an innocent African American man and a white woman. When a white mob subsequently accosts the man and prepares to lynch him for his crime, Christian steps into their path and argues for mercy. Playing his role in earnest, he pulls out a pistol and threatens to "kill or be killed" for his intervention.[30] Christian is quickly overwhelmed by the bloodthirsty mob, which, after disarming him, proceeds to lynch and mutilate the unnamed African American. From one perspective the scenario plays out like so many others in Griggs's novels, recounting the horror of lynching, the uncontrollable ferocity of the mob spirit, and the foolish simplicity of the crime. Yet Griggs maintains a firm sense of purpose and does not allow Christian's duplicity to go unrecognized.

Christian is haunted by the crime he instigated for personal gain. At night he dreams of the man he condemned to death: "The face [was] ploughed up with bullets, his eyes were bulging out, his stomach was ripped open, and his entrails were visible." Horrified by the spectacle, Christian attempts to turn away, but he notices a placard about the neck of the victim. Inching forward, he makes out the words "Thou art the man."[31] Seized by terror and seeking support lest his knees give way beneath him, Christian grasps the body of the dead man, which, from the added weight of his own body, falls and traps Christian's head beneath its mangled form. Steeped in the gore of the dead man, Christian presents a vivid image that connotes a history of racial violence between African Americans and whites. Through Christian's dream, Griggs reveals the national nightmare of post-Emancipation America. It is the white and aptly named Christian who is left with blood on his hands. Christian is a murderer, a politician masquerading as an interpreter of law and justice. He is a false friend who profits from African American men and women and trounces and traduces them in order to elevate his position.

Though he bears psychic scars, Christian fails to repent of his crimes, and he continues a pattern of misbehavior. Soon after allowing an African American man to be lynched for political gain, Christian seduces and defiles a young woman from one of the town's best African American families to satisfy his base desires. Following a series of narrative events, a political rival convinces Christian to alter his appearance with a makeover and the application of a special solution that enables the two to "go among the darky belles and have a good time." Following a night of drunken revelry in the African American side of town, Christian is taken to jail to sleep off the effects of his intoxication. As part of a complex plot, he is placed in the cell of a murderer, John Wysong, who, through a blurring of identities, is later removed from the cell, leaving Christian in his place. When he awakes, Christian remembers his ruse from the previous night and decides to continue to "play 'darky'" lest he be discovered by the white jailer and his behavior exposed, an outcome certain to ruin his political career. However, Christian soon discovers that he is no longer believed to be the inebriated African American man brought in for drunkenness but the murderer John Wysong, who is condemned to die that day. As he is led to the gallows, he realizes the full extent of his circumstances and, dropping the speech and behavior of an African American, begins to shout, "I am no Negro; I am a white man." His words only infuriate the jailer and the mob, who, insulted by his claims, "howled in derision." While Christian kicks, claws, and scratches to escape the noose, a black cap is placed over his head and the trap is sprung. His final words are "I am a white man, I killed a nigger; I am a white man, I killed a nigger."[32] Though the intended victim John Wysong escapes the noose, Christian's death provides justice.

Griggs turns the tables on not only Christian but also the mob. In its anger and its desire for vengeance, the mob cannot distinguish black from white or right from wrong. Griggs suggests that at some point the mob spirit can and will turn on whites as well. Because it acts on emotion, without logic, and in a space that does not adhere to due process of law, the mob is anarchic and results in the undoing of civil society. Prior to his death Christian is forced to confess his crime and to be judged for his previous transgressions. It is an ironic and chilling twist. Passing for black, the white Christian takes his final steps in another's shoes and experiences the most suffocating effects of life behind the veil.

While such episodes reflect the indirect consequences of white aggression, others examine how white racism and violence trigger direct responses from a new generation of African Americans. Griggs's *Imperium* protagonist, Belton Piedmont, is hardly a pacifist. His experiences with southern whites represent a range of indignities suffered by turn-of-the-century African Americans. When traveling through Louisiana to assume his position as president of the local African American college, Piedmont is accosted by a white mob and then thrown from a train for sitting in a first-class coach. When he refuses to pay for a meal at a restaurant where the white proprietor will not allow him to eat inside the establishment, Piedmont is arrested, fined, and forced to leave the city. While these confrontations were familiar to African Americans in the Jim Crow South, Griggs clearly indicates that white responses to African American behavior intensify when confronted by the appearance of New Negroes, whose advances in education and success in business or professional life display a freedom of mobility, thought, and action that threatens caste boundaries.

Like so many of Griggs's characters, Piedmont exemplifies not only the internal but also the external characteristics associated with the era's New Negro. In addition to his many internal attributes, Piedmont is recognized for his physical stature. Griggs describes him as a "fine specimen of physical manhood. His limbs were well formed, well proportioned and seemed as strong as oak." So striking is his appearance that he is said to have "excited interest wherever he was seen." Among those intrigued by Piedmont is Zackland, a local white physician who considers Piedmont the "finest lookin' darkey" he has ever encountered. Zackland is determined to gain possession of Piedmont's body in order to dissect it, and he approaches local "Nigger Rulers" to watch Piedmont and to find a reason to apprehend him. After securing a promise from Zackland of a keg of whiskey in return for their services, the men agree not to "burn [Piedmont] nor shoot him to pieces" for any transgression but to "kill him kinder decent" so that the doctor can have Piedmont's body.[33]

Soon after this conversation Piedmont helps a young white woman locate the proper page for a hymn during a Sunday church service. Incensed by what is perceived as Piedmont's "impudence," white townspeople call for him to be hanged. Eager to fulfill their promise to Zackland, the town's Nigger Rulers intervene in the fracas and carry Piedmont off for their sinister purpose. The following evening Piedmont is lynched, and a single bullet is fired into the base of his skull. The mob is certain that Piedmont is dead, and his body is delivered to Zackland and placed on a dissecting table. However, the wound proves superficial and the lynching unsuccessful, and Piedmont soon regains consciousness. While Zackland readies his instruments, Piedmont seizes a knife and plunges it into the doctor's throat. He then places the doctor's body on the dissecting board, covers him with a sheet, and leaves a note stating, "Doctors: I have stepped out for a short while. Don't touch the nigger until I come."[34]

The scenario is odd and uncomfortable and forces readers to ask, What is it about Piedmont that the doctor finds so intriguing? Is he to become a participant in one of Zackland's pseudo-scientific experiments? Is Zackland attracted to Piedmont's physical presence? Does he wish to punish Piedmont or to eradicate him for his attitude? Or is he a trophy to be added to Zackland's collection of oddities? While there are no clear answers to such questions, it is evident that Zackland's interest represents some degree of perversity among whites that stems from a fascination with African Americans and a desire to damage and destroy their bodies. Much like the scenario involving Christian's lynching in *Overshadowed*, in Piedmont's confrontation with Zackland there is a need to provide justice for the indignities perpetrated against African Americans. In this instance another prestigious member of the dominant class is made to experience the most severe treatment of minority members of society. Despite his intentions, Zackland is the only person "cut up" in this confrontation. After death at the hands of his would-be victim, Zackland is laid on the dissecting board, covered by a death shroud, and labeled a "nigger." Piedmont has offered the white South his other cheek during previous instances of harassment; now he shows that, when necessary, violence will be met with violence. In this episode he emerges from his violent negotiation having effectively silenced his oppressor.

However, not all violent responses from African Americans to America's racist environment are as easily justified in Griggs's novels as the one involving Piedmont and Zackland. In *Overshadowed*, Richmond's inhabitants prepare for a Labor Day celebration. The highlight of the festivities is to be a speech delivered by the Master Workman of the Labor Union of the United States. When the Master Workman appears, he steps into a carriage with the city's mayor. The driver of the hack is John Wysong, an African American who recently lost his job at the Bilgal Iron Works due to circumstances stemming from his inability to join the local labor union because of his skin color. Having lost his skilled position, Wysong struggles to find menial work in a city inundated by unskilled workers. It is only the unusual demand for transportation that enables him to make a few dollars on this day.

During the procession, Wysong overhears the Master Workman explain to the mayor that whites "cannot afford to enter into competition with the Negro" and that to ensure the prosperity of white families over that of African American families, the latter must be "crushed out." While Wysong listens attentively, the Master Workman suggests that African Americans have an "abnormal respect for constituted authority" and that because of their docile nature, they are unwilling to "throw off the hand of an oppressor." By way of contrast, the Master Workman argues, "the Anglo-Saxon has never gotten anything for which he did not fight." This is true with regard to the labor question in particular: "What we labor for WE MUST HAVE. We shall have it if we ignore all laws, defy all constituted authority, overthrow all government, violate all tradition. Our end MUST be attained, at whatever cost. If a foe stands in our way, and nothing will dislodge him but death, then he must die. That is the dictum of the Anglo-Saxon." The Master Workman's words unsettle Wysong, who, since his layoff, is unable to pay the mortgage on his home or to set aside money for his sister to attend school. As the parade ends, Wysong delivers the Master Workman and the mayor to City Hall, where they intend to view the city from the building's high tower. Unseen by onlookers, Wysong follows a crowd to the top of the tower. While the men look out the windows and wave to the people below, Wysong acts on violent emotions and pushes the Master Workman from a window. Though events immediately preceding the murder unfold quickly, the death of the Master Workman transpires in slow motion. People on the ground are "paralyzed with horror" while men in the tower scramble to grasp the falling man. Among the spectators, "voices were mute," "chills of terror" were widespread, and many "turned their heads away from the sickening sight." The Master Workman plummets fifty feet before striking a "protuberance" that causes his body to fall another two hundred feet, where it strikes "iron palings" that "ran their narrow shaped heads through his body as unconcernedly as though they were stationed there from all eternity to receive him."[35]

While the circumstances vary, the encounter between Wysong and the Master Workman shares important similarities with the one involving Piedmont and Zackland. The Master Workman does not attempt to kill Wysong in cold blood, but he does threaten Wysong's livelihood. The consequences of his Anglo-Saxon dictum have successfully displaced Wysong from economic viability and have relegated him to an inferior status that prohibits him from providing adequately for himself and his family. Not unlike the lynching episodes in which torture precedes an inevitable death, Griggs illustrates here the slow death that comes as a consequence of limited opportunity. Yet in this instance Wysong refuses to mask his emotions and suffer in silence. The murder of the Master Workman provides a literary outlet for the suppressed rage of countless African American victims of white racism and oppression.

Wysong's actions illustrate a dictum for a new generation of African Americans who, like the nation's white population, will fight to have the things that they must have. The death of the Master Workman is a warning to whites: discrimination breeds contempt. In this instance it is no longer the African American who is objectified and maltreated before transfixed observers, but a white man who dangles precariously over a precipice before being killed before a horrified audience. The scene reveals the psychological toll of suppressed emotion on African Americans and, in doing so, unveils a new state of terror.

As these examples reveal, radical responses to white oppression begin with *Imperium*, but they appear consistently in Griggs's novels. If anything, the examples in later works are more spontaneous and more violent than the organized responses in *Imperium*, and Griggs uses them in a manner meant to arouse the greatest fears of the white community. This idea is perhaps best illustrated by the character Gus Martin, who appears in Griggs's fourth novel, *The Hindered Hand*. Martin fought alongside his friends Ensal Ellwood and Earl Bluefield in the Spanish-American War, where he was wounded three times at the Battle of San Juan Hill. Despite noted acts of bravery, both Martin and Bluefield are unable to secure promotion due to their skin color. Martin is particularly stung by the rejection, and he returns to America disillusioned with the unfulfilled promise of civic equality. When friends question his faith, he tells them "cullud people" are "too jam full o' patience an' hope." Once a patriot, Martin now insists, "The flag aint any more to me than any other dirty rag. I fit fur it. My blood run out o' three holes on the groun' to keep it floatin', and whut will it do fur me? Now jes' tell me whut?"[36]

Soon after posing his rhetorical question, Martin seizes an opportunity to test the limits of American justice. Following the justifiable homicide of a white man, Martin attempts to turn himself in to law enforcement agents to avoid a lynch mob. He speaks with the local sheriff, the state governor, and even a White House official, but none is willing to guarantee his safety, confirming his belief that "there ain't no justice nowhere fur a black man." He then retreats with weapons and ammunition to the safety of a high tower, where he watches a mob gather. Moments later he is surprised by five white men hoping to overwhelm him. Despite their number, Martin kills them one by one. Eventually he is coaxed from his position and faces the mob. He looks fearlessly into the glaring white faces before him and at the "scores of pistols" the men level at his head. As the weapons fire in succession and each bullet finds its target, the unaffected Martin simply "smiled and died."[37]

With radical characters like Martin, Griggs presents readers with an early literary example of the New Negro that becomes more familiar following World War I. This New Negro sensibility is reinforced through the perspective of other characters such as Martin's friend Ensal Ellwood, who views Martin as "the child of the new philosophy that was taking hold of the race." His was a philosophy in which "every man was to act for himself, that each individual was himself to resent the injustices and indignities perpetrated upon him, and that each man whose life was threatened in a lawless way could help the cause of the race by killing as many as possible of the lawless band."[38] While there is no evidence to suggest a familiarity with Griggs's work, there is no doubt that echoes of Martin's radical masculinity are audible in later New Negro works such as Countee Cullen's "If We Must Die," published in 1919:

> If we must die, let it not be like hogs
> Hunted and penned in an inglorious spot,
> While round us bark the mad and hungry dogs,
> Making their mock at our accursed lot.
> If we must die, O let us nobly die
> So that our precious blood may not be shed
> In vain; then even the monsters we defy
> Shall be constrained to honor us though dead!
> O kinsmen! We must meet the common foe!
> Though far outnumbered let us show brave,
> And for their thousand blows deal one death blow!
> What though before us lies the open grave?
> Like men we'll face the murderous, cowardly pack,
> Pressed to the wall, dying, but fighting back![39]

Griggs's character Martin embodies a spirit of revolt within African Americans that has haunted whites since the period of slavery. Like Gabriel or Denmark Vesey, Martin's actions confirm the greatest fears of whites and even provide them with a new cause for alarm.[40] Though punished for his transgression, Martin robs the mob of its victory. He does not cower in fear, nor does he beg for restraint. He dies content; he dies smiling; and he takes his pound of flesh.

As these examples show, Griggs never turns away from a hard examination of the inevitable outcome of white violence and oppression. At one extreme, he delineates characters in textual moments that are filled with the pathos of tragedy. Readers are meant to sense their pain and frustration and to empathize with their hostility and rage. In such a context the violent responses of Griggs's characters are not declarations of war but pleas for justice, and the rhetoric of moral suasion seems to be imbedded within his narratives. At the other extreme, Griggs pens characters that find themselves hemmed in and hunted. Finding no legitimate outlet for their concerns, African American characters such as Wysong and Martin are forced to extreme responses. While these violent outbursts show that radicals exist on both sides of the color line, they also reveal a new boundary line being drawn by African Americans in response to racial violence, one that demarcates and identifies limits to provocation and promises severe consequences for offenders. At either pole, Griggs indicates that whites must demonstrate civility and abandon their savage behavior. Otherwise they will only reap what they sow.

The Great Divide

In 1849 an *American Whig Review* article claimed, "The study of man, physiologically, and psychically, is confessedly the noblest which can claim human attention; and the results of such study must lie at the basis of all sound organizations, social, civil, or religious." Interest in the subject was so pervasive, the author asserted confidently, that "ethnology is not only the science of the age, but also that it is, and must continue to be, to a prevailing extent, an *American science*."[41] Leading the American school of ethnological study were Samuel Morton, George Gliddon, and Josiah Nott. According to Bruce Dain, these men contributed to a midcentury ethnological racism that "tried to cement human diversity to a grimmer vision of nature's balance. Its supposed concreteness and objectivity claimed to discover natural truth, in an attempt not to make progress compatible with social hierarchy . . . but to segregate progress and restrict it to whites."[42] These men helped to affirm dominant cultural attitudes that justified the enslavement of blacks in the South and their social repression in the North, attitudes that Michael Omi and Howard Winant have shown reflect a centuries-old racial dictatorship in the United States, where "the origins of racial division, and of racial signification and identity formation" can be traced.[43] That these pseudo-scientific beliefs contributed to the creation of America's late nineteenth-century color line is indisputable. White Americans presumed themselves the physical, mental, and moral superior of blacks and other nonwhites.

They then used their superior position in America's racial hierarchy to maintain economic, social, and political supremacy. However, not all Americans fit easily in fixed racial categories, blurring the distinction between black and white and threatening the boundaries of caste.

Efforts to document the country's mulatto population began with the 1850 census. According to Jennifer Hochschild and Brenna Powell, "The ideological origins of particular classification schemes were buffeted by debate, resistance, and appropriation from competing normative commitments as well as by partisan and scientific motivations."[44] Further delineation within racial categories did not appear until the 1890 census, where enumerators were instructed to "be particularly careful to distinguish between blacks, mulattoes, quadroons, and octoroons." Though provided with no information on how to determine fractional differences among African Americans, enumerators were to utilize the following guidelines: "The word 'black' should be used to describe those persons who have three-fourths or more black blood; 'mulatto,' those persons who have three-eighths to five-eighths black blood; 'quadroon,' those persons who have one-fourth black blood; and 'octoroon,' those persons who have one-eighth or any trace of black blood."[45] Hypervigilance on the part of government officials and statisticians with regard to persons of mixed blood is better understood when viewed in the context of efforts by late nineteenth-century legislators to pass laws that mandated racial segregation.

Modeled after similar laws that existed in northern states prior to the Civil War, southern Jim Crow laws appeared in the 1880s and required separation of the races in practically all areas of public life. Legal segregation was another way southerners sought to reestablish white supremacy in the wake of Reconstruction. People of mixed racial heritage posed significant challenges to these new laws and to caste because many possessed physical features, light skin in particular, that made their ethnic and therefore racial affiliation difficult to classify. According to Hochschild and Powell, such challenges required legislators to provide further definition of racial categories: "Authorities presumably wanted to know how much the racial hierarchy needed to be further reinforced, which depended in part on whether the number of people blurring the line between the subordinated and the dominant races was increasing or decreasing, thriving or struggling, moving toward or away from whiteness."[46] Census records from the period suggest that an increase in the country's mulatto population provided whites with a reason for concern. According to census data, the country's mulatto population grew from

11.2 to 12 million between 1850 and 1870, to 15.2 million by 1890, and to 20.9 million by 1910. Additional census records indicate that even these numbers are conservative and that by 1910 as much as three-fourths of the country's African American population were of "mixed parentage." While the records indicate a clear concern that an increase in the country's mulatto population suggests "a continuous infusion of white blood" through contact between blacks and whites, a proportion of that increase cannot be determined without considering additional contact between mulattoes and mulattoes, mulattoes and blacks, or mulattoes with whites.[47]

These numbers also reveal that burgeoning mulatto populations are not bound by geography. According to records from each of the four censuses from 1850, 1870, 1890, and 1910, "the proportion mulatto in the Negro population has been lowest in the South, and at each of these censuses except that of 1850 it has been highest in the West."[48] Resolution of these dichotomies in identity, however imperfect, was codified in 1896, following the Supreme Court decision in *Plessy v. Ferguson*.[49] The Court upheld a Louisiana state law that segregated railway passengers according to race while traveling within state borders and, despite arguments that proved Homer Plessy was seven-eighths white and only one-eighth black, found him guilty of refusing to leave the white car. This ruling provided constitutional sanction for "separate but equal" treatment of African Americans and whites; for all practical purposes, it ensured that the status of any person with a discernible percentage of Negro blood was restricted and degraded within American society.

It is from within this marginalized space in American society that Griggs critiques the logic of the color line and, in particular, the effort among whites to prevent social equality between the races. In the pages of his fiction a rhetorical question consistently emerges on the subject: If the color line that separates African Americans and whites is necessary, to the point of being sacred, why is that line crossed regularly by whites to satisfy their most base desires? Griggs first examines the logic of a color line in *Imperium*, where he introduces readers to the mulatto woman who is the mother of Bernard Belgrave. Her appearance startles even the racist white schoolmaster Mr. Leonard, who sees at the school's entrance "a woman whose beauty was such as he had never seen surpassed." The woman is "tall and graceful. Her hair was raven black and was combed away from as beautiful a forehead as nature could chisel. Her eyes were a brown hazel, large and intelligent. . . . Her complexion was a rich olive, and seemed especially adapted to her face, that revealed not a flaw."[50]

Her femininity transcends her racial affiliation. Like so many of Griggs's African American female characters, she epitomizes beauty, charm, and sophistication and presents a figure more likely to be found in a museum than a second-rate schoolhouse.

Her history is equally intriguing. She is the product of a liaison between a white state governor and his African American servant. In order to prevent discovery of his affair, the governor sends the child to be raised in his sister's home, where she blossoms "into a perfect beauty" who "possessed a charming voice, could perform extraordinary skill on the piano, and seemed to have inherited the mind of her father, whose praises have been sung in all the land." When the child reaches the age of seventeen, the woman who cares for her dies, and the task of "attending" to the young woman's welfare falls to the dead woman's husband, a state senator whose name is "a household word throughout the nation." Despite his role as father figure to the seventeen-year-old mulatta, during her development "so many beautiful qualities appeared that she excited [his] warm admiration."[51] Acting on his desires, the connection between the two progresses from one of father and daughter to one of husband and wife. Soon after their coupling, the young woman gives birth to an illegitimate mulatto child, Bernard Belgrave.

A similar situation can be found in *Overshadowed*, where James Lawson, the son of a wealthy white politician, falls in love with Erma Wysong, an educated and industrious mulatto woman. Lawson stops at nothing to possess Wysong, destroying her family members' lives and forcing her into poverty. Lawson's advances are interrupted only when he discovers that Wysong is his half-sister, the result of an affair between his father and a young African American woman his father disgraced and abandoned as a young man.

In *The Hindered Hand*, Arthur Daleman Jr. is a member of a wealthy white family who, in addition to the family business, opens a number of loan companies operating under questionable practices. In the course of monitoring his operations, Daleman becomes enamored by Foresta, a beautiful African American still in her teens. Using both his position and his color to advantage, Daleman, who holds the notes on loans made by Foresta's family, threatens to send Foresta's mother to the penitentiary if Foresta does not agree to work as a servant in his home. Using a "significant tone" that conveys his true intentions, Daleman tells Foresta, "Be a good girl, and you won't have a better friend than I am."[52] Placed in an impossible position by the underhanded Daleman, Foresta acquiesces to his demands. However, unlike many of his contemporaries, Griggs does not perpetuate the tragic mulatto stereotype in his fiction. His female characters do not lament their existence, nor do their circumstances move them to hysterics. Despite repeated attacks on their character and person, they remain proud, determined, and resilient, and their actions effectively critique white male society and its proclaimed unimpeachable morality.

In addition these forays across the racial divide enable Griggs's critique of color barriers that whites have erected and transgressed since the seventeenth century. Contrary to contemporary pseudo-scientific claims that "the class of white men who have intercourse with colored women are, as a rule, of an inferior type," Griggs examines the profuse interaction between African American women and white men from middle- and upper-class society and among white men whose interest in African American women stretches beyond their yearning to experience a cultural taboo.[53] These interpretations also show that time has not curbed the appetite of whites with respect to their desire for African Americans, nor has it enabled whites to mature in their attitude toward or their treatment of African Americans. Thus the sins of the father and, in the case of Bernard's mother, the sins of family members are repeated and passed on, perpetuating a system of sexual slavery and concubinage between African Americans and whites.

Driven by egoism and desire, whites fail to recognize the widespread effects of their licentiousness. In some ways Griggs uses the previous examples to counter popular arguments among racist whites that African American men prefer white women and that to prevent such unholy interactions, white men are duty bound to intervene and to protect white womanhood. As Griggs ably reveals, white men rarely occupy the moral high ground. His fiction shows that it is not unusual for white men to leave white women for African American women. Griggs suggests that whether an affair is casual or protracted, illicit actions on the part of white men are an embarrassment and a slight to white women and to the ideas of white womanhood that white men are sworn to protect. Time spent with an African American mistress or mate is a loss to white women but also to white families, who require a father's presence and support. Griggs calls for white men to be held accountable for their actions. They can no longer blame the hypersexualized Jezebels conjured by their racist white imaginations for their indiscretions. As Griggs's examples forcefully illustrate, duplicitous white men prey on African American women of impeccable character. Time and again it is whites, not African Americans, who cross the color barrier with impunity. These transgressions allow Griggs to mock the implied superiority of whites and to suggest ironically that any white men who prefer the company of African American women to white women have not held up their racial responsibility to maintain the rigidity of the color line. Further, should a child result from one of these interracial affairs, white males need look no further than themselves to identify the party responsible for further diluting the gene pool that protects white supremacy.

From this perspective, Griggs critiques the color line as an artificial barrier created by whites to shield them from prosecution for their aberrant behavior. On the dark side of the color line, white men are free to abandon the mask of civility and to prey on African American women. Because their legal status identifies them as the social inferiors of whites, African American women, in the eyes of white men, have no rights that white men have to respect.[54] Such attitudes among white men place African American women in impossible positions. In many instances African American women are forced to endure verbal and physical assaults from white men in order to protect their jobs or their lives. According to Griggs, this power dynamic also upsets African American family structures because African American women face pressure to comply with unwanted advances in order to protect the men in their lives.

As Griggs's work consistently reveals, the mere suggestion of impropriety between African American men and white women is enough to justify punishment for those men by legal or extralegal means. Yet how are African American men to respond to white men who have ravaged their mothers, sisters, and daughters? Griggs argues that because whites dominate government at federal, state, and local levels, they are "as influential in what [they] will not do as in what [they] will do."[55] Because white lawmakers and agents of law enforcement fail to curb mob violence, Griggs argues, African American men are unable to uphold their most fundamental responsibilities, such as protecting the bodies, or even the lives, of their wives and daughters due to the ever-present threat of violence. Such scenarios place African American men in impossible positions, either emasculating them or forcing them to respond violently, options that are both likely to lead to destruction, whether physical or psychological. In either case African American women are forced to deal with the insult and the aftermath of white men's predatory nature.

Griggs also challenges demeaning stereotypes of African American women created by whites and seeks to elevate their status by transforming them from objects to subjects. In both his fiction and nonfiction, Griggs reminds whites that African American women "can be either the most valuable ally or the most deadly foe of the dreams of the white South." Because white men have shown repeatedly their inability to maintain the racial divide on which they insist, Griggs argues that the only obstacle preventing the amalgamation of the races is the "racial chastity" of African American women. As proof of his assertion, he states that if inclined, African American women need only loosen their morals "to the pressure directed against [them]" by white men in order to give birth to a "vast army of mulattoes."[56] As a result of continued fornication with white men, African American women could practically eliminate the dark complexion of African Americans and, with it, the color line that divides the races. If whites want racial purity, and if they demand separation between the races, then they must provide for equal protection on both sides of the racial divide. For Griggs there is no compromise nor any distinction based on gender. While "the world at large has heard that the problem of the South is the protection of the white woman," he writes, "there is another woman in the South."[57]

Common Ground

At the conclusion of *The One Great Question*, Griggs invokes as a warning to whites a parable from the Book of Esther. He compares the treatment of African Americans by whites living in the South to that of the Jews persecuted by Haman during the reign of Xerxes.[58] Motivated by pride and race hatred, Haman erects a gallows in order to hang Mordecai, a Jew and his enemy. However, Haman fails to recognize the political consequences of his actions and is himself hanged, an agent in his own destruction. The meaning behind this biblical story highlights a resonating political theme in Griggs's fiction. The solution to the problem of race in America is located within the hearts and minds of those who constitute a racial and a political majority. Whites must remove the obstacles that prevent full citizenship rights for African Americans. They must also abandon the attitudes and customs that perpetuate racist stereotypes of African Americans and sanction limits on African American social, political, and economic mobility. Rather than looking at a minority as the source of the country's ills, Griggs insists that whites must examine the source of their racism, their capacity for cruelty, and their contempt for African Americans before resolution can begin.

While the ultimate goal of Griggs's fiction was to solve America's race problem, he realized that there could be no resolution without interracial cooperation. Because whites occupied the dominant position in

American society, before making any concessions they would have to be persuaded that African Americans would agitate effectively to obtain the rights to which they were entitled. Griggs also believed that a united political front would show whites that African Americans were educated protesters who understood their power and purpose. He dismissed emigration or amalgamation as realistic possibilities for African Americans and was fixated on a solution that would enable them to remain in America with a status equal to whites.

These beliefs strongly influenced the creation of *Imperium in Imperio*. As countless critics have noted, *Imperium in Imperio* is a radical work. To imagine the existence of a black separatist government is a provocative concept, particularly for an African American Baptist minister residing in Nashville at the turn of the century. There is also no denying that Imperium president Bernard Belgrave's radical plans for secession and race war leave an indelible impression on the reader. What cannot be forgotten is that the novel does not end with war and race genocide. Berl Trout, who is influenced by Belton Piedmont's leadership and committed to finding an alternate solution to America's race problem, thwarts Belgrave's plans. This ending does not mean the novel is no longer radical in scope, but it does turn its emphasis away from extreme New Negro responses to white racism and toward a more moderate solution to the political differences between African Americans and whites.

Throughout the novel the New Negro is searching for points of resistance within the South in which African Americans can gain a foothold to challenge their subordinate status. The formation of the Imperium is a political end to that journey. Caroline Levander has noted that Griggs's selection of Texas as the site of the Imperium is not incidental but one of the "strategic locations on the nation's edges from which to productively rethink some of the founding assumptions governing the geopolitics of African American rights."[59] Waco clearly provides Imperium members a remote location apart from other southern cities examined in the novel such as Richmond and Nashville, where an organized body of African Americans could not escape the scrutiny of whites. However, Griggs was certainly aware that even borderland locations such as Texas provided only temporary sanctuary for his fictional Imperium and its members.

To imagine the feasibility of such a plan, Griggs needed look no further than the late nineteenth-century eradication of Native American territorial rights that begins with the Dawes Act of 1887. Rather than extending "the protection of the laws of the United States and the territories over the Indians," the Dawes Act, and subsequent acts extending its provisions, dismantled Native Americans' attachment to collective territorial possession and impoverished them individually as a way of decimating them collectively and politically.[60] While many tribes continued to fight the eradication of their territory and the destruction of their way of life by the federal government, their resistance proved futile.

On December 29, 1890, less than a decade before Griggs published *Imperium in Imperio*, American newspapers detailed a clash between federal soldiers from the 7th Cavalry and Sioux at Wounded Knee, South Dakota. By day's end twenty-five cavalrymen and an estimated three hundred Sioux, many of whom were women and children, lay dead. It was the last battle in a series of nineteenth-century Indian wars and among the greatest massacres of Native Americans by whites in their long history of racial violence. The Oglala Sioux leader Black Elk recalled the massacre in his oral testimony: "I did not know then how much was ended. When I look back now from the high hill of my old age, I can still see the butchered women and children lying heaped and scattered all along the crooked gulch as plain as when I saw them with eyes still young. And I can see that something else died there in the bloody mud, and was buried in the blizzard. A people's dream died there. It was a beautiful dream."[61] In *Imperium in Imperio*, Griggs appears cognizant of the historical similarities between Native American and African American struggles for survival within America's dominant white culture. In much the same way that Black Elk imagined the beauty of an independent Native American nation within America, Belgrave too envisions a beautiful dream: an African American Imperium in Imperio. However, Piedmont recognizes Belgrave's dream for what it truly is: a dream.

Piedmont realizes that whites retain both a numeric and a strategic advantage over African Americans. He is also able to imagine the senseless slaughter of African Americans at the hands of the superior forces they would face: federal troops whetted to a razor's edge by the Civil War, Indian wars of the West, Cuba, and other American imperial pursuits. There is no victory in annihilation. African Americans need only to survey the Native American reservations of the West to see their future after war. For Piedmont the Imperium provides a temporary space where African Americans can gather their ideological and material strength. In his vision for the Imperium, the political objective is not to exist apart from American society but to leverage their empowered position to enable entry into society as the equal of whites.

Piedmont is a southerner and a Unionist. He views the South as the spiritual center of African American life and believes the region has been consecrated by the sweat and blood of African Americans for generations. This is why he chooses to speak "in defence of the south" rather than accede to the separatist machinations of Belgrave and the assembled majority: "On her soil I was born; on her bosom I was reared; into her arms I hope to fall in death; and I shall not fear of losing popular favor to desist from pointing out the natural sources from which her sins arise, so that when judgment is pronounced justice will not hesitate to stamp it with her righteous seal." He also reminds other Imperium members who seek confrontation with whites through war or revolt that the Imperium was organized "to secure our rights within the United States" and declares that he will exert every effort to attain that end: "I love the Union and I love the South. Soaked as Old Glory is with my people's tears and stained as it is with their warm blood, I could die as my forefathers did, fighting for its honor and asking no greater boon than Old Glory for my shroud and native soil for my grave." He warns fellow Imperium members, "Hope and despair are each equipped with swords, the latter more dreadful than the former." He refuses to betray America by allying with foreign enemies or to witness the annihilation of any significant portion of the Imperium's African American constituency. He insists on a resolution that will "pull the veil from the eyes of the Anglo-Saxon" and allow the white population to discover the existence of the Imperium and to understand its collective strength. From this vantage point whites can no longer dismiss African Americans as docile, Old Negro caricatures but will be forced to see "the New Negro standing before [them] humbly, but firmly demanding every right granted him by his maker and wrested from him by man."[62] This display of race unity then becomes Piedmont's sword of hope, a veiled threat that suggests the possibility of violent response.

Despite its verve, Piedmont's voice falls on deaf ears, and he chooses to resign from the Imperium rather than participate in a course of action that will isolate him from his beliefs and decimate the region and the country that he loves. The decision is a death sentence at the hands of those he has worked so long to organize and instruct. However, it is also a victory for his New Negro politics. By choosing to "walk into the embrace of death," Piedmont proves himself a patriot, loyal to country and cause.[63] In turn his example influences Berl Trout, a member who exposes the existence of the Imperium and averts the impending race war. Piedmont's political ideas ultimately prevail and enable African Americans and whites to establish a dialogue that can bridge the country's racial division.

In *Imperium in Imperio*, Griggs goes to fantastic lengths to establish a New Negro identity that can challenge whites' political suppression of African Americans. His second novel, *Overshadowed*, pursues an even more radical position with which the New Negro contests his political status. Despite numerous obstacles, Astral Herndon and Erma Wysong, Griggs's idyllic New Negro couple, appear to have found solace in the marriage they have worked so hard to achieve. Removed from Richmond, at the feet of Nutall's Mountain, West Virginia, the two are raising their child beyond the city's polluted racist environment. However, their happiness is interrupted when a knock at the door signals the arrival of Erma's half-brother, John, who she thought had died years earlier for the crime of murdering a white man. Exhausted by his escape from a chain gang and his efforts to find the half-sister he left long ago, John dies. Overwhelmed by the tragedy of her half-brother's death, an inconsolable Erma then dies of shock, leaving Astral and their child alone. However, Astral is unwilling to bury his wife and her half-brother in American soil because the land is "overshadowed" by prejudice and racial violence.[64] He instead renounces his American citizenship and boards a boat headed into the Atlantic.

After committing his relatives' bodies to the ocean, Astral declares himself "A CITIZEN OF THE OCEAN," a title to "be entailed upon [his] progeny unto all generations, until such time as the shadows which now envelope the darker races in all lands shall have passed away, away and away."[65] It is an ending as curious as it is dramatic. If, as I have argued, *Imperium* provides us with a martyr to cause and to country in Belton Piedmont, *Overshadowed* presents a different kind of rebel altogether. Like Piedmont, Astral provides a damning indictment of white society, its crimes against humanity, its insufferable pride, and its unyielding dominion over those it deems inferior, but unlike Piedmont, Astral does not attempt to bridge the chasm that separates African Americans and whites. Astral leaves America, and by doing so he rejects an idealized construct, one fraught with racist attitudes and infiltrated by a suffocating atmosphere of contempt. His decision to leave America is a rejection of political accommodation and social conservatism. He refuses to abide; he will not wear a mask; and he refuses the path of least resistance. He rejects the warped social perspective that creates a Du Boisian double consciousness. Astral seeks a destination where African Americans can exhibit complete selfhood, unshadowed rather than overshadowed, free from beneath the veil.

From the scenario emerges a lingering, if rhetorical, question: Where does such an environment exist for people of African descent? Prior to Astral's departure, he is asked, "Are you returning to your fatherland?," to which he responds, "It too is overshadowed. Aliens possess it."[66] When pressed to provide a final destination, he offers no response. While one can assume that the "fatherland" referred to in this query is Africa, it is less clear whether Astral finds this destination unsuitable because much of the territory, like America, is in colonial (white) hands or because he feels no immediate or spiritual connection with natives of that continent. In such a context the conclusion of Griggs's novel becomes almost otherworldly. Independent and adrift, Astral is a modern-day corsair who rejects American citizenship and, by doing so, establishes sovereignty in a realm without boundaries where he (and ultimately his progeny) is free to move uninhibited across barriers of race, space, and time.[67]

In his final novels Griggs turns from the unknown and seeks solutions to America's race problem at home. Curiously critics such as Robert Bone argue that these novels, *Pointing the Way* in particular, suggest that Griggs returned to his work with a much more conservative political focus than he exhibited in previous works. As an example of what he calls Griggs's "conciliatory and accommodationist" position, Bone refers to Uncle Jack, "a minor character" who remarks, "Good white people kin lead de cullud folks ef dey will jes' gree ter do so."[68] On the surface Jack's simple dialect and the tell-tale "Uncle" label designate him as a dutiful "Tom." However, he, like most of Griggs's slave-era characters, is not so thinly drawn, nor is he the minor character Bone suggests.

Jack was born and raised in slavery, and after the Civil War he used his skills as a tenant farmer to support a family. Yet like so many newly freed slaves in the South, Jack faces an angry and impotent white community seeking retribution for the consequences of Reconstruction. His domestic serenity is interrupted when local Ku Klux Klan members attack his house. Following a hail of gunfire, Jack locates the deceased bodies of his two-year-old son, his one-year-old daughter, and his wife, who is shot through the head. When Klan members realize Jack has survived their raid, they beat and shoot him and prepare his lynching rope. Moments before Jack is lifted from the ground, he is saved from death by a neighbor who surprises the Klan members and kills them for their crimes. In the wake of his suffering, Jack is demure but not defeated. In order to function in a hostile environment, he dons a self-deprecating mask: "De elluphunt pertecks hisself wid his snoot, de dog makes his gitby wid his teef, de bee makes yer 'speck hisself wid er sting, an' de cullud man hez been takin' keer uv hisself wid er joke."[69] As evidence of how effectively he wears his mask, Jack earns the "Uncle" label from local whites, who view him as submissive and unthreatening. It is this side of Jack that

readers first discover upon his introduction to the novel and this image
that has garnered the censure of Bone and other critics.

At this stage, however, Griggs has just begun to develop Jack's purpose
in the novel. Soon after his introduction, he meets Eina Rapona, a race
woman who is a mulatto by blood but white to all observers. Despite her
ability to pass in white society and live a life free from restrictions, Rapona chooses to live as an African American and is committed to bridging the racial divide in the fictional city of Belrose, where she and Jack
reside. Enchanted by her beauty and her intellect, Jack introduces her
to his friend Baug Peppers, a young African American attorney whose
looks and sensibilities are equal to Rapona's. After a lengthy tête-à-tête in
which the two characters exchange ideas identified with the New Negro,
Rapona encourages Peppers to head a movement to eliminate race-based
inequalities: "Years of development since Emancipation have produced a
group of cleanly, cultured, aspiring people in the colored race. The first
step in the solution is for this group to take charge of and guide the racial
thought and life. It can be done, and the confidence of the people in your
character and ability point to you as the one man to weld this controlling
group and to link it on to the masses of the colored people."[70] The first
step toward their goal is to test a clause added to an Alabama state law
that disenfranchises illiterate African American voters but allows votes
from illiterate whites. To accomplish this task, they approach Jack and
ask him to cast his vote in an upcoming election.

Although it is an intimidating proposal for Jack, he recognizes it as an
opportunity to retaliate against the injustices he faced during the period
of Reconstruction:

> Times hab changed an'er cullud race we mus' stan' up now an' meet
> de diffunt qusshuns face ter face, face ter face. Wal' you young
> uns is able ter do dat. We ole uns wuz ignerrunt an' we jus' bowed
> an' scraped our way through ez bes' we could, tell yer all could git
> sense enough ter make er bettah stan. . . . Yer goin' ter see yer Uncle
> Jack comin' right back ter take up de cross yer young uns hez pur-
> pared fur him. Uncle Jack ain't feered. Nevah run frum nutthin' but
> er sperrit er ghost er sumpin' lak dat since I been bawn ter die.[71]

It is Jack's status as "Uncle" that enables him to enter the Birmingham courthouse unmolested. Election officials even invite the old man to sit and share
anecdotes from his slave days to pass the time. Jack shrewdly uses the audience
to his advantage. He wins them over with laughter and distracts them from
their focus. When the opportunity presents itself, he slips toward the election

box and casts his ballot before the election judge. "What have you done? You are not a registered voter," shouts the judge. In simple words and with a face that no longer hides his emotions, Jack responds: "I is er ill-littered man an' my granddaddy wuz er slave. Dey wouldn't put my name on de reg'stration books 'cause my granddaddy couldn't vote. Ez my granddaddy wuz kept frum votin' cause uv his color an' cause he wuz er slave, it is stretchin' color an' slavery down ter me terday fur me ter be shet out on 'count uv my grandaddy's shortcomin's. Ter stretch color an' slav'ry lak dat is pointedly 'gainst de constertution uv de United States. Ez I wuz shet out uv de reg'stration by unfair means, I done come straight ter de 'lection."[72] Enraged by Jack's impudence, the white election judge punches him in his face. The blow is so severe that the elderly man topples over, strikes his head against the wall, and loses consciousness. News of the disturbance reaches reporters, and Jack's decision to cast his vote in the election makes national headlines. Unfortunately Jack succumbs to his injuries and does not live to see Peppers argue successfully before the U.S. Supreme Court against the clause from the Alabama state law that he challenged. As a result of that victory, Peppers returns to Belrose, where he is able to eliminate the political warfare waged between African Americans and whites over equal treatment before the law and to institute reforms that produce opportunities for advancement without barriers of color. The final goal is for Belrose to serve as a model for communities across the country and to show the benefits of interracial cooperation.

What readers discover at the conclusion of *Pointing the Way* is an ending consistent with others in Griggs's repertoire, including *Imperium in Imperio*. Just prior to Jack's casting his vote at the Birmingham courthouse, he and Peppers are discussing the importance of political action by African Americans. Peppers reminds Jack that African Americans' citizenship rights "came to us amid the lingering passions of war and should not be taken as the sober sense of the American people."[73] Peppers, like Piedmont in *Imperium*, recognizes that whites are not committed to protecting African American equality. Each man also realizes that if African Americans tolerate any rollback of their rights, whites will perceive them as weak and undeserving of them. As representatives of the exceptional men among the race, they are responsible for focusing the potential and strength of men and women who constitute the masses among African American society. However, it is not enough for them to distinguish right from wrong or to think and talk about how to improve the status of African Americans, because those methods lead too often to social paralysis, and tasks remains undone.[74] For the New Negro, thoughts and words mean nothing without action. This ideology inspires Berl Trout to reveal the existence of the Imperium and motivates Jack to challenge the disenfranchisement of African American voters in Alabama.

By acting on their principles, men like Trout and Jack also play the role of hero and patriot. Their sacrifices enable the groups they represent to coalesce and achieve their stratagems. For Griggs it's a historical process Americans should recognize. The creation of the Imperium was influenced by the ideas of Jeffersonian democracy and the principles of republicanism. During his years at Stowe University in Nashville, Piedmont was recruited to the Imperium, where he served in the capacity of "chairman of the bureau of education" for the purpose of "educating the race upon the doctrine of human liberty."[75] *Pointing the Way* focuses on civic duty and the sacredness of the franchise. For African Americans in particular, political equality is needed for self-protection and for self-defense against racism and bias that is color-based. Griggs clearly suggests that whatever obstacles prevent blacks from voting in American society—property ownership, poll taxes, literacy tests—must also prevent whites of similar status from voting. He asks, How much better is an uninformed white vote than an uninformed black vote? Both sides must be pressed toward excellence, and none should be rewarded for ignorance. These ideas not only benefit local communities and state populations but are fundamental to the health of an enlightened democratic society.

Native Son

At the conclusion of *The Hindered Hand*, Ensal Ellwood travels from Almaville to the site where Bud and Foresta Harper were murdered. A white attorney named Maul, who helped prosecute those responsible for the crime, guides him to the location. Silently the two men survey the charred remnants before them. Breaking the silence, Maul observes, "They are dead—the trees I mean—and perhaps it is well. Time will now eat away their vitals and they shall no longer stand as monuments to the shame of our land."[76] Moved by a spirit of reconciliation, Ellwood asks Maul to join him on the steps of an African American church, where they discuss the possibilities for life in the South undeterred by issues of race.

Notably the chapter in which the conversation between Ellwood and Maul takes place is entitled "A Son of the New South." The symbolic value of this label reflects Griggs's selection of Almaville as a cover name for Nashville. What Griggs seeks is community between African Americans and whites. He wants whites to acknowledge their past sins and to work toward creating harmony in an environment that has nourished all of them. It is fitting that these two southern men, one African American and one white, stand with mutual respect upon a site that represents the horrors of a racial past and imagine a meaningful future. However, embedded within Griggs's visionary claiming of his southern home for members of both races is evidence of his ongoing radicalism.

For instance, "A Son of the New South" is a clear statement of inclusion, one that implies African Americans do not intend to vacate or abandon the South. In his discussion with Maul, Ellwood emphasizes that if white southerners, particularly radical southern Democrats, continue to persecute African Americans and prevent their attainment of citizenship rights, they will not only resist physically but also politically, by empowering opposing parties to ensure the isolation and impotence of the Democratic Party in national affairs. Ellwood insists that for the good of the South, and the nation, Maul must rally like-minded whites, those on the side of justice, to neutralize radical Democrats and exclude those preventing amity between the races.

Here, as in previous novels, Griggs questions whether whites respect the laws they endorse. If they do, he wonders why federal amendments are circumvented to prevent African Americans from obtaining full citizenship rights. Time and again he asks whether whites are able to make any claim to supremacy that does not require a demonstration of their cruelty or reveal their capacity for brute force? Are whites so insecure with their status that they are unable to face the prospect of African American equality? Griggs's novels repeatedly taunt and challenge white society: If whites are the superior race, if they are physical, moral, and intellectual superiors to African Americans, then what do they have to fear by enforcing equally the constitutional rights of America's citizens?

When pressed by Ellwood to declare whether or not he will enforce equal treatment before the law, Maul responds, "I would not have our nation live a lie and pollute the whole stream of our people's lives. If the nation is lawless it can hardly expect its citizens to be different."[77] His is a staunch defense of the concepts of liberty and justice and one that represents the moral revolution necessary to rebuild a New South. Because whites are the dominant (not superior) race, and because they constitute a political majority, Griggs calls on them to become defenders of African American men and women and of manhood rights and to search their consciences for a means to address the country's race problem. These imbalances must be corrected not only for the moral health of whites but also for the communities in which African Americans and whites are in regular contact.

5 / "Tried by Fire": The African American Boycott of Jim Crow Streetcars in Nashville, 1905–1907

All things come to them that wait, providing they hustle while they wait.
—CHARLES W. ANDERSON, *NASHVILLE GLOBE*, JANUARY 18, 1907

On August 27, 1905, sixteen African American men entered the downtown office of the county clerk in Nashville's Court House. Among the group were influential businessmen, politicians, and religious leaders from the city's African American community. The purpose of their visit was to file a charter of incorporation to establish the Union Transportation Company, a corporation authorized to "purchase automobiles, omnibuses, carriages, horses and run the same for conveyance of passengers and the transportation of goods, wares and merchandise, from one to another point in the city, or from one to another point in any county in the state."[1] Their decision to form a transportation company and to authorize twenty-five thousand dollars in capital stock created the first African American transit company in the United States. Significantly their decision to incorporate went beyond solely financial considerations.

For the previous two months the majority of Nashville's African American community members had boycotted city streetcars in response to state legislation that required the separation of passengers according to race.[2] While similar protests of streetcar segregation laws by African Americans occurred throughout the South between 1892 and 1907, the majority of them ended quickly.[3] However, Nashville's resolve was strengthened, due in no small part to the coalition that formed the Union Transportation Company, an assemblage of men who provided the financial backing and strong leadership that was absent from boycotts in other locations.

Seizing on enthusiasm for the new transportation venture, the Reverend Sutton E. Griggs rallied hundreds of African American citizens at the annual Labor Day celebration at Midway Park, where he urged continued opposition to Jim Crow streetcars. Griggs viewed the implementation of segregation laws as an effort by southern whites not so much to humiliate African Americans in the South as to control their movement, to force them beyond the region's borders, where they no longer posed a threat to white labor or social equality. Because Griggs saw the South as "an ideal home for the race," he argued that its African American citizenry must stand firm and remain "vitally interested in the standards that are to prevail." His words reflected basic New Negro attitudes toward political activism and the protection of manhood rights. Griggs argued that segregation laws had placed African Americans "in a furnace" where they were being "tried by fire" and that only sustained, organized resistance would deliver them "from the fire unscathed."[4]

According to August Meier and Elliott Rudwick, what made streetcar protests in the South so significant was that they "lasted as long as they did" or that "they had ever taken place" at all.[5] Although Nashville's African American community was unsuccessful in overturning laws that segregated streetcars, their two-year boycott (1905–7) proved to be the longest and most successful protest of streetcar segregation laws in the country. The protest showed that African Americans in Nashville, at a time of extreme racial violence, could freely meet, organize, and establish economic and rhetorical positions of resistance without the kind of reprisals likely to occur elsewhere in the South. The movement also produced the *Nashville Globe*, a significant secular African American newspaper that became a successful medium for sustaining the ideas and sensibilities that went into organizing the boycott and establishing alternative transportation opportunities. This sensibility identified Nashville's African American community as economically as well as politically and socially independent and had several implications for Nashville's development as a significant New Negro cultural and intellectual center of the New South from which African Americans exerted sustained and organized resistance to white supremacy in the age of Jim Crow.

Dividing Lines

In January 1899 Tennessee's General Assembly discussed extending laws that segregated public transportation to include streetcars.[6] Although the proposal never made it beyond the House Judiciary Committee, groups of white citizens from different parts of the state continued to press officials to pass legislation that segregated streetcars. A similar proposal seeking "to require separate street cars for the white and colored races" appeared on January 30, 1901, but like its predecessor, it was defeated.[7] The topic, however, remained a popular subject of debate within the legislature and among Tennessee's white population. In the months following the latest vote for segregation of the state's streetcars, whites began to agitate more effectively for their cause. The pages of local papers across the state, providing a forum for discussing streetcar segregation, reflected racist public opinion: "There can be no doubt that many of the negroes who travel on streetcars are very offensive to the white passengers, and as the latter are the mainstay of the system, they feel that they are entitled to some protection. Those negroes who are offensive are very offensive indeed. Negro women of this kind will crowd into seats where there is no room for them, sometimes almost sitting on the laps of white women; and it is the conduct of these creatures that has aroused such a sentiment against the negro generally."[8]

In February 1903, with the support of such racist sentiments, Tennessee passed a streetcar segregation act.[9] Introduced by A. K. Hancock of Shelby County on January 13, 1903, Senate Bill 37 included "all street railroads and street railways in any county in the State of Tennessee having one hundred and fifty thousand inhabitants or over, as shown by the Federal census of 1900, or any subsequent Federal census." Although a number of cities had been included in the original provisions, the final version of the law meant that only Memphis, located in Shelby County, met this population requirement. Memphis streetcar company owners, however, were unwilling to enforce the law. Despite public pressure from local whites who voiced their concerns about riding integrated streetcars, streetcar companies, like the railroad companies before them, were unwilling to create separate cars for the transportation of African Americans because they felt that the flow of traffic during any given period was unpredictable, making the cost to haul empty cars prohibitive. Rather than face the financial burden of trailing a second car or refurbishing existing vehicles to accommodate the separation of its customers by race, the Memphis Street Railway Company challenged the constitutionality of the statute. The railway company's appeal cited five "assignments of error," including an assertion that the 1903 Act was "repugnant" to the Fourteenth Amendment, which guaranteed "equal protection of the laws."[10] Based on a legal technicality stemming from improper phrasing, the Tennessee Supreme Court upheld the railway company's appeal, requiring lawmakers to reconsider their approach to what had become an extremely sensitive issue.

The question of whether African Americans were to be separated from whites by trailer or separate compartments continued to be debated in Tennessee. When a number of white Nashvillians complained about the odor emitted from the bodies of African American employees who worked at a local fertilizer plant, the Nashville Railway and Light Company added an extra car to the West Nashville Line to appease its white patrons.[11] One African American weekly suggested that whites fearing contamination from contact with African Americans should lobby their legislatures for "the building of parallel roads, under separate and distinct companies and entirely different cars," with "gigantic screens all along the line so the respective race passengers cannot see each other."[12] This response highlights fear of disease as an additional motive whites had for segregation. Because streetcars moved through multiple areas within Nashville, many whites saw them as a conduit for disease. According to Don Doyle, it is "more than coincidence that the systematic reign of Jim Crow emerged in law and practice at the same time that the germ theory was gaining popular acceptance." Doyle believes segregation of toilets, restaurants, fountains, hospitals, and streetcars was not only an effort to establish white supremacy across the South but also a way to "protect the white race from contamination" by isolating contact in places where whites were wary of practical health concerns.[13]

Among the greatest of these concerns for local whites was the threat of tuberculosis, which was responsible for 16 percent of all deaths in Nashville between 1885 and 1915. Although tuberculosis did not discriminate by race among the urban poor, the death rate of African Americans was three times that of whites, providing statistical evidence that enabled several communicable diseases to become "laden with moral and racial connotations."[14] These beliefs seem impractical, if not absurd, given the contact between whites and African American domestic laborers in a number of settings, including the homes of many whites, where African Americans worked in various capacities as cooks, servants, and caretakers. Nevertheless anxieties related to possible contagion persisted among the urban white population.

The physical distance that would be created by streetcar segregation laws was emblematic of the public dividing line in spaces over which African Americans and whites would wage a battle against the urban politics of Jim Crow. Such legal maneuverings sought to cement a division between the races that had become more fluid since African Americans began migrating to city centers in recent decades. In the antebellum urban South, large numbers of African Americans often lived in simple, shanty-like communities known as "back-alley" settlements. Primarily occupied by domestic workers, these houses could be found behind the more impressive homes of their white employers. Legal constraints and social convention during the antebellum period ensured African American inferiority and subjugation; however, once the fetters of bond slavery no longer bound them, African Americans challenged those practices and customs that had previously held them in place. According to the psychologist Kenneth Clark, "The most intimate relationships have been approved between Negro and white so long as the status of white superiority versus Negro inferiority has been clear. Trouble comes only when Negroes decide not to be servants or mistresses and seek status equal to that of whites. When Negroes start to assume symbols of upward mobility, then a pattern of residential segregation develops."[15] A decided shift in the segregation of residential communities, coinciding with the influx of African American migration to urban centers, began at the close of the nineteenth century. As a result wealthy whites began to move from the center of the South's major cities to suburban areas. The urban settlement of African Americans began on the outskirts of locations newly settled by whites. Because land at higher elevation was considered most valuable, African Americans generally lived in "damp, poorly drained lowlands," or bottomlands as they were called in many cities. According to John Kellogg, white landowners were quick to take advantage of African American migrants by designating "only the poorest land" for agricultural or residential purposes.[16] These practices often limited space to areas considered undesirable to whites, such as vacant lots near railroad tracks, cemeteries, or city dumps. These practical economic considerations and a desire by many African Americans to reside near people of their own color also exacerbated the chasm between African American and white communities.

Nashville's African American community was among the fastest growing in the South, having expanded from a population of 31,331 in 1880 to 46,710 in 1910, an increase of 49 percent.[17] In 1900 Nashville's white elite began moving from the city center of Capitol Hill to the suburban West End area and its adjacent Richland and Harding Pike communities.[18] The majority of African American residents occupied the same areas established by migrants twenty years earlier: Black Bottom, located between Broad and Demonbreum; Trimble Bottom, near Central Tennessee College; Fort Negley–Edgehill, south of Lafayette Street and both sides of Franklin Road; Hell's Half Acre and Smokey Row, located in the Crawford-Gay Street area; and near Fisk University, just south of

Jefferson Street.[19] Because of the separation between residential communities, streetcars became one of the few places African Americans and whites were in proximity.

Of particular concern to Nashville's white streetcar-riding population was the predominantly African American area located to the southeast of Nashville's city center known as Black Bottom, "a sprawling slum in a flood-prone area near the river."[20] Demands to clean up the area, which encompassed portions of Sixth, Fifth, Third, and Second avenues and their connecting cross streets and alleys, began as early as the 1880s. These demands were due in part to a decline in property values that occurred when legitimate businesses found themselves surrounded on all sides by "a conglomeration of dives, brothels, pawnshops, second-hand clothing stores," and other "disgraceful and sickening" locations which ran through "the hideous heart of Black Bottom." Many white Nashville residents lamented the migration of African Americans into a vicinity that had once been occupied by a "respectable population." According to one white inhabitant, "The English language is not sufficiently versatile or strong to characterize 'that untidy looking and unsavory spot.'"[21]

To combat what they perceived to be a bacterial adversary associated with the presence of African Americans, white Nashvillians formed numerous organizations during this period to address the revitalization of what they perceived to be downtrodden areas that were responsible for the spread of disease. Claiming that "sweet smelling roses cannot be grown upon a dunghill," Nashville's Civic Improvement Committee sought to raze entire blocks and their buildings to create a central park, modeled after the one in New York City, in order to "furnish wholesome breathing and resting places for the people."[22] Citing the "evil of expectoration," women of the Nashville Centennial Club lobbied the board of health to enforce a city ordinance that would ban people from spitting on streetcars and in public.[23] The overwhelming attitude of Nashville's white community was that the "microscopical demons" responsible for spreading typhoid and tuberculosis be destroyed where they were bred, and the location repeatedly identified as the source was the Black Bottom home believed to be "their jungle, their paradise." Proclaiming the district a "plague spot," many whites were unwilling to ride a streetcar through the locale.[24] The increasing popularity of these beliefs only exacerbated the gap between African Americans and whites, further justifying their forced separation.

A Place in the Sun

On April 4, 1905, Tennessee's General Assembly enacted House Bill 87, which sought to "promote the comfort of public travel by providing for and securing the separation of the white and colored passengers on street cars."[25] The streetcar companies were given until July 5 to be in compliance. Although the language of the document provided exceptions for African American nurses who might be tending to sick or elderly whites or African American nannies who were watching over the children of white passengers, Tennessee's streetcar segregation bill demanded separation according to race and insisted that signage be created and displayed to designate appropriate spacing of passengers. Failure to take one's assigned place would result in a misdemeanor fine that carried a twenty-five-dollar penalty. Failure to comply with such regulations also led in most cases to forcible removal and additional violence.

Confrontations between African Americans and whites were neither rare nor limited by an African American's age or gender. According to one African American resident in Memphis, "Many of our people, through fear of maltreatment [at the hands of streetcar conductors] are walking while not a few prefer to walk rather than comply with the 'Jim Crow' requirement."[26] In Jacksonville, John Wallace argued that granting southern streetcar employees, who were almost exclusively white, police-like authority was a matter certain to "cause friction and disturbance" among "law abiding" African American citizens.[27] Drawing a parallel between the class to which white streetcar employees belonged and that from which the "white hoodlums" so often responsible for white-on-black violence emerged, the *Richmond Planet* editor John Mitchell Jr. argued that segregation laws, particularly the right of streetcar conductors to carry weapons, empowered streetcar employees and created a volatile environment in cities where white conductors were already "universally feared" for their "overbearing and insulting conduct."[28] In Nashville an African American woman informed the *American* that her "'sensibilities' and 'feelings' had been crushed so often that she actually hated to get on the cars any more."[29] Yet to members of the city's white population, streetcar segregation was a way of ensuring peace in public spaces.

Just weeks after the passage of Bill 87 on April 4, 1905, Nashville newspapers reported the appearance of Jim Crow signs. According to white papers, enforcement of the new law had caused "no friction whatever" between African Americans and whites, evidenced by the lack of complaints received at Nashville's police headquarters and the main offices of the Nashville Railway and Light Company.[30] The only visible encumbrance mentioned was that borne by the conductors, who were responsible for the "necessity" of "changing passengers from one seat to another."[31] Nashville's streetcar conductors, like many across the South, quickly realized that discontented African American customers were not their only concern. White conductors often argued with white passengers who did not like being told where they must sit. In Mobile a white dentist leaped dangerously from a moving car after being told he must abandon his regular section. A white woman in Little Rock threatened to report a conductor to the streetcar company's general manager for expecting her to "give up her seat to a negro."[32] Many times white men returning home from jobs that caused them to become sweaty or soot-covered chose to sit in sections marked "colored" rather than sit next to white women. Passengers, white and black, wanting to smoke their pipes or cigars while traveling to and from their destination were required to use one of three rear rows of seats.

By not segregating these smoking sections, Nashville's streetcar company forced its white passengers to choose between their vices and their racist beliefs. Edward Ayers describes the indeterminate space on streetcars that separated African Americans from whites as a "twilight zone," where constantly shifting attitudes and enforcements regarding race and identity reflected those sweeping across cities of the South.[33] These examples represent only a few of the inconveniences that were common throughout the South as a result of streetcar segregation laws. Ayers points out that because of these laws, conductors were required to make immediate judgments about an individual's racial identity. According to Isaiah B. Scott, editor of the *Southwestern Christian Advocate*, "determining who is white and who is colored" was particularly challenging in New Orleans, where the existence of a large Creole population left a conductor "with more than he can possibly do."[34] Situations arising from this process of delicate decision making often forced conductors into unwanted "altercations, lawsuits, and fistfights" with out-of-town travelers who were unfamiliar with local ordinances or with local workers deemed unrecognizable because of sullied clothing or dirty faces.[35] Nashville's streetcar company sought to avoid such incidents by instructing its conductors not to engage noncompliant customers but to locate a police officer when possible and have the offender "placed under arrest."[36] Most Nashville papers tried to deflect any negative occurrences associated with the new laws, choosing instead to stress that the number of African Americans riding Nashville's streetcars was "small in comparison" with the number of whites riding. Most passengers "would not know" that Jim Crow laws were even in effect.[37] Hoping to alleviate any confusion for those people "not yet accustomal [sic] to it," local newspapers included helpful reminders that encouraged "white people to the front, colored people to the rear."[38]

By July 5, 1905, when the streetcar segregation laws went into effect, even the white papers could not ignore signs that the city's African American community members had begun a boycott of local streetcars. The *American* noted an immediate "falling off in the number of negroes riding," and the *Banner* reported that "quite a number" of African Americans had "determined to walk rather than ride under the new law."[39] One white businessman experienced the determination of boycotters personally when his cook informed him that she must quit because "she had to walk too far now and she said she could not ride on the cars." Likely hoping to alleviate concerns regarding the possibility of a concerted movement by African Americans, white papers were quick to point out that Nashville's African American population did not appear to have held any "mass-meeting" or established any "union or concert in their action." White papers also focused their readers' attention on the fact that "laboring men" had to travel long distances to reach work sites and that most African Americans would soon "tire of walking" and would be "compelled to ride on the cars."[40]

Despite their knowledge of widespread streetcar boycotts from southern African Americans in response to segregation laws, editors of Nashville's papers refused to acknowledge any motive on behalf of the city's African American population. The *American* claimed that Nashville's African American community was "under the erroneous impression" that the segregation policy was discriminatory. In defense of the law's fairness, the article stated that, though the law prohibited "negroes from sitting by whites," it also kept "whites from sitting beside negroes," suggesting that each race was entitled to some degree of privileged space.[41] In general the articles published in the days following the city's implementation of streetcar segregation laws expressed opinions on the matter that were similar to those of a white Nashville resident who was quoted as saying, "As a rule, [African Americans] are easy to manage and bidable," and therefore they would accede to "existing conditions."[42] Opinions from whites about the ability of African Americans to sustain meaningful boycotts against streetcar segregation laws were bolstered by reports similar to those of Erwin Craighead, editor of Mobile's *Daily*

Register, whose May 1905 article declared, "The negroes . . . have invariably declared a boycott, and heroically abandoned their greatest delight, i.e., riding the cars, but time plays them a trick. They discover that walking is not as amusing as it is said to be. . . . Consequently, they resort again to the street cars, finding to their surprise, that separation law is actually a very fair provision. . . . Then the boycott falls and the negroes patronize the cars as before. About 2 months' time is necessary for this conversion from ignorance."[43] Craighead fails to mention the intimidation tactics or the instances of violence used by Mobile's whites to force the city's African Americans into compliance with local ordinances or state laws; however, his timetable for the disintegration of African American boycotts proved accurate for the majority of efforts prior to 1905. Not surprisingly most whites in Nashville believed that African Americans would not forfeit their opportunities to work and that they would not risk upsetting the white community through widespread demonstrations.

Had white Nashvillians paid closer attention to the concerns of the city's African American community regarding the discriminatory nature of streetcar legislation, they would have seen the coming storm. Prominent representatives from the city's African American community, such as James A. Jones, pastor of the St. Paul A.M.E. Church, had also been speaking to reporters prior to the law's enactment. Addressing the possibility of Jim Crow streetcars, Jones argued, "The day the separate street car law goes in effect...that day the company will lose nine-tenths of its negro patronage and there will be practically only one class of colored passengers to content [sic] with....The self-respecting, intelligent colored citizens of Nashville will not stand for Jim-crowism on the streetcar lines in this city. The shoe stores and livery stables will very likely profit by this move on the part of the City Council."[44] Similar to previous comments made by Griggs, Jones's words emphasize the New Negro's determination and his commitment to protest any infringement of civil liberties in the public sphere. Other influential African American leaders echoed Jones's sentiment, including the Reverend Edward W. D. Isaac, editor of the *Nashville Clarion*, who encouraged his readers to "trim their corns, darn their socks, wear solid shoes...and get ready to walk."[45] Many African Americans viewed streetcar segregation as another attempt by whites to visibly put them in their place. Others objected to the lack of partitions that defined appropriate spaces for passengers of either race. And still others commented that they could not stand the "bull-dozing of the conductors," who were repeatedly blamed by African Americans for their rough and unfair treatment.[46] George T. Robinson, an African American lawyer and former editor of the *Star*, was one of many African Americans angered by the consistent passage of laws by white southern legislatures that denied African Americans full citizenship. In response to what he viewed as a blatant attempt to display African American inferiority, Robinson told reporters he had "one request to make of white people of the South, and that is to get out of our sunshine—in other words, let us alone."[47]

Wheels of Progress

On August 1, 1905, Nashville Negro Business League members, including Preston Taylor, R. H. Boyd, and Sutton Griggs, assumed a leadership role in the boycott and began organizing members of the African American community.[48] A meeting at Clarion Hall, located on the corner of Second Avenue North and Locust Street, was advertised as "the most important meeting of the year by far." Although the need to elect delegates for representation at the national convention in New York City on August 16 was a pressing matter, leading members Griggs and Taylor sought to "inaugurate a movement" that would join similar efforts by African Americans in Tennessee's other major cities and would pressure legislators to repeal Jim Crow laws that applied to streetcars during their next session. Committee members cited the work of African American citizens in Memphis who had already raised five thousand dollars for the cause, and they pressed Nashville's African American citizens to raise equivalent monies. Leading Business League members specifically urged Nashville's African American community to avoid riding streetcars "except under cases of absolute necessity."[49]

Following a course of action previously employed by African American boycotters in Jacksonville, New Orleans, and Richmond, who encouraged protestors to avoid riding trolley cars by providing alternative transportation, organizers also encouraged express wagon operators to "do all they could" to support the streetcar boycott and, when possible, to cart their fellow African Americans to locations across the city. In an effort to deflect white criticism of the boycott, Taylor stated that protestors bore "no feeling of animosity in this affair" and that the reaction of many African American community members could be explained as a "simple case of protecting our own rights."[50] News of an organized boycott quickly spread throughout Nashville's African American community, and people were determined to respond to the new segregation law by showing a united front. Their reactions highlight the importance of race pride and race solidarity as key components of New Negro activism.

By the end of August, Nashville's African American population proved just how resourceful it could be.

The Union Transportation Company of Nashville sought to carry "passengers, merchandise, traffic and freight" across the city and eventually to locations throughout the state.[51] When the announcement reached local papers, Boyd was in Tarrytown, New York, where he placed an order for five steam-propelled vehicles, each with the capacity to transport ten to eighteen passengers. Apparently he also reserved the option to purchase an additional twenty cars if necessary.[52] Boasting "experienced men" as conductors and a transfer system identical to that of their white competitor, the company confidently asserted that operations would begin by the middle of September "at the very least."[53] As both a political and an economic maneuver, the venture characterized the progressive agenda of the New Negro.

Inspired after hearing about Nashville's creation of an African American transit line, John Mitchell Jr. called for "electric motor cars in every Southern city where the infamous Jim Crow street-car law is in practice."[54] Only in Richmond, where pledges of financial support from the city's four African American banks were extended, was there discussion of creating another African American transit line. Although no such line ever materialized outside of Nashville, southern boycotters defiantly relied on hack service, wagons, and even undertaker "bus" delivery systems in an effort to avoid riding streetcars. Nashville's African American incorporators avoided questions from whites about the timing of their newly formed venture, saying that they were only seeking a profitable business opportunity. Despite the feigned indifference of these entrepreneurs, white papers informed their readers that many of these same men had been responsible for calling a meeting of the Business League to declare that "they would use every effort to keep the colored people as far as possible" from using the lines of Nashville's white-owned streetcar company. In a subtle jab directed at newly implemented segregation laws, Union officials happily announced that for only a five-cent fare, they looked forward to transporting both African American and white customers "from one end of the city to another."[55]

In an effort to sustain momentum for the new transportation venture and the boycott of Nashville's white-owned streetcars, Preston Taylor presided over an open stockholders meeting, where an announcement concerning the routes for the newly arriving omnibuses was made. After a motion to delay submission of the bylaws, Boyd assessed the running expenses and announced that seven thousand of the subscribed twenty-five thousand dollars in stock had been raised. A portion of these funds had already been allocated for a "carry-all" drawn by four horses that was being used by the company to meet passengers arriving by train at Nashville's Union Station.[56] Amid a series of applauses, President Taylor interjected that "considerable stock" had been acquired from "colored citizens" from Louisville, Kentucky, and as far away as New York.[57] His words encouraged local community members that they were not alone in their struggle. Nashville protestors were well aware of the financial limitations that had caused enthusiastic protests in the cities of Alabama and Arkansas to dwindle within weeks.[58] Taylor's words also recalled those of Griggs, who, two weeks after the Labor Day celebration, insisted that an effective response to streetcar segregation would require support that transcended class lines and included a visible role for the city's masses.

Additional money for the transportation company was also collected that evening from those in the swelling crowd who paid five cents for a button bearing a picture of one of the streetcars. In an effort to impress upon the crowd the company's desire for fiscal responsibility, Taylor notified those gathered that, despite being "flooded with applications for positions," the company sought to move forward with the "most economical plan possible." According to Taylor, Union officials planned to "devote their labor free of charge" and sought to add "something like ten men" until the organization was fully operational. To further boost support of the new transportation company, Entertainment Committee Chairman D. A. Hart informed the crowd that ten thousand tickets were being printed for a dedication ceremony to be held at Watkins Park, where each attendee would receive a complimentary ride in the new vehicles. Before adjourning, Luke Mason, chairman of the Route Committee, unveiled the proposed routes, which had been selected based on "the condition of the streets, the grades and the length."[59] Mason also announced that a fifth car would remain in reserve in the event of mechanical failure or heavy traffic. As the meeting adjourned, company officials announced that the cars should arrive the following week and that the line would be operational within three weeks.

The steady resolve of Nashville's African American community stunned many white citizens who were certain that an organized boycott would cease within weeks. As weeks passed, rumors began circulating among African Americans and whites that the Nashville Railway & Light Company was experiencing significant financial losses as a result of the boycott. The *Voice of the Negro*, an African American periodical published in Atlanta and later in Chicago, reported that Nashville's boycott of the local streetcar company had caused losses totaling "$7,500 per month," and was expected to reach "$90,000 per year."[60] Despite citywide evidence of a reduction in African American traffic on streetcars and a decline in the African American patronage of white-owned businesses, Nashville's Railway & Light Company executives published an article claiming that the boycott had "not in the least" affected their revenue. The company claimed that, in fact, earnings since the beginning of the boycott showed the same "percentage of increase over last year." Company officials pointed out that because "negro patrons are not nearly so numerous as before the 'Jim Crow' law became effective," the "number of white passengers must therefore have been increased."[61] With the looming arrival of the Union Transportation Company's cars, it was becoming clear that all eyes were on the new venture, particularly those of white business owners who feared that the revenue losses from the streetcar company might begin to significantly affect their own businesses should the boycott continue. (See figure 10.)

Despite having generated enormous support from Nashville's African American community, however, the Union Transportation Company was forced to delay its opening ceremonies on several occasions without explanation. To avoid drawing negative attention to these setbacks, company officials encouraged boycotters to continue using their "temporary system of horses and wagons."[62] They also flooded weeklies with positive information regarding their newly erected garage on Cherry Street, located just behind the transfer station at the Colored Odd Fellows Hall on Fourth Avenue North. Company officials lauded the new station, with its carefully arranged seating and its café that served food "at all hours."[63] However, the delays frustrated those who had invested in the company, and the uncertainty created by the setbacks stifled momentum among supporters of the boycott, particularly those who were forced to travel considerable distances on foot.

After several weeks without word of a Union Transportation Company opening, officials were forced to admit that the five cars they had purchased were "utterly incapable of standing the rough usage and cannot be used at all by the company." The power generated from the steam automobiles was simply inadequate for navigating Nashville's hilly landscape. In an effort to remedy the situation, Taylor left for St. Louis, where he promised to "spare no expense to get the best" before his return. During this lull, rumors began to spread that African American passengers were beginning to return to the white-owned streetcars. Apparently many had become "exasperated with the dilatory methods" of the

NASHVILLE'S MANLY PROTEST AGAINST JIM-CROWISM

The Union Transportation Co., with Rev. Preston Taylor at its head,
by establishing a line of motor car,, has delivered the Negroes of
Nashville from the humiliation and friction,that will attend their
riding in the Jim-crow cars.— News Item.

FIGURE 10 "Nashville's Manly Protest against Jim-
Crowism," *Voice of the Negro* 2 (1905): 828.

Union Company and its failure to efficiently handle its business obliga-
tions.[64] Fears of waning interest prompted community leaders to call a
meeting that would again rally the city's African American population
around the boycott and would help them discover alternative means of
resistance.

A Battle with Baal

An answer to any doubts among supporters in the African American
community came quickly, when, in December 1905, many of the same
leaders affiliated with the Union Transportation Company organized the
Globe, a weekly newspaper intended to provide boycotters with a forum
for protest. *Globe* founders, including Boyd, J. O. Battle, Chas H. Burrill,
and D. A. Hart, understood that although Nashville was "the greatest

printing center of the race and sent out more different periodicals than any other city in the country," it did not have a practical news outlet that served the larger needs of the African American population. They also knew that Nashville's white papers had begun to treat their protest against streetcar laws with indifference. Years later *Globe* representatives reflected on their decision to incorporate: "In the struggle to success-fully maintain the opposition to the 'Jim Crow' laws, the leaders of the movement and others connected with it found that they were greatly handicapped in that they possessed no public-spirited, secular news medium through which they could reach the masses of our people."[65] The motives for creating the *Globe* reflect the New Negro sensibilities of its organizers. As part of the culture politics in the fight against discrimination, the paper was another symbol of African American ingenuity and enterprise. It provided an outlet to counter perceptions of the protest as recorded in the white press and was able to sustain popular support for both the Union Transportation Company and the protest movement.

The first edition of the *Globe* appeared on January 14, 1906, arguing that "self-reliance and racial solidarity" provided Nashville's African American community with their best opportunity "to succeed and prosper within the confines of the Jim Crow South."[66] The paper provided a steady stream of articles that covered Union Transportation Company operations.

Even before the news could be read in the *Globe*, word of mouth had already spread throughout the community that Taylor had returned from his travels, not only making arrangements for the transportation of nine new electric vehicles to arrive within weeks but also bringing an expert with him who would be responsible for the "reconstructing of the old machines" to navigate Nashville's steep grades and hills.[67] The failure of the initial five cars might have been a tremendous blunder, shaking the faith of supporters who had invested their hard-earned savings in the venture, but following that setback, subscription to stocks were reported to have risen from ten thousand to twenty-five thousand dollars.[68] These funds were added to the nine thousand dollars that had already been raised. It is possible that this boost in support was attributed in some manner to reports that at least one white councilman attempted to have the Union Transportation Company's charter revoked, a sign that boycotters were probably costing the Nashville Railway & Light Company or other white businesses more money than they were willing to admit. The accumulated funds, however, also represented a broad base of New Negro support that included money from a professional class of

African Americans as well as "the cooks, the hod-carriers, the man with the pick and shovel and the wash women."[69] In the following months news of Nashville's streetcar boycott garnered national attention for its determined stand against Tennessee's segregation laws, but local papers eagerly catalogued what seemed like a never-ending series of obstacles for African American protesters.

In a bitter irony, Union Transportation Company officials soon realized that the only way to charge the large batteries in their new electric cars was to purchase electricity from the charging station of their competitor, the Nashville Railway & Light Company. Not long after conceding to this awkward arrangement, Union officials were told of a "horrible accident" in which the batteries of their fourteen cars were ruined after being overcharged by attendants working for the white-owned company. White newspapers eagerly spread reports of mishandling on the part of the African American–owned company and suggested that its irresponsible decision making was the source of the company's misfortune. Despite the dubious circumstances surrounding the destruction of the batteries, a tragic event that cost the company precious dollars and time, Union officials purchased new batteries, but they also installed their own "dynamo and electric-generating equipment" at the facilities of the Nashville Baptist Publishing Board.[70] Financial problems were compounded when, in April 1907, Nashville's all-white city council members passed a "privilege tax" of forty-two dollars on all electric cars.[71] While there can be no certainty that the appearance of this new tax coincided with news reports of the Union Transportation Company's vulnerable financial position, it is clear that the funds needed to cover the tax contributed to the company's decision to temporarily halt operations.

With the Union Transportation Company's finances stretched, Taylor and Boyd urged all "ministers, pastors, churches and officers of lodges" to make announcements and post notices regarding dates and times for public meetings to discuss the company's future.[72] In a series of meetings held in the following months, company officials discussed openly the "failure of many of the subscribers of stock to pay up their shares." It was also announced that in an effort to "relieve the pressing embarrassment" caused by the dearth of liquid funds, Union officials had decided to settle a portion of the company's outstanding debt. Taylor cited some "dozen letters of inquiry" from firms in New Orleans, Memphis, and Owensboro, Kentucky, but he then announced that eight of the electric vehicles had been sold to a St. Louis firm representing buyers in Virginia who intended to run the cars between Norfolk and Jamestown for an upcoming exposition. Because officials were able to negotiate the cars' purchase at their original mortgage price, only $734.26 remained unpaid on the company's original $20,000 debt.[73]

Despite this negative information, the majority of the company's stockholders stated that they were "well pleased with the slow progress that ha[d] been made by the company" since its inception and that the temporary suspension of the cars' operation had "by no means" weakened their confidence "in the management and the officers, who have been handicapped by lack of finances." A *Globe* reporter asked Taylor whether it was the company's intention to "dispose of all the cars," but Taylor confidently asserted, "We have put the cars here for the benefit of the colored people. They want them."[74] Taylor was eager to collect the outstanding money owed to the company to purchase new batteries and to service the cars adequately, but at subsequent meetings he soon realized that interest in the transportation venture was waning. In one of the company's final meetings Taylor acknowledged the dedicated contributions of its female African American stockholders, who, as the majority stockholders, continued to show "a deep interest in the affairs of the company." He also chastised all but "three or four men in Nashville" who had "borne these [financial] burdens," pointing out that countless other citizens had failed to follow through on their financial commitments.[75] The *Nashville Globe* lamented the demise of the Union Transportation Company, claiming the city's African American population "would be lost . . . without a method of transportation in keeping with the rapid march of progress."[76] In stern defiance of the segregation laws, however, the paper also declared that "the boycott [was still] a powerful weapon" and that there were "hundreds of Negroes in Nashville who have never 'bowed their knees to Baal' [Jim Crow law]."[77] Unfortunately for the majority of the city's African Americans, two long years of battling both the streetcar segregation law and Nashville's powerful white interests had proved too difficult to continue active protesting.

A Righteous Cause

It is essential to remember that there were no successful attempts to thwart streetcar segregation within the traditional boundaries of the South.[78] Meier points out that fundamental changes were possible only in border states such as Kentucky, where the Reverend W. H. Stewart, a friend of Booker T. Washington and editor of the *National Baptist*, successfully organized a protest in Louisville that was directly responsible

for preventing the passage of a local ordinance.[79] Yet although the boycott in Nashville did not result in a change of policy at the local, state, or
national level, the movement can hardly be viewed as a failure. The issue
is not whether the boycott succeeded but what roles Nashville's African
American community members were able to assume in promoting the
boycott and in competing with whites. Under the leadership of Griggs
and others, Nashville's African American community was able to sustain a collective, two-year protest against the discriminatory practices
of Jim Crow laws. Their efforts challenged not only the state legislature
and the white community but also the monopoly on transportation and
electric power maintained by Nashville's Railway & Light Company. It is
significant that it took Nashville's white community two years to defeat
the Union Transportation Company and ultimately the collective protest
against streetcar segregation laws, and that it had to do so through economic subterfuge, not overt violence. Clearly this showed that African
Americans could organize and form independent economic and rhetorical positions without their being violently aborted.

Nashville protesters also overcame many obstacles experienced by
African Americans elsewhere. In smaller southern cities like Augusta,
Georgia, and Pine Bluff, Arkansas, few transit alternatives existed, and
the number of boycotters was unable to affect significantly the revenue
of white-owned streetcar companies, whose riding population was overwhelmingly white. The transportation resources available to Nashville's
African American community in the form of hacks and express wagons and the Union Transportation Company enabled them to sustain
their movement and prevented whites from simply waiting out African
American resolve, tactics that proved successful in cities such as Atlanta
and Mobile. The unity among Nashville's African American community
and the number of boycotters probably prevented the intimidation and
violence perpetrated by whites that contributed to the cessation of protests in cities such as Chattanooga and Savannah. Another crucial factor
in Nashville's success was the broad support across class lines, the lack
of which was detrimental to movements in Memphis and Richmond,
where the decision of clergy members to abstain from participation in
the boycott greatly undermined success.

Moreover those involved in the streetcar protest did not end their agitation against segregation because of a single defeat. Along with Griggs,
the protesters played essential roles as speakers and organizers in the
formation of racial solidarity among Nashville's African American community members. These men and women also contributed significant

time and financial resources to future causes. The boycott validated the independent and entrepreneurial spirit of Nashville's New Negroes and showed that accommodation and deference were characteristics of a different era. These examples indicate the economic, cultural, and intellectual factors that distinguish Nashville as an exemplary site of New Negro life and activism in the South. They also reveal the factors that enabled the city's African American community to sustain radical responses to white supremacy in subsequent years and to play a critical role in reshaping definitions of African American identity in moments of crisis that include the Fisk University protests in 1924–25. Finally, the response of Nashville's African American community to streetcar segregation laws at the turn of the century, and similar efforts by African Americans living in other southern cities, provided a blueprint for future generations of African Americans who participated in the transit strikes of the 1950s and influenced methods of protest against racist policies throughout that civil rights movement.

6 /   "Before I'd Be a Slave": The Fisk University Protests, 1924–1925

Before I'd be a slave
I'd be buried in my grave.
— AFRICAN AMERICAN SPIRITUAL

W. E. B. Du Bois arrived in Nashville on June 2, 1924, to deliver the Fisk University commencement address before students, faculty, alumni, and members of the administration. It was not the first time he had been given such an honor, having delivered a commencement address in 1898 and participated as an alumnus speaker in 1908. However, for Du Bois this occasion was both personal and political. He sought to witness the graduation of his daughter Yolande and to indict a system of inequality he believed existed at Fisk. His opening lines revealed a guilty conscience: "To my long continued silence, Conscript Fathers, which I have made use of in these days, not on account of any fear, but partly from grief, partly from shame, this day brings an end and also a beginning of my speaking according to my former custom what I think and what I know." Invoking Cicero's oration in defense of Marcellus, Du Bois lashed out at the autocratic administrative practices of Fisk president Fayette McKenzie, claiming "never to have known an institution whose alumni on the whole are more bitter and disgusted with the present situation in this university than the alumni of Fisk University today."[1] His speech surprised many in attendance, particularly members of the administration, and provoked negative responses among Nashville's white community. For Fisk students, and for the majority of the city's African Americans, Du Bois's words were a welcome surprise. The contents of the speech articulated the suffocating influences of missionary paternalism and emphasized the discontent among African American men and women wearied by academic practices that prohibited their individual and spiritual development. Within days of the speech, tensions between African American students and white administrators and benefactors quickly polarized the citizens of the Nashville community along racial lines and initiated a campus standoff that would have national implications for the future of African American education and the boundaries of caste.

Lines of Color

Questions regarding the role to be played by African Americans in their educational future were concomitant with the creation of African American schools and colleges in various forms by freedmen's aid societies and white northern religious institutions in the generations following the Civil War. According to James McPherson, African Americans engaged in debate with whites about their role in their own education was not aimed at a "restructuring of the methods, content, or purposes of education" but was an effort to "achieve greater participation in it as teachers, deans, presidents, and trustees."[2] Responses to questions regarding increased participation of African Americans in universities established for their education only intensified in the later decades of the nineteenth century, as scores of graduates from these colleges proved capable of filling numerous roles in the education of their race. Among those seeking greater visibility for educated African Americans was Francis Grimke, who insisted that race prejudice and selfishness among whites prohibited widespread institutional advancement of African Americans:

> The time has come, it seems to me, for black men to speak out, and to direct attention to this evil; to let these pseudo friends,—many of whom have allied themselves with negro institutions only for what they can get out of them, under the pretence [sic] of being actuated by philanthropic motives, know, that we understand their true character. . . . If this is philanthropy, then I, for one, think we have had quite enough of it. If this is the treatment we are to continue to receive from our friends, then it is time for us to begin to pray to be delivered from our friends.[3]

As members of the Niagara Movement would argue twenty years later, it was time to end the white monopoly on access and administration at the college level.

Disagreement over control of African American education and the guiding influences in its institutions led many African American educators and community members to act on their separatist impulses. Exercising their commitment to home rule, the African Methodist Episcopal and Zion churches established a number of distinct African American colleges. African American communities throughout the South also pressed for the creation of numerous southern African American agricultural and mechanical and land grant colleges.[4] While these educational outlets increased opportunities for African American administrators, staff, and faculty, they also exposed many hardships associated with expansion. Among the most significant obstacles faced by these institutions were financial difficulties, maintaining educational quality on par with similar white institutions, and, specifically in the case of agricultural and mechanical colleges, being beholden to white-dominated state legislatures for funding, exposing the limitations of their control.

However, even at prominent African American universities such as Fisk and Howard, where educational standards were rigorous and economic support was sufficient, the most significant and divisive questions among African Americans and whites remained focused on leadership and participation within the institutions. To whom did the schools belong: the white liberal interests that founded and maintained the institutions or the African American students and communities that the institutions served? At times differences between the two sides erupted in fractious campus incidents.[5]

In general, student protests from this era were short-lived and failed to establish sweeping institutional changes or academic practices. However, many of these events signaled a shift in consciousness among African American students that sought to alleviate the "deadening influence" of white authority.[6] Although he does not use the term *New Negro* to describe this change, one African American editor identified an emerging sensibility that was evident among protesting students at Roger Williams University: "The Colored People of the South are rising in morals and courage. The fact that the students of Roger Williams rose up, condemned two of their instructors of dishonesty and immorality, proves that the coming generation stands firm in the path of manhood."[7] The majority of students at these universities were certainly cognizant and respectful of the historical role whites played in the establishment and maintenance of many African American schools and colleges. However, succeeding generations also recognized that "what has been liberal in name and intention has not always been liberalizing in effect."[8]

In the early twentieth century most African American students who challenged the paternalistic attitudes of whites were not militants; their protests were not motivated by separatist impulses. These men and women demanded recognition as individuals and as adults. Their search for manhood on college campuses was but an aspect of their larger quest toward the fulfillment of a federal promise, one that began with the Thirteenth Amendment by acknowledging African Americans' basic human rights and evolved through the passage of the Fourteenth, Fifteenth, and Nineteenth amendments, which invested African Americans with citizenship rights.[9] In this respect education was another channel through which they sought integration into American society. Alain Locke perhaps best expresses this dimension of African American consciousness in his 1925 essay, "Enter the New Negro": "The Negro mind reaches out as yet to nothing but American wants, American ideas. But this forced attempt to build his Americanism on race values is a unique social experiment, and its ultimate success is impossible except through the fullest sharing of American culture and institutions."[10] African American students sought a college experience that did not mirror their status beyond campus grounds, a white-dominated environment in which code and custom rendered them second-class citizens.

While experiential similarities between African American and white students in the 1920s existed, African American students faced restrictions unknown to their white counterparts. Although it was not uncommon at white universities during the 1920s, compulsory chapel was the norm for African American students, whether attending institutions such as the Agricultural and Technical College of North Carolina or liberal arts colleges such as Fisk. Except at military academies that required uniforms, dress codes for white college students were rare, but they were widespread at African American colleges. At West Virginia Collegiate Institute, for instance, the dress code limited the number of items one could own, the fabric from which they were constructed, and even the color they were dyed. At some institutions, such as Lane College in Jackson, Tennessee, dress codes determined even the undergarments worn by attending students.[11] Unfortunately for African American students of the period, invasive practices did not end with regulation clothing.

At Storer College in Harpers Ferry, West Virginia, and Tougaloo College in Mississippi, incoming mail was subject to inspection, and even disposal if deemed inappropriate by university officials.[12] At Fisk male students were forbidden to walk beside female students on campus, day or night. Students were also not allowed to sit on campus grounds in groups of more than three. At most African American colleges women were prohibited from having male visitors, and students of either sex had to be in bed with lights out by 10 P.M. Restrictions applied even to leisure

restrictions faced by African American students

activities, where smoking, dancing, and card playing were prohibited at a number of colleges, including Hampton, Tuskegee, and Atlanta University. Unable to achieve egalitarianism and motivated by significant sociocultural changes, African American student activism intensified in the 1920s.

In previous decades many African American students were forced to work while attending college, a situation that proved a difficult balance of time and focus and often lengthened time to graduation. Following the First World War improved economic conditions enabled African Americans, particularly those in the middle class, to attend colleges in unprecedented numbers and to attend institutions with better facilities and higher academic standards. Between 1920 and 1933 the number of graduates from Negro colleges grew from 497 to 2,486, a 400 percent increase. Between 1926 and 1936 there were more African American college graduates than in the previous one hundred years.[13] African American students not only attended colleges in greater numbers during this period but also provided campuses with geographic diversity, a trend resulting in a college student body with a wealth of life experiences that reflected the period's significant cultural awakening.

Fed from a diverse musical reservoir, the 1920s witnessed the flowering of jazz and blues. Their rhythmic tones emanated from vibrant cultural centers such as New Orleans, Kansas City, Chicago, and New York City. For the first time listeners heard commercial recordings from Bessie Smith, Gertrude "Ma" Rainey, and Victoria Spivey. They thrilled to the notes of James P. Johnson, Louis Armstrong, and Thomas "Fats" Waller and stepped to the beats of the Charleston and the Black Bottom. In America and abroad audiences lauded the diverse talents of Roland Hayes, Josephine Baker, and Paul Robeson. In the realm of visual arts, Meta Vaux Warrick Fuller and Aaron Douglas reimagined a cultural experience that validated Afrocentric themes to a mainstream marketplace.

The period also witnessed a proliferation of news and literary outlets that included the *Crisis* (1910), the *Messenger* (1917), and *Negro World* (1918), publications that espoused diverse philosophical perspectives and openly engaged the social, economic, and political ramifications of African American life in a segregated society. In the realm of literature, Jessie Fauset, Locke, and Du Bois drew attention to the renaissance of African American art and to New Negro artists such as Langston Hughes, George Schuyler, Claude McKay, Countee Cullen, Zora Neale Hurston, Rudolph Fisher, and Wallace Thurman. Through verve and visibility

African Americans definitively shaped 1920s America, emerging from the margins of cultural life to establish a modern aesthetic for a new generation.

While African American students of the 1920s reflected attitudes seen in their white counterparts, they also exhibited responses specific to their race. According to V. P. Franklin, "Student activism was an important element in itself and as a part of larger social reform movements." Franklin argues that students of the period "sought even more personal freedom to accept or rebel against the social conventions and cultural conditions they inherited from the generations that spawned the 'Great War.'"[14] Paula Fass views 1920s American youth in a similar context, as "the product of change and the agents of change, because they existed at a strategic point in history when their actions really did make a difference." Fass emphasizes that 1920s youth proclaimed their allegiance, "broad or narrow, to a different sort of God, as they invested a kind of religious devotion to their leisure pursuits, to sports, dating, and song."[15]

That college campuses provided an ideological battleground between forces old and new, traditional and modern comes as little surprise. In his work on 1920s college environments, Herbert Aptheker observed, "The decade was one of considerable uneasiness for college and university authorities in general," noting in particular that by spring 1924, white students had "rocked campuses at Brown, Temple, Amherst, and the University of Tennessee" with a series of strikes.[16] Though the impetus for these strikes varied from dress codes to restrictions on campus social life and from parietals to curriculum concerns, at the core each protest challenged the authoritarian control of college officials.[17] Franklin's work on student activism in the twentieth century reveals similar anxiety among African Americans: "To a very great extent, the black college rebellions in the 1920s were generated by the cognitive dissonance black collegians experienced when they left the real world of the 'New Negro' and entered the Victorian environment maintained on campus by white and black administrators."[18] African American responses reflected shifting sociocultural changes unique to their peer group. Whereas in the late nineteenth century it was African American students who were often unprepared for their college experience, in the early twentieth century it appeared colleges were unprepared for a new type of African American student.

In 1885 Francis Grimke referred to African American colleges as sacred ground, constituting "the soil in which will be grown the men and women who are to labor among the masses," as well as those "who are to take rank among the great scholars of the land."[19] Echoes of Grimke's

words resonated well into the twentieth century and were further delin-
eated by Du Bois's concept of the talented tenth. Each reflects basic New
Negro attitudes regarding racial progress and achievement and raises
critical questions regarding race and representation for a new generation
of African Americans. In the 1920s these exceptional college-age men
and women had come of age under the imposed segregation of *Plessy v.
Ferguson*, had fought for democracy on the battlefields of World War I,
responded to systematic racial violence in the riots of summer 1919, and
embraced the emerging cultural renaissance that defined the decade. If
college campuses of the 1920s were training grounds for the next era of
race leaders, they would have to accommodate a New Negro generation
poised for determined responses to retrogressive measures.

The decision by Fisk's African American students to openly challenge
the paternalistic structure of their university's white administration
and the autocratic practices of President McKenzie between the years
1924 and 1925 was a watershed in African American sociopolitical and
cultural history. These student demonstrations had significant and far-
reaching effects on the future of African American higher education and
the perception of the New Negro in America. Far from just a local skir-
mish that tested the boundaries of racial equality and racial tolerance
in a city of the Jim Crow South, the Fisk protest catalyzed a national
movement that questioned the role of whites in the personal and professional development of African Americans. In particular they questioned
how historically black universities could act in the best interest of their
African American students, supporting parents, and invested community members when directly controlled by a white president, a majority
of white trustees, and a predominantly white faculty and when they were
influenced by northern philanthropy and beholden to popular southern
sentiment.[20]

The Guiding Hand

The focal point of Du Bois's commencement attack was fifty-two-year-
old Fayette Avery McKenzie, then in his ninth year as Fisk president.
Based on his professional background, McKenzie did not appear to be
an obvious choice for the presidency of an African American university.
A native of Montrose, Susquehanna County, Pennsylvania, and a graduate of Lehigh University, McKenzie had taught at Juniata College and
the University of Pennsylvania before spending two years as an instructor at a Shoshone reservation in Wyoming. Native American studies

profoundly influenced McKenzie, who returned to the University of Pennsylvania, where he completed his doctorate in sociology with a dissertation entitled "The American Indian in Relation to the White Population of the United States." In the years prior to his appointment at Fisk, he worked in various government agencies on issues related to Native Americans, helping to organize the Society of American Indians in 1910, before finally returning to teach economics and sociology at Ohio State University.[21] Upon his appointment at Fisk, McKenzie had neither served in an administrative capacity at a university nor had experience working with African American issues, but it appears that Fisk's predominantly white board of trustees made little distinction between the experience of working with Native Americans and working with African Americans.[22] While McKenzie had lived in the North and in various western locations, his move to Nashville would be his first time in the South and would serve as his initial exposure to southern race relations. *inexperienced for pres. job @ HBCU*

Still, when McKenzie delivered his inaugural address in November of 1915 he appeared to represent the university's mission well. Believing that a "cultured man" would make a more "useful citizen," he endorsed the "education of the mind rather than the hands."[23] This "new type of young, scientific philanthropist" sought to use Fisk graduates as mentors who would return to their hometowns and rural locations to educate and train succeeding generations of African Americans and serve as community leaders abroad in their capacity as business or professional men and women.[24] McKenzie was confident that eliminating illiteracy and ignorance among the South's African American population would ensure their economic and spiritual growth and also transform the region in which they lived. To achieve his ambitious plans he initiated a campaign to raise a one-million-dollar endowment. Although collecting the necessary funds would be an unprecedented achievement for an African American university, McKenzie seemed willing to lead the charge as he thundered, "Let us dare to be big!" "Let us dare to be a university!"[25] (See figure 11.)

Soon into his tenure, however, the enthusiastic support McKenzie had enjoyed from many African American students, faculty, and outsiders was replaced by chagrin. According to McKenzie, in order to instill the students of Fisk with "culture," it was necessary to begin the "forcible tearing up of the weeds of idleness and ease."[26] Among the many casualties of his cultural landscaping were a number of outlets that had championed student spirit and complimented assertive individuality. McKenzie suspended the Fisk Herald, the first student newspaper published by an

FIGURE 11 Fayette McKenzie in his office at Fisk University, ca. 1920. Courtesy of Tennessee State Library and Archives.

African American university.[27] While he claimed the *Herald*'s suppression was the result of financial difficulties, he was able to locate the funds necessary to assume control and distribution of a new journal, entitled *Fisk News*. No longer a forum for student creativity and expression, the new journal became a mouthpiece for the university and represented its larger goals. McKenzie's suspension of the *Herald* effectively silenced student voices, a decision at odds with the democratic fervor of his inaugural speech and one suggesting that the public voice of Fisk was dictated by the university's white, male, authoritarian principles.

Instead of feeling as though they would play an important role in the future of their race, Fisk students felt threatened by a series of gradual changes from McKenzie's administration that suppressed their initiative through legislation. McKenzie dissolved the student government and informed students that dissent was forbidden. Although an NAACP chapter had been operating in Nashville since 1919, McKenzie denied student requests for their own chapter on campus. Students were dismayed that Fisk, which publicly represented a successful partnership between African Americans and whites, would not allow the presence of an organization known to defend the civil and political liberties of African Americans. McKenzie even ordered the university librarian to inspect the NAACP organ, *Crisis*, and remove any articles deemed radical. Although they were welcome at universities across the country, representatives from the International Youth Movement were not allowed to speak with Fisk students. When organizations representing African American fraternities brought their "Go to High School, Go to College" campaign to campus, they too were turned away.[28] Reinforcing McKenzie's belief that "the iron ploughshare of discipline both in conduct and in study is the only effective instrument for the man who aspires to real education and real culture," additional rulings prohibited men and women from walking together on campus; lights had to be turned off in dormitories by ten o'clock at night; smoking was not allowed; attendance at meals was mandatory; and a dress code was established whereby conservative fabrics in brown, black, blue, and gray replaced silk and satin low-neck or short-sleeve outfits, which were deemed flashy or excessive.[29] Under McKenzie's rule, the Fisk campus quickly began to mirror the racially segregated society beyond, where code and custom suppressed African American movement and expression.

Given Nashville's history as the cauldron of the New Negro sensibility, it retrospectively seems inevitable that McKenzie's rule would meet with open confrontation on a veritable canon on New Negro principles, and it is also not surprising that a leading figure in the event would be Du Bois, one of the most prominent and influential New Negroes to have emerged from Fisk. Because Du Bois believed that higher education played a vital role in the development of leadership among African Americans, he refused to be a silent witness to changes in Fisk policy that, he believed, would fix rather than alter the social and political inequalities between African Americans and whites in the South.

Among these changes were damaging reports that McKenzie was responsible for organizing Jim Crow events involving students and faculty. At a downtown performance by Fisk's Jubilee Club, audience members bought tickets at separate windows, depending on their race, a practice that caused Bishop Isaiah Scott of the Methodist Episcopal Church to be "refused service and insulted" by white booth operators. Once African American audience members, including teachers, were admitted, they were required to sit apart from white audience members and faculty while viewing the performance. According to Du Bois, there were other events arranged by McKenzie that bordered on spectacle.

He accused McKenzie of parading "girls from some of the best Negro families in the United States" to what he called "the Grotto, a former Rathskeller." McKenzie was said to have funneled these students down an alleyway and through a servant's entrance, to perform before "Southern white men as these men smoked and laughed and talked."[30] It was an event, Du Bois claimed, that would have caused Fisk's first president, Erastus Cravath, to "rise from the grave and protest."[31]

Du Bois viewed McKenzie's affiliation with the Shriners as another example of politicking meant to ingratiate himself with Nashville's white elite. McKenzie had already assumed membership in a number of organizations, including the Nashville Kiwanis Club and the local Chamber of Commerce, continuing a pattern of community membership he had established in Columbus, where he served as president of the Philanthropic Council, director of the metropolitan Chamber of Commerce, and chairman of the Universities and Social Welfare Section of the State Conference of Charities and Correction.[32] Du Bois saw these affiliations as not unlike those of Booker T. Washington, who had served as a board member at Fisk from 1909 until his death in 1915 and who had used his relationships with powerful white interests from the North and South to provide a source of revenue for the school. Du Bois refused to allow Fisk's integrity to be compromised or to allow acquiescence and accommodation to be promoted among the university's African American students.[33]

Well aware that politics in the North and the South had historically sanctioned a doctrine of white supremacy that endorsed the economic and social repression of blacks, Du Bois challenged the burgeoning relationship between McKenzie and his powerful contributors. He argued that Fisk was not taking "an honest position with regard to the Southern situation" because it had "embraced a propaganda" that "overpraised the liberal white South" as a ruling elite, while teaching that the "only thing required of a black man is acquiescence and submission." He charged that a "Corrupt Bargain" had been struck between white philanthropists and McKenzie in which, "either openly or by implication," McKenzie had sold "the white south the control" of Fisk University in exchange for creating a curriculum and an atmosphere that would guarantee the servility of its African American students. Rather than equating monetary gain with success (like the majority of whites supporting McKenzie's administration), Du Bois detected undertones of modern or industrial slavery in these power relationships by which African Americans were being sold to the highest bidder. These powerful interests were supplying the financial stake that would leave African Americans beholden to dollars at the expense of their spiritual selves. Should such a bargain have been accepted by McKenzie's administration, either "consciously or unconsciously, openly or secretly," Du Bois clamored that he "would rather see every stone of [Fisk's] buildings leveled and every bit of its activity stopped" before such concessions were tolerated by any African American.[34]

As evidence of what he viewed as McKenzie's inability to work within racial lines to promote equality and foster goodwill among northern supporters of Fisk, Du Bois recounted a fund-raising trip to Cleveland, Ohio, in June 1923. On this occasion, McKenzie, Paul Cravath, the president of the board of trustees for Fisk, and Wallace Buttrick, chairman of the General Education Board, were honored guests of E. M. Williams, president of the Cleveland Board of Education, and each spoke to a number of influential white citizens about possible contributions to Fisk.[35] Cleveland should have been an ideal location for a fund-raising event. The city had no segregated institutions, had a number of African American councilmen, and was home to many prominent citizens, including Charles W. Chesnutt. Astoundingly no African Americans were invited to attend the event, nor were any consulted about affairs that directly influenced either the Nashville or Cleveland communities.

The following day the fund-raiser was front-page news in Cleveland papers, and several quotes provided damning evidence in support of Du Bois's claims of "Jim Crowism" within the McKenzie's administration. The *Times Commercial* headline declared, "Negro Problem Solution Seen in Segregation." Highlighted in the accompanying article was Cravath's statement, "The only solution to the negro problem is complete segregation, and the building up of a separate negro society." To support his claim, Cravath insisted, "The negro of today patronizes negro tradesmen, doctors, lawyers, goes to negro church, his children attend negro schools. As fast as leaders are supplied, he is becoming a separate social unit." In closing, Cravath emphasized that the role of Fisk and similar African American institutions was to develop leaders capable of building and maintaining a segregated African American society: "Nobody wants anything else. It is the only possible solution. Assimilation would be out of the question."[36] Cravath was followed by McKenzie, who publicly endorsed Cravath's speech. McKenzie later claimed the comments were meant to reflect opinions concerning race relations in American society and not the university community. However, the episode damaged his standing among a majority of African Americans in both North and South. In particular they were offended by the sweeping and patriar-chal spirit of words that implied a self-segregation on the part of African Americans without acknowledging the realities of life behind the color line as imposed by *Plessy v. Ferguson.*

Du Bois's vocal criticism of McKenzie's administration drew media attention from across the country. The *Gazette Times* of Pittsburgh labeled Du Bois a "propagandist" and cautioned Fisk's students to think about their future and realize they "will be heard at the right time, if they have a message."[37] The *Chicago Whip* considered Du Bois's speech an "unwarranted, malicious verbal attack" on McKenzie meant to dis-credit his administration and, ultimately, to thwart its efforts to raise a one-million-dollar endowment. Participating in a melee of speculation and rumor regarding Du Bois's motivations, other papers suggested his speech was a ruse by which Du Bois hoped to step in and fulfill his own "desire to take the presidency."[38] Many papers, such as the *Springfield Massachusetts News*, condemned Du Bois's attitude toward the presi-dent's policies as "extreme," and at least one article claimed that outraged Nashvillians had "literally burned the radical editor in effigy" following his visit and suggested it would be unsafe for him to return to the city.[39]

In Nashville white newspapers used the opportunity to bolster sup-port for McKenzie's administration. The *Banner* praised the financial contributions of white Nashvillians, who had added fifty thousand dollars to the endowment drive, the first occasion "any such sum has been contributed to Negro education by any single city in the South." As evidence of its success as a leading institution of African American education, the article cited Fisk's ability to foster those "proper relations between the races," which operated in the "best interests of the com-munity, the state and nation."[40] The *Tennessean* noted the overwhelming support of charitable organizations in the North such as the Rockefeller General Education Board, the Carnegie Corporation, the John F. Slater Fund, and the J. C. Penney Foundation, as well as individual contribu-tions from philanthropists in Chicago, Philadelphia, Cleveland, Boston, and New York. Espousing a position similar to that of the *Banner* edi-tors, those at the *Tennessean* hoped additional funds would be used to "educate young Negroes *in the way they should go.*"[41]

A Call to Action

By the time classes began in fall 1924, tension between the students and the administration was palpable. In October a student committee provided board members with a list of grievances. Among them, students catalogued rules and regulations implemented by McKenzie that they deemed excessive. They also questioned the commitment of faculty members, many of whom they considered untrained. There were also allegations of a spy system from which unnecessary disciplinary measures resulted. Students called for the participation of African Americans within the institution so that they would have mentors invested in their educational and spiritual development. In closing, they voiced concerns regarding the direction and quality of Fisk's curriculum. Despite the sincerity of the student committee members and the fact that they had observed protocol, their petition was largely ignored.

In November 1924, however, Fisk students openly displayed their discontent. When board members arrived during the second week of November for their annual meeting, they were met by what newspapers later referred to as a "tin pan riot."[42] Students marched across campus banging on pans and trash can lids and shouting, "Away with the czar!" and "Down with the tyrant," indicting McKenzie's oppressive administration and protesting his suppression of student rights and organizations.[43] Faculty members quickly removed lists of grievances that had been posted on campus bulletin boards and attached to doorposts. At one point a large group of students locked themselves inside one of the dormitories, turned out the lights, and demanded a meeting between faculty members, McKenzie, and student representatives to discuss policy changes. Only when T. W. Talley, an African American professor, assured students they would have the opportunity to seek alterations to restrictive guidelines did they agree to cease their demonstration and leave their dormitories.

In the days following the student demonstrations, sympathetic reverberations were apparent citywide. Daily papers revealed that tags reading "We are for the boys and girls of Fisk" were worn by hundreds of students at Nashville schools.[44] Those activities were highlighted on Sunday, November 19, during a special Founder's Day celebration at Fisk's Memorial Chapel. Students from Fisk, Meharry Medical College, and other local institutions waited until McKenzie, board members, and noted guests Julius Rosenwald and Mrs. Booker T. Washington were seated, and then filed demonstrably into the chapel. Many of the

supporters were established community members who had participated in the trolley strikes twenty years earlier and subsequent protests
in defense of equal rights. Their tags of support emphasized solidarity
among peers, but their presence signified participation from a community that was attuned to affairs that affected their progress as a race.

Additional support came from Du Bois, who, following his commencement address, had begun his own campaign to sway public
opinion in favor of the student body. According to Du Bois, his June
commencement address was "only the first gun of a long campaign"; the
next step was to "gather the facts in careful shape."[45] Within weeks of his
return to New York, he met with members of the New York Fisk Club to
discuss an organized response to conditions at the university. The members agreed to carry out an orchestrated campaign against the McKenzie
administration on behalf of current students. Du Bois and Fisk Club
members contacted numerous alumni by mail, particularly those who
had graduated during McKenzie's tenure. Each was informed that many
fellow alumni found conditions at Fisk intolerable and that a change of
leadership was necessary to return Fisk to its former glory. The decision
to have the letters come from numerous Fisk Club members was made in
part to prevent criticism from outside agitators that Du Bois was acting
alone. The letters acknowledged that an "unpleasant battle" was certain
to follow but asked whether or not the individual would care to make
a statement regarding McKenzie's administration.[46] Du Bois offered
anonymity to those uncomfortable with becoming involved in a public
dispute.

In order to give the protest movement a platform from which to
speak, Du Bois restored the *Fisk Herald* and printed it from his office in
New York City. The first volume reproduced his speech from June 2 and
included an editorial announcing that the collective clubs "have begun
the emancipation of the Fisk Spirit."[47] To show their solidarity, former
Fiskites were asked to make a contribution and to sign the following
addendum: "Hereditary bondsmen! Know ye not, who would be free,
themselves must strike the blow? The situation at Fisk is critical. It must
be changed. We are the ones to change it. This will cost money. What
will it cost you? The education of our children is fundamental. Shall we
surrender it? Never. Then sign and send today."[48] Motivated by Du Bois's
inquiries and by news of recent events at Fisk, responses from current
students and alumni were overwhelming and reaffirmed that the university was in crisis. Several respondents expressed difficulty communicating their experiences to family and outsiders. J. W. Fowler, like many

under the current administration, was a legacy student. He lamented, "Father knows only the one Fisk," a pre-McKenzie era that occupied a fairy spot in his parent's memory. In deference to parental wishes, Fowler noted that he and others "gritted their teeth and pushed on toward their goal" of graduating. However, daily life, infused with "a minimum of happiness and an overdose of unpleasantness and humiliation," had transformed the historic Fisk into a "Beautiful Hell." An acquaintance of Du Bois's daughter Yolande while at Fisk, Fowler pleaded, "listen to the charges from the lips of your own daughter, and have faith to BELIEVE her," that Fisk must be judged according to its current status, and not its previous condition.[49]

Most prevalent among those responding were conditions that stifled student autonomy. Upon arrival at Fisk, students were required to agree in writing to "obey all present rules and all rules that hereafter shall be made."[50] One respondent noted that even the university chaplain "urg[ed] us to do all sets of indefinite things . . . to see that the rules are kept."[51] With no student council, no student-edited periodical, and no special committees free from faculty influence, students felt they had no outlet to share opinions concerning university life. What student activities were allowed had to be supervised or directed by faculty or members of the administration. Students were particularly upset that they were not allowed fraternities and wondered whether McKenzie perceived a threat from "the results of organized effort from students?"[52] Their distress reflected a New Negro concern with issues of manhood. Forced to operate within this suffocating environment, one student lamented, "We are not treated as men [and] are not considered as being able to think for ourselves."[53]

Compounding student concerns regarding self-expression were repeated allegations that McKenzie implemented a spy system to ensure student adherence to university policies. Many recounted being monitored while on campus and suggested that such policing created an antagonistic relationship between students and faculty. When Minnie Carwin, a popular female student, was unable to explain her possession of a five-dollar bill, one of the "faculty spies" accused her of theft and had her "dismissed peremptorily." Once her innocence was proved, "no retraction of the miserable charge was ever made."[54] In another scenario, two students were reported and subsequently placed on probation for presenting a departing professor with a gift purchased by students from their own funds. Because the event took place during chapel, special permission was required but had not obtained.[55] Such negative interactions between faculty and students exacerbated feelings of suspicion and discontent and caused one student to exclaim, "We have to be watched and guarded in every move we make [so that] we do not know who to trust."[56] These negative emotions carried into the classroom, affecting student attendance and performance. Blame for the internal rift repeatedly fell on McKenzie. In the eyes of students and alumni, he not only failed to address campus factionalism; he created it.

Rather than a puritanical concern with discipline and morality, many detected racist overtones in McKenzie's oppressive regime. Several students claimed that African American teachers were being forced out by McKenzie and replaced by "immature white undergraduates" who were "unfit for a position anywhere else."[57] Another source claimed the university was "honeyed . . . with whites" from the South and implied it had become a "'training school' for white students who desire to teach after graduation from Vanderbilt University."[58] John Wesley Work Jr., a Fisk alumni, former faculty member, and sitting president at Roger Williams University, who recalled that since McKenzie's arrival at Fisk, his "policy" was to gradually "replace all colored men" with whites, supported these statements.[59] More frequently these authority figures tended to be of southern descent. Among those criticized were two white faculty members, a physics teacher named Parch, and a biology teacher named Cook, who were considered the president's "handy men."[60]

While the inexperience and the malleability of youthful instructors might be expected, racist attitudes could not be overlooked. Parch, a graduate of Millsaps College in Mississippi, was reportedly overheard saying he "hates [the] Negro," whom he deemed "incapable in every respect."[61] Another graduate reported that such limited perspective was to be expected when one considered the university's leadership model. During a business trip to Nashville in spring 1924, a Mr. Allison met with McKenzie to discuss the "general conditions" of the student body on behalf of Fisk alumni. Allison recalled that while McKenzie praised enthusiastically the financial contributions from whites that supported Fisk's future, he simply "could not understand why more of the Fisk boys did not take to trades like carpentry, plastering, and bricklaying."[62] For many Fisk supporters Allison's encounter with McKenzie confirmed their greatest fear: that white philanthropy was shaping African American college curriculum in a manner least threatening to the dominant white majority and in a direction that ensured the economic subordination and intellectual subjugation of future generations. (See figure 12.)

The Chemistry classes must suffer the inconvenience of reciting in the laboratory, due to overcrowded conditions in the Science Building

FIGURE 12 Fisk University students attending chemistry class, ca. 1920. (Courtesy of Tennessee State Library and Archives.)

Unable to endure the strictures of McKenzie's "Iron rule," many Fisk students sought opportunities elsewhere.[63] This movement was particularly noticeable among males, who appeared less willing to tolerate McKenzie's moralizing and had more economic opportunities beyond campus than female students.[64] Noting the recent trend in departures, one student estimated that in the past four years, the number of men attending Fisk had decreased "by no less than thirty-five percent."[65] Livingstone Hall, the men's dormitory, filled to capacity just a few years earlier, was half-full by 1925. Another Fiskite commented that so many students had left Fisk for Howard and other universities, that surely "someone should suspect" that this was no coincidence.[66]

Based on responses from alumni and students, many, including McKenzie, were aware of the exodus. According to numerous accounts, the president viewed a student's decision to leave Fisk as an unpardonable offense and a personal insult. In one instance, two male students unhappy with McKenzie's policies attempted to transfer to Howard, but McKenzie refused to grant them an honorable dismissal. The students appealed to G. M. McClellan, a former teacher and director of academics at Arkansas Agricultural, Mechanical & Normal School. McClellan sent numerous letters and appealed to McKenzie for resolution but was ignored. Incensed by McKenzie's "unspeakable egotism and zaristic [sic] spirit," McClellan hired a lawyer to intervene on behalf of the students.[67] Faced with the unwanted publicity of a public trial, McKenzie relented and released the students to Howard by telegram.

However, not all students had the relationships or the resources to challenge McKenzie's authority. According to Fowler, students were "living under the strain of a white man's eccentric rule; living like slaves. . . . We were Negroes, yet were not particularly wanted in a University for Negroes."[68] In many cases those opposing McKenzie found their records smeared for minor infractions.[69] Any suggestion of impropriety on the part of students was punished by suspension or expulsion, their credits were reduced, or they were prohibited entry to another university. With such measures McKenzie forced students to either acquiesce or face an indeterminate status that forestalled future social and economic mobility.

Incensed by an immediate and, to many, spiritual crisis at Fisk, alumni drew on their vast relationship network to rally support for the students and bolster race solidarity nationwide. Letters of inquiry poured in from all cardinal points, including Los Angeles, Kansas City, Tuskegee, and Boston. Concerned by "questions" surrounding Fisk leadership, Morehouse College's president John Hope warned, "An institution of learning is such a delicate organism . . . the slightest touch sometimes disturbs its healthy function."[70] R. C. Bailey, a Georgia insurance executive, echoed Hope's concerns, claiming, "[Without] very necessary and radical reforms . . . we can hope for nothing else but the loss of this great institution to our people as far as its usefulness is concerned."[71] In several respects Fisk's success as an educational institution was for many African Americans emblematic of New Negro pride and progress in a national age of self-determination: "Fisk University has sent from its walls some of the ablest men and women in the race; its graduates are serving in almost every capacity, wherein valuable and helpful service is required. Its graduates are among our ministers, doctors, lawyers, teachers, businessmen, etc."[72]

Among Fisk's exceptional graduates was Charles H. Wesley, a Howard University professor, who closely monitored the recent events at his alma mater. Like many of his classmates, Wesley viewed Fisk's predicament as a threat to other African American institutions under majority white control. Wesley agreed that "to save the traditions of Fisk" was in "the best interests of our group." He also recognized that support from Fiskites alone was not enough to tackle the pivotal crisis before them and that "any action to be effective must be united."[73] Wesley's sentiments reflected fundamental New Negro beliefs about political awareness and activism and were shared by a number of respondents who felt, "The time has passed when white men like Thomas Jesse Jones and others can speak for the Negro."[74] Among those responding to calls for a united front was John Wesley Work Jr., who garnered support among faculty at Roger Williams and promised to "take up the matter with the Meharry group." Work supported Du Bois's involvement, claiming, "You are making a great fight for Fisk University and our people, and you deserve the full support of us all." However, he entertained no delusions regarding the enormous challenge before them and admitted, "Blowing one's brains out is a great sight easier than some of the things we have to do and stand."[75]

By January 1925 the movement had gained momentum, and Du Bois organized a three-session meeting for Fisk Club members from across the country. The invitations requested the attendance of Fisk graduates as well as former students who had attended Fisk in recent years but chose to leave. It is possible that Du Bois hoped to gain allies among those in the latter group who left because of dissatisfaction with administrative personnel or university policies. The meeting took place in New York City on January 2 and 3. It was decided that each club and its members would vote to form a united organization headed by an executive committee of which Du Bois would serve as chair. In this capacity Du Bois's primary responsibility was to speak on behalf of the newly formed association at various locations in the North and South in an effort to raise awareness of Fisk's problems.[76]

In an effort to keep Fisk's concerns in the national news, Du Bois maintained contact with various African American members of the press. In one cable he urged N. B. Brascher of the Associated Negro Press to "get into this Fisk fight on the right side" and publish developing information, for which Du Bois agreed to "personally stand responsible." Among the first accounts he shared was a report from Miss Cashin, a Fisk University English professor. Cashin recounted that she was required to have her majors complete a five-thousand-word thesis entitled "Reasons Why Dr. McKenzie Should Be Retained at Fisk University."[77] According to Cashin, the most favorable essays were published in the *Fisk News* as evidence of student support for McKenzie. Du Bois assured Brascher that this was not the sentiment of Fisk students and that it was another

instance of McKenzie influencing faculty behavior and improperly placing students in a conundrum where their only choice was to accede to
unscrupulous demands or face the possibility of failure or expulsion.

Du Bois also directed press members to scrutinize the university's
General Regulations, which stated, "The university is open only to such
students as are intellectually and morally prepared, and who are happy
and content to abide by the spirit and the letter of all the regulations and
requirements of the University." Also highlighted in the regulations was
the ominous reminder, "A student may be sent away at any time if considered unsatisfactory, without any definite charge being preferred."[78]
Du Bois wanted the public to be aware that such regulations left students
at the mercy of the administration, which had been empowered as the
sole arbiter of what constituted proper attitudes or modes of behavior.
Because of these rulings Fisk students had to sacrifice rights and privileges that most African American colleges offered and that were often
unquestioned at white universities.

A Coming Storm

After further attempts to reconcile grievances by student and faculty
committees failed, trustees spoke with McKenzie during a visit to New
York at the end of January about a compromise that might alleviate student hostilities. However, the collective response to student complaints
became public upon McKenzie's return to Nashville on January 31, when
he told reporters, "A complete ignoring of the charges made against the
administration will be the policy of the Board of Trustees of Fisk University."[79] When McKenzie used a February 4 chapel speech as an opportunity to press his views on discipline and concluded the service with an
ultimatum for students to either "abide by the rules of Fisk University" or
"get out," embittered students organized a vocal response.[80]

While student accounts of their activities on the evening of Wednes-
day, February 4, vary dramatically from those of Fisk's administration,
there is no dispute that the events of that night transformed a simmering
local conflict into a heated national debate. According to student narratives, the male residents of Livingstone Hall gathered for a demonstration around 10 P.M. Just prior to their display, the students were careful
to assure the matron of Livingstone Hall, Miss Boyton, and McKenzie's
secretary, Miss Herbst, who also lived in the building, that their actions
were a civil response to the policies of President McKenzie and that no
harm to any person or to the university grounds was intended. Over the

next two hours the men moved deliberately through dormitory halls and onto the athletic field, beating pans with sticks while singing, "Before I'd be a slave, I'd be buried in my grave."[81] Amid the echoing spiritual rejoinder, intermittent shouts of "Du Bois! Du Bois!" were also heard by observers.[82] These words signified their connection to a black vernacular laden with radical historical implications and evoked a defiant and determined sensibility identified with the New Negro of the twentieth century. After an hour transpired, Fisk's male students concluded their circuitous protest and returned to their beds.

Approximately thirty minutes after returning to Livingstone Hall, students claimed, they were awakened by pistol shots.[83] Those sounds were followed by loud footsteps later identified as belonging to some eighty Nashville policemen. The officers, who were armed with riot guns, were responding to a phone call made by McKenzie to the chief of police. Police officers found the Livingstone hallways silent and the eighty-six resident students in their beds. Unprovoked, police began knocking down doors and tearing out transoms until they had awakened every student in the building. However, the police were not seeking to arrest those who had participated in the demonstration that evening; they already had a list of seven names: George Streator, J. B. Crawford, Edward Taylor, Victor Perry, Charles Lewis, E. L. Goodwin, and R. R. Alexander. Only five of the men were identified that evening. Streator, who lived off campus, could not be located, and Crawford lived in the home of a white family in the West End area. It was no coincidence that the seven names on the list given to police by McKenzie included the same students who had presented objections to his administration and its policies throughout the previous year and who had visited with the board of trustees just three months earlier.[84]

The five men who could be located were taken under armed guard to the president's house, where he refused to see them and instead requested that they be moved immediately to the police station on Second Avenue.[85] Once they were removed by a police wagon, the president ventured out, under armed guard, and had the remaining students brought into his office one at a time. There they were asked to sign a paper promising "to obey to the letter" all Fisk University rules and regulations "on pain of being arrested or expelled."[86] The first to be interrogated by McKenzie was Senior Class President Ernest Crossley, who flatly refused to sign any document and was then given less than two hours to catch the last train home to Chicago. Under the strain of McKenzie's tactics, some students did agree "to obey to the letter all present rules of Fisk University and all that should be made," yet most refused to sign or surrender the fight.[87]

In Black and White

It took little time for white newspapers to pick up the story of student demonstrations and turn them into reports of widespread rioting. Local and national headlines featured the frightening "revolt" carried out by "a band of fractious," "unruly," and "rebellious" Fisk University students. Amid the reports were supposed phone threats to McKenzie's home that "it would be dangerous" for him or faculty members to appear on campus that evening. Others recounted "25–50" pistol shots raining from the windows of Livingston Hall. Foreboding black-and-white images of Livingstone Hall's chapel, where rows of benches were overturned, chairs smashed, and windows broken, accompanied some articles and appeared to verify exaggerated accounts of property destruction. It was also from this location that "ringleaders" were said to have instigated the riot and armed students, who then started toward McKenzie's home two blocks away. Purportedly fearing for his safety, and the safety of those faculty members visiting his home, McKenzie "called police headquarters for protection." Only when "an army" of police officers arrived, dressed in full riot gear and armed with machine guns, did the "band of negroes retreat," and order was restored.[88]

Each article from white papers excoriated Fisk students in its own manner; one in particular accused participants of the "complete abolition of the ideals and policies of supervision and discipline which have done so much to make Fisk graduates noticeable and notable wherever they have gone." However, readers were reassured that those responsible for the riot had been arrested and that police with riot gear "remained in charge of Fisk University campus."[89] Rather than portraying these events as a civil demonstration common to university campuses nationwide, white newspaper accounts characterized the demonstration as a contemporary slave revolt, playing on white fears of an African American uprising.

McKenzie's decision to call police to Fisk rather than handle differences among administrators, faculty, and students through dialogue only verified what many African American critics of his administration had argued: that McKenzie was an unreasonable man who exercised his authority with impunity, and worse, that his treatment of students was discriminatory. The journalist A. L. Jackson was angry that McKenzie

understood so little about procedure after a decade of southern exposure: "No man, white or black, who knows anything about the South and
southern attitudes could help but know that such a move would bring
anything else but trouble and lots of it."⁹⁰ Part of that trouble derived
from an expectation of fair play between McKenzie and the student body
whom he was supposed to represent. African American onlookers could
not but wonder whether an army of riot police would flood a white university campus to engage demonstrating students over policy issues. If
Fisk men and women were college students of standing equal to their
white counterparts across town and around the country, then they must
be accorded identical treatment in such circumstances.

While their collective action exhibited a racial spirit, Fisk students
also exercised a democratic one. This parallel was not lost on a journalist from Jacksonville's *Florida Sentinel* when he argued, "In fighting
for their rights as men and women—American men and women, the
students of Fisk have a just cause, and those who are concerned with
education should realize that they must insist that those things which
are due us be given us."⁹¹ His words echo those of Grimke and other New
Negroes who insisted that African Americans would not submit to inferior treatment or apologize for public demonstrations that protested any
restriction of their rights. McKenzie's contrary response prohibited the
very individual and intellectual development the college system should
foster. It was particularly troubling to Fisk's burgeoning student body,
which, like so many of their generation, embraced a new race consciousness and demanded a new self-respect concomitant with the New Negro.

Many African American observers felt that by trampling on these ideals, McKenzie brought upon himself, and the institution he represented,
a volatile attack. Leading the charge was the *Chicago Defender*, which
left little doubt about the consequences of McKenzie's actions: "Declared
war? Indeed, war; open wicked war against your own. You called in the
enemy to curse, tread down, denounce, violate the sons and daughters
of fathers, of mothers too long violated—called in from the city the dirt
and filth of it that have boasted that they would get Fisk and bring it to
its belly. You ordered machine guns turned on children. Is this war? By
God and by His teachings, this is war: war against children. You have
made Fisk a Belgium and invited the Huns to play hell."⁹² While allud-
ing to a past fraught with racial transgression, the quotation resonates
with an equally inflammatory, though more contemporary reference. Six
years earlier, the Treaty of Versailles formally concluded World War I, a
struggle in which over 350,000 African Americans, many on the front

lines of Western Europe, dutifully served their country.[93] History and legend have made the Hun synonymous with barbarism, but when connected to Imperial Germany the Hun was widely understood as a threat to democracy—a threat patriotic African Americans recognized. When, in 1917, Woodrow Wilson asked Congress for a declaration of war on Germany, he argued that Americans were "champions of the rights of mankind." In the face of violent aggression, Wilson argued that neutrality was unrealistic and that a temperate course of action was required: "Just because we fight without rancor and without selfish object, seeking nothing for ourselves but what we shall wish to share with all free peoples, we shall, I feel confident, conduct our operations as belligerents without passion and observe with proud punctilio the principles of right and of fair play we profess to be fighting for."[94]

The analogy was clear: by referring to Fisk as a battlefield, the *Defender* ceded the (moral) high ground to the students. It was their organized and peaceful demonstration that was assaulted by an insidious foe, a police horde assembled at the behest of McKenzie, a brutish master. Two generations removed from slavery, demonstrating Fisk students showed that submission to white domination was a past practice. Their response was heralded by Du Bois, who, upon hearing of the demonstration and the ensuing police debacle, clamored, "I thank God they did [respond]. I thank God that the younger generation of black students have the guts to yell and fight when their noses are rubbed in the mud."[95] Their responses played an important role in their own identity formation, but they also helped to reshape public perception of the New Negro for both African Americans and whites.

McKenzie's handling of the student demonstration became national news, dividing Nashville and citizens around the country along racial lines. Even more significant, his actions highlighted questions posed by many African Americans about the role of whites in traditionally African American colleges, a repository for representatives of a new racial era. For most African Americans who witnessed McKenzie's response, the answers had become clear: "You turned loose the Nashville police on our young women: on the mothers of our future: our sisters, on the lone hope of a Race that, by God, comes now to take a stand and live or die! You called the Black Mariah—the whistle blew and the clang of the bell was heard in the city streets! Mac, you went crazy!"[96]

Trial

On Thursday, February 5, the City of Nashville transferred its case against the five defendants to the Second Circuit Court for deliberation. The trial began at two o'clock in a courtroom overflowing with white and African American observers, many of whom were spurred to attendance by intensive media coverage. Although warrants had been issued for George Streator and J. B. Crawford, they had not been arrested. The two men worked closely with fellow students Van Taylor, Stanley Hemphill, Frank Williams, and Ernest Crossley to contact Fisk alumni in Tennessee and sympathetic African Americans in Nashville and to raise 150 dollars in cash and secure twenty thousand dollars in bonds. The accused were charged with a felony, which meant incarceration if convicted, so the allotted funds were used to hire a former Tennessee governor, Albert H. Roberts, a formidable defense counselor.

In a move that surprised many in attendance, prosecutor John DeWitt asked Judge Roscoe Matthews to dismiss the case against the five students. DeWitt was pursuing a course of action shared publicly by McKenzie with a handful of local white reporters just two hours earlier. McKenzie's "leak" not to prosecute "unruly students" was likely a political maneuver seeking to establish his control over recent campus events and to appear magnanimous in his treatment of the accused students.[97] However, defense attorney Roberts vehemently objected to the dismissal. He was aware of DeWitt's thin case. In particular Roberts knew that the prosecution could produce no witnesses to support the charge of inciting a riot. Capitalizing on his clients' strong position, he wanted proof of their innocence on record. In response to Roberts's objection, Judge Matthews altered the felony charge of inciting a riot to a misdemeanor count of disorderly conduct.[98] The five defendants invoked their constitutional right not to testify. The court then called a series of arresting officers to the stand. Under cross-examination from Roberts, none of the officers could identify any of the defendants. In testimony damning to the prosecution, officers admitted under oath that the only reason they had arrested the five men was that President McKenzie had provided them with a list of specific names. When it was McKenzie's turn at the stand, Roberts asked him why he had supplied police with the names of the accused. He responded, "It's a long story, your honor. These men have spoken against my administration and my policies all during the year. While I had no actual proof that they were in the disturbance, I felt that they might be behind this or anything of its nature."[99] Following

McKenzie's startling testimony and the inability of the prosecution to provide witnesses to corroborate the charge of disorderly conduct, the case was dismissed and the defendants discharged. To affirm the victory, the prudent Roberts made sure that their case was filed with the court.

Mass Meeting

On February 9 members of Nashville's Negro Board of Trade attempted to quell a raging storm by communicating with McKenzie on behalf of the students to discuss resolutions proposed by the student body. McKenzie countered their offer with a proposal to create an impartial committee of eighteen individuals. The committee would include six of their number, six from the Chamber of Commerce, and six members representing local universities—Vanderbilt, Peabody, and Ward-Belmont (all white), and Walden, Meharry, and State Normal (all African American)—to act as jury for the recent student allegations of Fisk's excessive rules and regulations. However, McKenzie stressed that the proposed committee's purpose was merely to provide "advice" to Fisk administrators and to aid "the quieting of the public mind." While open to community feedback, McKenzie emphasized, "A college can never submit its integrity or its authority to agencies beyond itself."[100] Rather than participating in what they viewed as a biased committee, Negro Board of Trade members organized their own mass meeting of concerned African American citizens to form a definite plan of action.

When C. L. McKissack, president of the Nashville Negro Board of Trade, called the 7:30 meeting to order that night, he saw an imposing sight. An estimated three thousand African American community members crowded Saint John African Methodist Episcopal Church to share grievances over the unrest at Fisk.[101] Visible amid the throng were New Negroes whose activism could be traced to the streetcar strikes decades earlier and who overwhelmingly supported student interests: E. W. D. Isaac, editor of the *Clarion*, one of Nashville's African American newspapers; T. Clay Moore and Dr. J. T. Phillips, former Fisk Alumni Association presidents; pastors R. W. Nance, former president of Alcorn College, and Noah Williams, a former army chaplain; J. A. Martin, Colored Methodist Episcopal School Board secretary; Dr. J. T. Barnes, a dentist and Fisk alumnus; and Meredith G. Ferguson, bookkeeper at Citizens' Savings Bank and a veteran who served as an officer in the First World War. Also visible were a handful of McKenzie supporters, including Dr. J. A. Napier and Dr. W. W. Sumlin, conservative citizens from two of the city's best-known African American families.

The majority of the men and women present were not passive observers but active participants in the student rights struggle. When reports of rioting appeared in local papers, many of those attending the mass meeting were from neighboring streets who submitted signed affidavits stating they were "not in the least terrorized or even unusually disturbed by the student demonstration."[102] Others in attendance were local residents incensed by the police presence summoned by McKenzie to prevent "outsiders" access to the university campus in the days following the demonstration. Word had spread among community members that McKenzie, in an effort to stem student departures, halted campus mail delivery and asked white merchants not to cash student money orders.[103] In response to acts that were viewed as further evidence of McKenzie's intimidation tactics, African American families from across Nashville boarded displaced students in their homes and provided much needed financial support.[104] Among those providing assistance was Meredith Ferguson, who defiantly cashed student money orders from a car parked adjacent to campus and allowed displaced students to phone parents from his home—a gesture that increased his bill to an estimated eight hundred dollars monthly.[105] Aware that sentiment among the crowd was anti-McKenzie, McKissack called for "no waving of the bloody shirt, no fire-brand speeches . . . only sane logical thinking."[106]

The first to speak was George W. Streator, one of the five students previously suspended by McKenzie. Streator repeated student demands for representation by a council of their peers, reinstatement of a school paper informed by student contributions, the creation of an athletic association, and the ability to join fraternities and sororities like students in other institutions. Streator told the audience that after sharing these requests with McKenzie, the president warned that he was "sending his soul to hell in asking for things the president did not think desirable." It was an anecdote that illustrated McKenzie's autocratic behavior, and a tone, Streator claimed, with which he and other students were familiar in numerous lectures by McKenzie about loyalty and the consequences of disobedience. He excoriated the white press for characterizing the demonstration as a riot and for exaggerating damage to school property. He also refuted claims by white newspapers that students were "paid agents of Du Bois" and insisted that "after much persuasion" from students during his spring visit, Du Bois had consented to support their efforts to find a suitable replacement for president of the university. Before ceding the floor Streator also emphasized that McKenzie's replacement did not need to be "a Negro president or a white president but a president."[107]

After similar statements regarding student demands from Charles S. Lewis, another of the five students suspended by McKenzie, a student protester named J. Anrew Simmons took the stage. He apologized for his late arrival, explaining that he had just come from Union Station, where he had helped thirty-three striking students board trains for home. The announcement was met with thunderous applause. Simmons argued that by demonstrating, he and other students were defending Fisk University, not destroying it. He reminded the audience that despite contributions from whites, Fisk did not get its reputation as "the greatest Negro school in the world by just sitting on a hill out there"; it was the physical and financial contributions of African Americans that enabled its success.[108] He focused on aspects of racial progress and uplift associated with the New Negro, and insisted, "Fisk today was the Fisk of 1870," but that the "times and the people had changed." Neither slaves nor servants, students should no longer be treated as "a bunch of boys and girls, but [as] men and women."[109]

While responding to contemporary events at Fisk, Simmons's statement addressed educational questions African Americans had posed for decades: Was an institution such as Fisk established as "a Negro college" or "a college for negroes"?[110] Were African American students merely participants in an educational process administered by paternalistic presidents and backed by a board of trustees committed to a policy of racial uplift yet blinded by their own inherent prejudices? Or were students active agents whose individual voices might be raised until the collective reverberations transformed autocratic administrations into empathetic democracies? At issue were not only New Negro concerns regarding manhood but also ownership and management of institutions created for their advancement. Before stepping down, Simmons demanded an administration of "people who are in sympathy with the institution regardless of race, color, or creed" and who would treat the students as responsible adults.[111] His comments echoed the concerns of a new generation that sought to move their race forward without hesitation or retreat to achieve intellectual freedom and individual success.

Following the student representatives, voices in the crowd called for a motion to draft resolutions for the university's board of trustees. Dr. James A. Napier, present on behalf of McKenzie, perceived the crowd behaving as judge, jury, and prosecutor. Rising to his feet, he shouted, "How many of you are going to uphold mob law?"[112] The crowd responded to his question with a flurry of catcalls and hisses, forcing him to sit. Dr. W. W. Sumlin, another McKenzie supporter, attempted to speak, but the hissing crowd rendered his statements inaudible. In an attempt to restore order, McKissack ruled that student testimony could be rebutted only by members of the faculty, and since none were present, additional arguments were inadmissible. Seizing on the momentary silence, Napier protested the ruling and asked students, "If the conditions there have been intolerable, why haven't they left before now, like men and women?" He was again met with a flood of jeers and shouts. Infuriated by the partisan response, Sumlin rushed to the front and shouted dramatically, "Now you are showing the true Negro mob spirit. Come on, you mobsters, if you have got the nerve. Put the rope around my neck and string me up!" Cries of "sit down" and "make him sit down" filled the church.[113] When Sumlin attempted a rebuttal, he was silenced, and then retired.

Without further deliberation, the Negro Board of Trade passed the following resolutions:

(1) That we regard the things prayed for by the students as reasonable and practicable.

(2) That the requests of the students have not been given a respectable hearing.

(3) That having been denied a respectful hearing, the board of trustees of Fisk be and is hereby petitioned by the citizens in mass meeting assembled, to give their case a full hearing and impartial investigation.

(4) That the president, Dr. F. A. McKenzie, has shown his inability to govern the school by calling in police to stop a demonstration which was easily within the power of him and his faculty, and by causing the imprisonment of five students, against whom his accusations were subsequently withdrawn for lack of evidence.

(5) In view of his inefficiency as evidenced by the facts herein stated, it is our firm opinion that his usefulness as president of Fisk University is at an end.[114]

The Beginning of the End

McKenzie's indifference to criticism from the African American community damaged his symbolic status as an instrument of racial cooperation. His behavior also suggested that paternal attitudes of the dominant white majority trumped minority voices with regard to the substantive experience of African American education. McKenzie acknowledged that his decision to involve police brought "much adverse criticism from colored people," but countered that whites had "endorsed the act with a great deal of enthusiasm." On February 6, one day after the trial, McKenzie was greeted by an ovation from Kiwanis Club members while attending a regular event. He recalled that in the days following the Kiwanis Club dinner, "everywhere I receive very strong commendation." Emboldened by community support that, in his eyes, appeared most consequential to Fisk's continued success, he mused "whether I shall ever be so much admired here or anywhere else again in my life." Apparently feigning modesty, McKenzie initially turned down an opportunity to speak at Nashville's Exchange Club, fearing "the danger of too much applause." However, in correspondence he recalled accepting the invitation and that, upon his introduction, "everybody in the room rose to his feet and a great many yelled as well as a great many cheered with their hand clapping."[115] At Nashville's Hawaiian Club, McKenzie was "wildly cheered" on his way to the speaker's seat. The vocal response prompted the removal of the club's attending black wait staff before McKenzie reiterated his Fisk policies and urged the continued support of Nashville's white community.[116] In the following days McKenzie appeared confident, even grandiose, stating at one point, "Somehow I feel that never before in the United States has a white man had such a hold upon a city as I now have upon Nashville."[117] However, despite public enthusiasm among whites, McKenzie's actions unsettled the university's trustees.

Of increasing concern was the widespread student absenteeism. While McKenzie basked in the public spotlight following the trial, Fisk students organized a strike that began on Friday, February 7, at 10 A.M. To ensure unanimity, a larger meeting of diverse student groups was held on the evening of February 6, where it was decided that there would be "no attendance at chapel, church, classes or any of the official or semi-official university exercises." Frustrated that McKenzie failed to reach an agreement with the Negro Board of Trade's arbitration committee, students reached out to Paul D. Cravath, president of the Fisk board of trustees, with the following resolutions:

1. The right to student government
2. The right to organize and maintain an athletic program consistent with an advanced institution
3. The right to have a student publication

4. The right to join recognized Negro college fraternities and sororities

5. Freedom of expression

6. Revision to the Fisk code of law, a thing promised by the trustee board

7. Reinstatement of the five suspended students without penalty.[118]

Strike leaders also indicated to board members that within the next twenty-four hours, at least one-third of the student body would depart campus in protest.

When McKenzie rose to address the chapel attendees on Sunday, February 8, he witnessed the determination of the student strikers. According to a student committee poll monitoring the protest, 35 of 146 women were present, while only 2 of approximately 86 male students remained. Among high school attendees at Fisk, only 5 of 50 appeared, along with 26 of the approximately 100 day students. McKenzie appeared discomfited, warning those present not to "move on the spur of the moment and to move in masses on emotion rather than upon the basis of careful thinking." He reassured the audience that having fewer students would allow those remaining to "become better acquainted and get a better sense of the human, heartfelt affection that exists between us."[119] While it is impossible to discern just how many students were open to McKenzie's gesture toward harmony, there is evidence that many of those in attendance had much to lose by striking.

Among those in limbo were students attending Fisk on scholarship and those only months away from graduation. Still, George Streator claimed that as many as forty of those attending chapel were "pledged to the strikers," including members of the senior class who, along with Streator, planned "to enter Howard University." Streator claimed that as McKenzie spoke, a student representative was on the way to Howard to "make arrangements for the large exodus." Proving that Streator's words were no empty boast, Howard University issued a formal press release announcing that "no new students can be admitted until March 14" and that "seniors entering from Fisk cannot be graduated in June" because any transferring student "must remain in residence one year before the degree is conferred." Ever defiant, McKenzie claimed, "Even if the number of students at Fisk University gets as low as ten, we are going on with the classes as usual."[120] Faced with an escalating crisis, the board was forced to intervene.

On February 9 Hollingsworth Wood, vice chairman of the Fisk University Board of Trustees, responded to student resolutions from the previous weekend. Wood indicated that Cravath was traveling in India and would be unavailable, but that he would arrive in Nashville on February 11 to "see justice done to all parties."[121] Wood arrived as promised and told the student audience gathered in Livingstone Hall to "promptly return to their classes and endeavor to support the president and faculty in carrying out their duties to the university and the country." While Wood appeared to stonewall student requests that he investigate not only their concerns but also the escalating concerns among Nashville's African American community regarding McKenzie's authoritarian regime, he expressed a very different opinion behind the scenes. According to a *Nashville Banner* reporter, Wood was overheard following his arrival at Nashville's airport saying that he was inclined to view recent student responses as no more than "youthful pranks." Only after he was pressed to elaborate by the reporter, who reminded him of the outrage among white Nashvillians over what they viewed as inexcusable student behavior, did Wood offer a formal vindication of McKenzie on record, stating, "The trustees stand absolutely behind Dr. McKenzie in his unflinching stand for the maintenance of law and order."[122] However, it was becoming clear to board members and McKenzie that their relationship had reached an impasse.

Immediately following Du Bois's June 1924 commencement address, McKenzie had sent a complete report to the trustees, who replied that they would issue a statement of endorsement on his behalf. Perhaps under the assumption that there would be no further controversy, the endorsement remained undrafted. As communication between McKenzie's administration and the student body deteriorated in fall 1924, McKenzie again requested backing from the board. After a delay of several months a statement was received, but it was not signed by Dr. Thomas Jesse Jones, who was out of the country, or Dr. William N. DeBerry, who was unwilling to provide a complete endorsement of McKenzie.[123] (See figure 13.)

Following the February demonstration McKenzie requested the physical presence of board members on campus as a show of solidarity, but they refused. Adding to McKenzie's frustration was the discovery that board members Wood and Baldwin were "meeting with the Du Bois group in hopes of bringing about better relations" rather than "holding up the hands of the president and cheering those on the job."[124] Incensed, McKenzie initiated a new media campaign, pitting letters of support for his administration against those of students and their supporters.[125] The only result from this effort was to prolong the standoff between the two sides and to draw even more negative attention to a crisis that was clearly beyond McKenzie's control. Increasingly aware that his effectiveness at

FIGURE 13 Fisk University Board of Trustees, ca. 1920. Among those identified at bottom from the left are Dr. Thomas Jesse Jones, Dr. Beard, Dr. Fayette McKenzie. In the top row from left are Reverend William N. DeBerry, Paul D. Cravath, chairman of the board, and James C. Napier. (Courtesy of Tennessee State Library and Archives.)

the university had reached its end, McKenzie tendered his resignation to the board on April 15.[126]

Because the controversy involved a white university president and an African American student body, it was easy for many to view differences between the two sides as racially inspired. That race played a distinct role is a matter of little doubt, but the manner in which race was interpreted and incorporated into the controversy was, at times, overly simplistic. It was not a matter of race in terms of removing a white president in order to substitute an African American president. However, because of the way the matter was publicized, this is how many perceived the matter, relegating Du Bois and McKenzie to symbolic status.

In the eyes of whites, Du Bois was the African American radical and agitator. The white press viewed his "Diuturni Silenti" speech on behalf of Fisk alumni and students as an insult, an affront to many whites' sense of propriety. In at least one instance, the *Crisis* editor was burned in effigy and threatened with physical violence if he returned to Nashville.[127] Du Bois was attacked verbally and even accused of crafting a scheme in which he intended to suggest a suitable African American replacement for McKenzie and ultimately unseat the white president for his own personal advancement.

To a majority of African Americans, McKenzie epitomized white supremacy; in particular he reflected the white South's dominant views of African American inferiority. The *National Baptist Voice*, the organ of the National Baptist Convention of America, labeled the atmosphere at Fisk "too serious a Race affair to try and hide its ugliness."[128] Members of the African American press reiterated this message, a position that was easily reinforced following the police raid on campus. In the wake of that decision by McKenzie, African American papers across the country featured articles with photographs of the strike leaders under the heading "Martyrs at Fisk."[129] Given the emotions on both sides, it comes as little surprise that African American and white citizens of Nashville, and ultimately communities across the country, overwhelmingly aligned themselves along racial lines. Yet, blinded by a limited understanding of the ways race affected the events at Fisk, most community members, regardless of race, missed the protest's deeper implications.

The Fisk controversy was not about individuals; it was about caste. It was not simply about the color of those involved but the degree of control they were allowed to exercise. According to McKenzie, he was "under attack from bolshevistic, if not anarchistic, elements of society."[130] He repeatedly blamed Du Bois for provoking student behavior rather than acknowledging his own neglect of Fisk's viable and vocal student community. McKenzie believed that the situation at Fisk "could not have been saved" because trustee members had not "in some way compelled the students and the alumni" to understand that no "methods and machinations of outsiders and of students against the discipline and authority of the institution" would be tolerated.[131] His mentality was very much "us against them," superiors versus inferiors. However, in his missionary paternalistic zeal, McKenzie was blind to his own prejudices. Looking down at students from his administrative heights, he believed "the college should be the torch-bearer and the touchstone of what was best; and the 'streets' should lift themselves to college level, and not the latter descend to the streets."[132]

Like many of his predecessors, McKenzie saw a right way and a wrong way to educate African Americans. He believed whites were able to best administer African American students and to negotiate and distribute the benefits derived from white capital. As McPherson has argued, "Subjectively, some missionaries shared (perhaps subconsciously) the widespread conviction that black people were deficient in organizational and executive skills" and were particularly "hesitant to entrust Negroes with outright control of funds" contributed by white northern philanthropists.[133] African Americans too were aware of this financial relationship. When rumors surfaced that an African American president would replace McKenzie, T. Clay Moore, a former Fisk Alumni Association president, acknowledged, "It is all tommyrot. . . . We know, just as everyone else knows, that the whites supplying the funds for Fisk will not give hundreds of thousands of dollars to the institution if a colored president is placed in charge. We know too that the people among whom we live would not like it."[134] McKenzie, like many liberal whites, did not perceive as racist the dynamic that existed within African American educational institutions because such a dynamic reflected inherent societal beliefs among whites of African American inferiority during the period.[135] However, McKenzie underestimated the importance of maintaining successful relationships on both sides of the color line, an error that ultimately led to his undoing.

When the controversy between Fisk students and McKenzie escalated in November 1924, McKenzie's administration had not eradicated $150,000 in debt that would enable completion of the university's well-publicized one-million-dollar endowment. When McKenzie failed to resolve differences between the two sides and tensions increased during the 1925 school year, Fisk's debt doubled to approximately $300,000.[136] Donations from alumni and parents had dwindled since the beginning of the 1924 school year, and trustees soon recognized that despite white Nashville's enthusiastic support of McKenzie following the campus "riot," community members indicated their loss of faith in McKenzie, and Fisk's future, by refusing to fulfill their endowment pledges in 1925. In addition to members of the Nashville community, several white northern philanthropists failed to submit the remainder of pledges, supporting the opinion that McKenzie was incapable of effectively managing his administrative duties as president of Fisk.

Once exposed, Fisk's financial concerns compounded existing fractures within McKenzie's administration. From the outset of the disputation, Du Bois had attacked McKenzie, but in doing so he addressed the inherent problems of missionary paternalism. He acknowledged, "The time [has] come when the claims of colored men for the presidency of our Negro schools should be considered and considered on the same terms as the claims of white men," but he also reiterated consistently in *Crisis* and elsewhere that he did not care "whether the next president of Fisk University is black, white or green."[137] While directed at McKenzie's administration, Du Bois's concerns focused on administrative failures that were manifested in Fisk's harsh disciplinary system, its suppression of student initiative, its unwillingness to solicit alumni support, and the suggestion that in exchange for financial support academic standards were lowered to conform with white expectations of African American achievement. Ultimately, as a result of recent student demonstrations, trustees acknowledged many of Du Bois's criticisms and recognized something that McKenzie did not: the need for amelioration between the two sides.

Board members lamented accusations of irresponsible paternalism at Fisk, and McKenzie himself openly conceded that "the situation might have been saved" if he had been more receptive in "granting concessions to the students."[138] The board members bristled at suggestions of racism within the university hierarchy and emphasized publicly that they "most desired a President who will maintain a sympathetic and liberal attitude toward Negro education."[139] In addition the board submitted an editorial to the *New York Times* that claimed "a careful study conducted by the trustees and by representatives of the alumni developed that no race issue was involved" in the student demonstrations.[140] The position of the board members was difficult. While they did not agree with McKenzie's handling of the dispute, they feared that in firing him, students would overestimate their influence with regard to policymaking decisions beyond the limits of their control. Yet board members also realized that they were the ones with the most to lose. No longer could administrators reign supreme over a silent African American majority. Though they were deemed current with regard to Native American education, McKenzie's policies proved inadequate for the New Negro student. His demise initiated a shift in the administration of African American colleges and signaled the end of missionary paternalism.

A New Fisk

With Fisk's administrative reconfiguration, changes to the university were profound. An interim committee was appointed to handle administrative duties following McKenzie's departure and to communicate with the faculty members who were responsible for daily decision making.[141] Among their first resolutions was reinstating those students suspended during student demonstrations. Publication of the *Fisk News*, a faculty organ implemented by McKenzie, was suspended, and the student-led *Fisk Herald* was reestablished and provided with a five-hundred-dollar subsidy.[142] After careful deliberation, the committee recommended a white president to maintain a positive rapport with Nashville's white community and white philanthropy; at the end of the year trustees offered the position to Thomas Elsa Jones, a thirty-five-year-old Quaker who was completing his dissertation at Columbia University.[143] Like McKenzie, Jones lacked experience in race relations. However, he was young, enthusiastic, and an experienced educator. In addition to his domestic exposure, Jones had worked abroad with diverse student populations from England, Japan, and Siberia. From the moment of his arrival in February 1926, Jones was eager to mollify existing tensions between students and the university's administration.

Students returning to Fisk in the wake of McKenzie's resignation witnessed a number of changes to their campus community. The first of these was the creation of an athletic association that was to be regulated by a joint committee composed of alumni, faculty, and students. A student council was also installed and was given the authority to monitor student behavior both on and away from campus. Although each of these organizations required faculty supervision, students were allowed to adjudge and implement policy. Students were pleased by the return of their beloved *Fisk Herald* and enthusiastically organized a joint committee of students and faculty to tackle original projects. It would be another year before students enjoyed the recognition of sorority and fraternal organizations on campus and slight alterations to the previously stringent code of conduct, but gradual changes were made. A committee composed of faculty and students was instituted to determine an appropriate, though much more lax dress code for men and women. The campus became a more welcoming social space for students. It was no longer forbidden for opposite-sex students to meet and walk together on campus without the "presence and permission of the dean of women or a teacher."[144] After much debate the men were allowed a smoking room in the campus chocolate shop, although rules prohibiting women from smoking would not change until 1935.[145] Students were even allowed "a few well chaperoned and carefully managed" campus dances.[146] Having reconciled a number of student concerns, Jones then worked to establish better communication between faculty and alumni.

Jones enacted systematic changes that definitively altered Fisk's institutional landscape. In June 1926 trustees recommended the permanent representation of three alumni members to the board, a maneuver that significantly bolstered African American representation at the administrative level.[147] He also dramatically reshaped the racial composition of the faculty. Between 1926 and 1936 he increased the number of African American faculty by 50 percent. Under his leadership African American faculty penetrated the glass ceiling that previously prohibited organizational advancement at Fisk. In 1927 a history professor named Alrutheus Ambush Taylor was appointed dean of men. That summer Jones promoted another faculty member, Ambrose Caliver, to dean of the university, making him Fisk's first African American dean. Juliette Derricotte became Fisk's first black dean of women just two years later.

These positions were complemented by a stunning array of artists and educators assembled under Jones that made Fisk the center of African American cultural and intellectual life. This list includes Zephaniah Alexander Looby (economics), Charles S. Johnson (sociology), St. Elmo Brady (chemistry), Alain Locke (philosophy), Lorenzo Dow Turner (English), Arna Bontemps (poetry), Aaron Douglas (art), and the inimitable James Weldon Johnson. Jones helped to create not only a more diverse faculty but one that was better educated. Between 1925 and 1930 the number of faculty holding a PhD increased from two to ten, and those engaged in study beyond the MA rose from zero to twelve. These changes enabled Fisk to offer advanced degrees in history, English, and chemistry, innovations that made it the leading African American university, on par with the best private universities in the country.[148]

According to the historian Joe Richardson, the assemblage of such a talented and diverse research faculty led many observers to herald the birth of a "New Fisk" under Jones's tenure.[149] These changes in leadership were part of the work that enabled Jones to reestablish ties between Nashville's African American and white citizenry and to complete the one-million-dollar endowment project McKenzie began. While Jones endured many challenges as the president of Fisk University, he enjoyed a successful twenty-one-year career, highlighted by his strong support for African American expression and advancement. Under his tenure Fisk became "the first historically Black College and University to receive a Class A rating from the Southern Association of Colleges and Secondary Schools" and the "first HBCU to attain status on the Association of American Universities' approval list."[150] Following his departure in June 1946, the board appointed Charles S. Johnson, who became Fisk University's first African American president.

Agents of Change

While Fisk students were not the first in the history of African American higher education to challenge autocratic administrations or to rebel against stifling paternal practices, their unified and sustained demonstrations during 1924–25 were the catalyst for a series of strikes and demonstrations that followed at more than a dozen colleges across the country and epitomized New Negro student activism. The men and women of Fisk garnered national attention and provoked responses that inspired African American students at similar institutions during the era to challenge unsatisfactory conditions, reshape curricula, and seek the agency denied them by institutional power structures.[151] While none of the student demonstrations were identical in method or result, each responded to student repression (often race-based) under conservative and (largely white) autocratic administrations.

In May 1925, just weeks after McKenzie's retirement at Fisk, demonstrations at Howard erupted over the suspension of five students who had violated the university's compulsory ROTC policy. Though the students were eventually reinstated and the ROTC requirements adjusted, a constellation of issues among students, alumni, faculty, and university administration emerged in the following months.[152] Many of these issues, such as requests by student council members for the removal of faculty members deemed unfit for their positions and a desire for an African American dean of men, reflected a growing New Negro sensibility among students invested in race solidarity and an emerging race consciousness. Like those at Fisk, Howard students collectively challenged dictatorial policy and sought greater participation in the direction of their institution, demands that placed them in confrontation with faculty, administration, and trustees. Motivated by student agitation and in conjunction with increasing disagreements with alumni and faculty over management of the university, J. Stanley Durkee resigned in March 1926, enabling the election of Mordecai W. Johnson, the university's first African American president, in June 1926.

Discontent among African American students of the period was not limited to colleges supporting a liberal arts curriculum. In 1927 another significant protest occurred at Hampton Institute, touted publicly as the "model for all institutions devoted to the education of the mind and will through the education of the hand."[153] Student unrest emerged after an incident at Ogden Hall that led to the adoption of legislation that segregated public entertainment statewide. By October additional campus clashes between students, administration, and board members occurred. Hampton students presented their administration with a list of seventeen grievances. Among their concerns was a desire to improve Hampton's academic curriculum, to loosen stringent regulations, and to diversify and strengthen university faculty. Students also refused to sing Negro spirituals, particularly in the presence of whites, because they deemed the practice demeaning and reminiscent of old Negro plantation stereotypes. In response to what he deemed insolent behavior, Principal James Edgar Gregg suspended dozens of students and, with the board's consent, closed Hampton "until further notice."[154]

Unlike Fisk students, those at Hampton did not enjoy critical assistance from alumni or community members to sustain their opposition. Hampton students also faced an administration, backed by figures in state government, that was dedicated to the institute's industrial and agricultural model. However, during the late nineteenth and early twentieth century, the primary question regarding the future of African American education was no longer an antagonistic one pitting an industrial Hampton-Tuskegee model against a traditional collegiate one. By 1925 that discussion was becoming obsolete. Hindsight revealed that both educational models were needed to serve various elements of a burgeoning African American population, whether rural or urban. In fact the years 1924 and 1925 provided Tuskegee and Hampton, respectively, with their first graduates from a traditional course of study, suggesting that even industrialized education for African Americans was being augmented in a manner that redefined the practical needs of modern American society. Ultimately students reenrolled after signing a pledge of "loyalty and obedience."[155] They continued to challenge repressive rules and regulations at Hampton, behavior that contributed to the resignation of Principal Gregg in May 1929.[156]

In his discussion of African American college rebellions during the 1920s, August Meier argues, "Because students were dominated by white bourgeoisie values and aspirations, it can scarcely be said that the student rebels were part of the New Negro movement."[157] However, issues that were central to demonstrations at several colleges, such as those at Fisk and Howard, were motivated by a move toward autonomy, physical and spiritual. These demonstrations were contests of manhood, each tinged by the need for a reevaluation of self—from within and without—to move beyond "a world that looks on in amused contempt and pity" to one that recognizes the assertion of race pride, race consciousness, and a vision of the self-made man.[158]

Students' participation in demonstrations against their established educational institutions was a bold undertaking. It was a widely held opinion in African American communities of the period that earning a college degree was "a sacred and difficult attainment."[159] From this perspective it is not difficult to understand why some parents of Fisk students supported McKenzie throughout the demonstrations. The chance to attend Fisk was viewed as a privilege. To become labeled as an agitator or to be summarily dismissed for participation in demonstrations against college administrations placed the future education of each participating student in jeopardy. In light of such consequences, Herbert Aptheker considered such demonstrations "so outrageous as to border on the sacrilegious."[160]

One must also recognize that despite public attributions, men were not the only "ringleaders" and "martyrs" of these contests. Fisk provides an excellent example. The majority of women at Fisk had already chosen a side, whether or not they marched among their male counterparts in November 1924 or in February 1925. They spoke in absentia when they chose to miss chapel exercises, to vacate the classrooms following the trial of suspended students, and to board trains for home during the spring protests. Through these orchestrated demonstrations Fisk women revealed a spiritual alignment with their male classmates and a consciousness that defied societal expectations of African American women of the 1920s.

Fisk students were men and women representing an era influenced by new ideas. Their generation had tired of patriarchal attitudes, and they demanded recognition of their own perspectives. They wanted an education equal to that of white students, one that prepared them for professional opportunities rather than for supplementing a serving class. Unwilling to be stifled by outdated rules and regulations proscribed by those who deemed them members of a childlike race, Fisk's New Negroes utilized collective responses to initiate an end to race-based treatment and paternal authority in the higher education of African Americans. In doing so they helped reimagine race relations for a modern era.

Epilogue

The concept of the New Negro has now become as archaic as the word *Negro* itself, so much so that we may be in danger of losing sight of its historical importance. If this study has added some understanding to the origins of the New Negro, it is also important to note the legacy of that figure in its nineteenth-century southern context. Although the New Negro was no Black Panther, the autonomy of that Oakland community in the 1970s may have owed as much to the independence of African Americans in Nashville as did the Black Arts movement to *Imperium in Imperio* or the Montgomery Bus Boycott to the Nashville streetcar strikes. In many ways the Union Transportation Company anticipated Marcus Garvey's Black Star Line, and Nashville's postbellum black entrepreneurs were the precursors of Jesse Jackson's Operation PUSH.

Whatever the legacy, we know for certain that the South played a critical role in the construction of the New Negro. While a small minority of African Americans left the South for new opportunities in the decades following the Civil War, the majority remained in the South well into the twentieth century. There, in the nineteenth century, premier institutions of black learning emerged, and W. E. B. Du Bois was educated at one of them. The first New Negro novels were written in the nineteenth-century South, and black enterprise, journalism, publishing, engineering, and design all flourished there, long before they did in Harlem or Chicago.

Nashville's unique role at the forefront of this history has also faded from recent memory as the city has become more and more a site first on the Dixiecrat and later on the conservative Republican map. Today it is much more distinctive as the epicenter of country and western music than of African American initiative.

In the nineteenth century, however, Nashville was unique among a number of southern cities that fostered the New Negro sensibility. With institutions such as Morehouse, Spelman, Morris Brown, and Clark Atlanta University, Atlanta was an important educational center that contributed significantly to generations of empowered, race-consciousness students. But Nashville's educational institutions were the earliest and among the foremost of those founded to educate African Americans. In particular Nashville was the first to offer legal and medical training for African Americans in the South at institutions considered the best in the region and arguably in the nation. As institutions committed to a liberal arts education, Fisk and Roger Williams exemplified the progressive and reactive sensibility identified with the New Negro. The list of graduates from Nashville's African American educational institutions is a who's who of African American history that ranges from Du Bois to Oprah Winfrey.

As an important economic center lauded for its finance and insurance enterprises, Durham, North Carolina, in many ways symbolized the possibilities for African American business and commercial development, but the most successful African American business in the country, the National Baptist Publishing Board, was founded in Nashville. Known for its powerful newspaper and a host of influential citizens, Richmond, Virginia, had long been considered an important African American site of bourgeois respectability, but the first black transportation company, first black doll manufacturer, and a host of additional transformative race ventures were in Nashville. Most important, all these economic, political, intellectual, and artistic elements came together in Nashville.

Therefore it is not surprising that Nashville remained an important center for African American intellectuals well into the twentieth century. Although each of the following men established a New Negro reputation before arriving in Nashville, Charles S. Johnson, James Weldon Johnson, Aaron Douglas, and Arna Bontemps are among the many African American intellectuals and artists who made their way to Nashville following the demise of the Harlem Renaissance. This fact is causally related to the development of Nashville as a significant center of African American cultural life prior to the twentieth century.

In 1927 Charles S. Johnson joined the Fisk faculty to lead the Department of Social Research. Johnson's early work included recognition for his analysis of the causes and subsequent impact of the race riots in

Chicago in 1919. After becoming the secretary of Chicago's Commission on Race Relations, he worked as the director of research for the National Urban League, where he founded and edited *Opportunity,* an important vehicle for racial debates and for the literary success of many Harlem Renaissance figures. Johnson thrived in Nashville, completing a number of sociological works, such as *The Negro in American Civilization: A Study of Negro Life and Race Relations in the Light of Social Research* (1930) and *The Collapse of Cotton Tenancy: Summary of Field Studies and Statistical Surveys, 1933–35* (1935). He won the 1930 William E. Harmon Gold Medal for distinguished achievement among blacks in the field of science and service, headed the Institute of Race Relations at Fisk, and became Fisk's first African American president in 1946.[1]

Johnson used his influence among African American intellectuals and artists to continue the legacy of the New Negro movement in Nashville. Among those he brought to Nashville was James Weldon Johnson, who taught classes in creative writing and American and African American literature at Fisk University from 1931 until 1938, when he was killed in a car accident. Johnson's time in Nashville enabled him to pursue the "contemplative life" that he had always dreamed about and offered him a different venue from which to pursue his goals for addressing the country's race problem. Like Charles Johnson, James Weldon Johnson coupled teaching responsibilities with writing. Viewing Nashville as "favorable ground" on which to develop a "racial strength" that would provide him with "fresh forces against bigotry and racial wrong," he completed a number of works, including his autobiography, *Along This Way* (1933), and *Negro Americans, What Now?* (1934) during his years at Fisk.[2]

Charles Johnson was also responsible for bringing Aaron Douglas and Arna Bontemps to Nashville. Douglas, arguably the preeminent African American artist of the period, came to Fisk in 1930 when commissioned to paint a set of murals for the library. After a stint as a part-time instructor while completing a master's degree, he accepted a full-time position as an art professor and remained at Fisk until his retirement in 1966. From 1943 until his death in 1973, Bontemps resided primarily in Nashville, where he served in varied roles from librarian to writer in residence at Fisk and continued his work as one of the most important editors and writers in African American culture.[3]

The very intellectual and cultural history in Nashville that fomented the New Negro, however, also helped facilitate the migration of African American artistic and cultural production to urban communities in the

North and, later, in the West, which since the mid-1920s have been the chief sites of African American production, competition, and debate. As prestigious, traditionally white institutions became more accessible to minorities, especially since the 1960s, historically black colleges have become less able to compete for the most talented black students and less able to fund their missions.

Today Fisk, like many historically black colleges and universities, faces a number of significant financial challenges. In a story that made national headlines, the university attempted to sell a portion of its Alfred Stieglitz art collection in order to remain open. Initially Fisk was prevented from selling the collection, estimated to be worth $70 million, because the donor, Georgia O'Keeffe, stipulated that the collection must never be sold. However, after several years in the Tennessee court system, Fisk was allowed to partner with Crystal Bridges Museum of American Art in Bentonville, Arkansas, for a 50 percent stake in the collection for $30 million dollars. Even with this financial infusion, however, Fisk has been forced to cut staff and faculty salaries, to require unpaid furlough days, and to endure probationary status with the Southern Association of Colleges and Schools over its financial concerns. Compounding these issues are a downturn in enrollment and a dearth of alumni support. While recent administrative restructuring brings the prospect of sweeping changes, the battle to maintain Fisk, and many other vibrant and historically significant institutions, is far from over. The fact that neither Fisk nor Nashville may ever be able to return to its centrality in black intellectual and artistic life, however, should not obscure the foundational role they played in creating the successes of African Americans in the twentieth century or the possibilities open to them in the twenty-first century.

Notes

Introduction

1. Alain Locke, "The New Negro," in *The New Negro: An Interpretation*, ed. Alain Locke (New York: Albert and Charles Boni, 1925), ix.

2. Henry Louis Gates Jr., "The Trope of a New Negro and the Reconstruction of the Image of the Black," *Representations* 24 (1988): 131–32.

3. Henry Louis Gates Jr. and Gene Andrew Jarrett, eds., *The New Negro: Readings on Race, Representation, and African American Culture, 1892–1938* (Princeton: Princeton University Press, 2007), 1–2.

4. Kenneth Warren, "The End(s) of African-American Studies," *American Literary History* 12.3 (2000): 643.

5. Robert Reid-Pharr, "The Slave Narrative and Early Black American Literature," in *Cambridge Companion to the African American Slave Narrative*, ed. Audrey Fisch (New York: Cambridge University Press, 2007), 137.

6. St. Clair Drake and Horace R. Cayton, *Black Metropolis* (New York: Harcourt, Brace, 1945), 12.

1 / The New Negro Genealogy

1. "A Merciless Planter, and Two Generous Negroes," *London Magazine, or Gentlemen's Monthly Intelligencer* 56 (1745): 495, http://hdl.handle.net/2027/mdp.39015063697257. The article recounts the story of a slave named Arthur, who, after failing to escape his cruel master and join a mountain Indian tribe, is forced to submit to three hundred lashes. Among those forced to deliver the blows is a "new Negro" who refuses to enforce the punishment after recognizing Arthur as a kinsman who had saved his life in tribal warfare prior to their enslavement. To punish the insubordinate "new Negro," the slave master demands that he too must receive three hundred lashes. Rather than witness his fellow slaves as participants and victims in the American slave system, the "new Negro" stabs the slave master in the heart and

then takes his own life. His decision is an intriguing act of loyalty, but it is also notable as a final statement of independence and manhood. Henry Louis Gates Jr. was the first to bring attention to this article in the context of interpreting the term *New Negro* in "The Trope of a New Negro and the Reconstruction of the Image of the Black," *Representations* 24 (1988): 133.

2. Gates, "The Trope of a New Negro," 133, 135.

3. "Negro," s.v., *Concise Oxford English Dictionary*, 11th ed., ed. Catherine Soanes and Angus Stevenson (Oxford: Oxford University Press, 2008).

4. Orlando Patterson, *Slavery and Social Death: A Comparative Study* (Cambridge, MA: Harvard University Press, 2007), 8.

5. Gates, "The Trope of a New Negro," 131, 132.

6. Henry Louis Gates Jr. and Gene Andrew Jarrett, ed., *The New Negro: Readings on Race, Representation, and African American Culture, 1892–1938* (Princeton, NJ: Princeton University Press, 2007).

7. Established in 1910 as the organ of the NAACP, the *Crisis* sought to "place consistently and continuously before the country a clear-cut statement of the legitimate aims of the American Negro and the facts concerning his condition." W. E. B. Du Bois, *The Autobiography of W. E. B. Du Bois* (New York: International, 1968), 260. According to its editor Du Bois, publication of the *Crisis* began in November 1910 with 1,000 copies, a number that climbed to an estimated 100,000 sold by 1918.

8. Gates, "The Trope of a New Negro," 135.

9. Anna Julia Cooper, "One Phase of American Literature," in *A Voice from the South* (Xenia, OH: Aldine, 1892), 225, 222, 223, 227.

10. Frances E. W. Harper, *Iola Leroy* (Boston: Beacon Press, 1987), 116; Victoria Earle Matthews, "The Value of Race Literature: An Address Delivered at the First Congress of Colored Women of the United States" (1895), in *With Pen and—Voice*, ed. Shirley Wilson Logan (Carbondale: Southern Illinois University Press, 1995), 146.

11. W. E. C. Wright, "The New Negro," *American Missionary* 48.1 (1894): 10, 11.

12. W. E. B. Du Bois, "The Talented Tenth," in *The Negro Problem: A Series of Articles by Representative Negroes of To-day* (New York: J. Pott, 1903), 10.

13. Wright, "The New Negro," 12.

14. J. W. E. Bowen, "*An Appeal to the King*: The Address Delivered on Negro Day in the Atlanta Exposition. October 21. 1895," in Gates and Jarrett, *The New Negro*, 32.

15. Booker T. Washington, introduction to *A New Negro for a New Century*, ed. Booker T. Washington et al., (Chicago: American, 1900), 3.

16. Fannie Barrier Williams, "The Club Movement among Colored Women of America," in Washington et al., *A New Negro for a New Century*, 382, 404.

17. John H. Adams Jr., "Rough Sketches: A Study of the Features of the New Negro Woman," *Voice of the Negro* 1.9 (1904): 324, 323, 325–26.

18. John H. Adams Jr., "Rough Sketches: The Negro Man," *Voice of the Negro* 1.9 (1904): 447, 450, 452.

19. Gates and Jarrett, *The New Negro*, 2.

20. William Pickens, *The New Negro* (New York: AMS Press, 1969), 15.

21. Ibid., 238, 239, 15.

22. *Crisis* (1910–present), monthly organ of the NAACP, originally edited by Du Bois; *Messenger* (1917–28), socialist weekly that claimed to be the "only radical Negro magazine in America," initially edited by A. Philip Randolph and Chandler Owen;

Negro World (1918–33), created and edited by Marcus Garvey as the weekly voice of the Universal Negro Improvement Association and African Communities League; *Crusader* (1918–22), Afro-communist periodical published by Cyril Briggs, founder of the African Blood Brotherhood; *Liberator* (1919–24), leftist magazine published Max and Crystal Eastman to support the Bolshevik Revolution and later edited by Michael Gold and Claude McKay; *Opportunity* (1923–33), organ of the National Urban League (1910) and edited by Charles S. Johnson; *Worker's Monthly* (1924–27), communist publication created when *Liberator*, *Labor Herald*, and *Soviet Russia Pictorial* merged to provide a new platform for communication.

23. Rioting and racial conflict occurred in major cities, including Atlanta, Baltimore, Charleston, Chicago, New Orleans, Memphis, New York, Philadelphia, and Washington, D.C., and in smaller locations such as Bisbee, Arizona; Coatesville, Pennsylvania; Hattiesburg, Mississippi; Longview, Texas; Newberry, South Carolina; and Texarkana, Texas.

24. Barbara Foley, *Spectres of 1919: Class and Nation in the Making of the New Negro* (Urbana: University of Illinois Press, 2003), 31–32. For additional connections between the New Negro and communism, see William J. Maxwell, *New Negro, Old Left* (New York: Columbia University Press, 1999).

25. Stanley B. Norvell and William M. Tuttle Jr., "Views of a Negro during 'The Red Summer' of 1919," *Journal of Negro History* 51 (1966): 214, 216.

26. James Weldon Johnson, *Along This Way* (New York: Da Capo Press, 2000), 341.

27. Norvell and Tuttle, "Views of a Negro during 'The Red Summer' of 1919," 216.

28. Rollin Lynde Hartt, "The New Negro: When He's Hit, He Hits Back!," *Independent* 15 (1921): 59, 60.

29. Claude McKay, *A Long Way from Home* (New York: Lee Furman, 1937), 31.

30. Claude McKay, "If We Must Die," *Liberator* 2 (July 1919): 21.

31. W. E. B. Du Bois, "Let Us Reason Together," *Crisis* 18 (September 1919): 231.

32. "Following the Advice of the 'Old Crowd Negro,'" *Messenger* 2 (September 1919): 16. In "A New Crowd—A New Negro," A. Philip Randolph describes the Old Crowd Negro as a conservative who "lacks the knowledge of methods for the attainment of ends which it desires to achieve." In addition to Du Bois, Randolph indicts a number of educators, writers, and politicians as members of the Old Crowd, including Kelly Miller, James Weldon Johnson, Chas W. Anderson, and George E. Haynes. Similar to the Bolsheviks who united to topple the Russian crown, Randolph believed New Crowd Negroes, "young men who are educated, radical and fearless," were needed to create a new society in America—"a society of equals, without class, race, caste or religious distinctions." *Messenger* 2 (September 1919): 26–27. Despite his role as a race leader and seasoned activist for African American equality, Du Bois was viewed by many at the *Messenger* as an Old Crowd Negro because he was "subsidized" by Old Crowd whites. Among the examples provided in support of this claim was that even in his capacity as editor at the NAACP, Du Bois was not a policymaker, a task that was left in the hands of primarily white board members. "Du Bois and *The Crisis*," *Messenger* 2 (September 1919): 9–10.

33. "The New Negro—What Is He?," *Messenger* 2 (August 1920): 73–74.

34. "The 'New Crowd Negro' Making America Safe for Himself," *Messenger* 2 (September 1919): 17. Further emphasizing the poignancy of the cartoon statement was a quotation above it: "Force, Force to the utmost—force without stint or limit!" The

quote is part of a speech delivered by President Woodrow Wilson in the Fifth Regiment Armory in Baltimore on April 6, 1918, for the Third Liberty Loan Campaign. In his summation Wilson exclaimed, "Germany has once more said that force, and force alone, shall decide whether justice and peace shall reign in the affairs of men, whether right as America conceives it or dominion as she conceives it shall determine the destinies of mankind. There is, therefore, but one response possible from us: Force, force to the utmost, force without stint or limit, the righteous and triumphant force which shall make right the law of the world and cast every selfish dominion down in the dust." John T. Woolley and Gerhard Peters, *The American Presidency Project*, http://www.presidency.ucsb.edu/ws/?pld=65406.

35. Jessie Fauset, *There Is Confusion* (New York: Boni and Liveright, 1924).

36. "Harlem: Mecca of the New Negro," *Survey Graphic* 6 (1925): 622–724; Alain Locke, "The New Negro," in *The New Negro: An Interpretation*, ed. Alain Locke (New York: Albert & Charles Boni, 1925).

37. Locke, "The New Negro," 3.

38. Ibid., 6.

39. Ibid., 3, 4.

40. Ibid., 10, 12, 15, 9.

41. Gates and Jarrett, *The New Negro*, 8.

42. Foley, *Spectres of 1919*, 5.

43. Arnold Rampersad, "The Book That Launched the Harlem Renaissance," *Journal of Blacks in Higher Education* 38 (2002–3): 90.

44. Wilson J. Moses, "The Lost World of the Negro, 1895–1919: Black Literary and Intellectual Life before the 'Renaissance,'" *Black American Literature Forum* 21.1–2 (1987): 63.

45. Gates and Jarrett, *The New Negro*, 9.

46. "The Negro in Art: How Shall He Be Portrayed," *Crisis* 31.4 (1926): 165. For additional responses to this topic see the following 1926 issues: March, 219–20, includes responses from H. L. Mencken, DuBose Heyward, and Mary Ovington; April, 278–80, includes responses from Langston Hughes, J. E. Spingarn, Walter White, Alfred A. Knopf, John Farrar, and William Lyon Phelps; May, 35–36, includes pieces by Vachel Lindsay, Sinclair Lewis, and Sherwood Anderson; June, 71–73, shares responses from Jessie Fauset, Benjamin Brawley, Robert T. Kerlin, and Haldane MacFall; July, 193–94, includes Georgia Douglas Johnson, Countee Cullen, and J. Herbert Engbeck; September, 238–39, has essays from Julia Peterkin and Otto F. Mack. The final segment of this symposium appears in the November issue, 28–29, and is contributed by Charles W. Chesnutt.

47. Gates and Jarrett, *The New Negro*, 2.

48. W. E. B. Du Bois, "The Younger Literary Movement," *The Crisis* 28 (February 1924): 161; Jean Toomer, *Cane* (New York: Boni and Liveright, 1923).

49. Alain Locke, "Negro Youth Speaks," in *The New Negro: An Interpretation*, 47, 50.

50. Benjamin Brawley, "The Negro Literary Renaissance," *Southern Workman* 56 (1928): 177–84.

51. Allison Davis, "Our Negro 'Intellectuals,'" *Crisis* 35 (1928): 286.

52. Lloyd Morris, "The Negro 'Renaissance,'" *Southern Workman* 59 (1930): 82, 86.

53. Martha Gruening, "The Negro Renaissance," *Hound and Horn* 5.3 (1932): 505, 508.

54. Langston Hughes, "The Negro Artist and the Racial Mountain," in *African American Literary Theory*, ed. Winston Napier (New York: New York University Press, 2000), 30.

55. W. E. B. Du Bois, "The Sorrow Songs," in *The Souls of Black Folk* (New York: A. C. McClurg, 1903), 250–64; John W. Work, "The Negro Folk Song," *Opportunity* 1.10 (1923): 292–94.

56. Greenville Vernon, "That Mysterious 'Jazz,'" *New York Tribune*, March 30, 1919; "Jazzing Away Prejudice," *Chicago Defender*, May 10, 1919.

57. Rollin Lynde Hartt, "The Negro in Drama," *Crisis*, June 1922, 64.

58. Alain Locke, "The American Negro as Artist," *American Magazine of Art* 23 (1931): 220.

59. Romare Bearden, "The Negro Artist and Modern Art," *Opportunity* 12 (1934): 372.

60. For recent studies of the New Negro, see Davarian L. Baldwin, *Chicago's New Negroes: Modernity, the Great Migration, and Black Urban Life* (Chapel Hill: University of North Carolina Press, 2007); Elizabeth Anne Carroll, *Word, Image, and the New Negro* (Bloomington: Indiana University Press, 2005); Rebecca Carroll, ed., *Uncle Tom or New Negro?* (New York: Broadway Books, 2006); Foley, *Spectres of 1919*; Gates and Jarrett, *The New Negro*; Cherene Sherrard-Johnson, *Portraits of the New Negro Woman: Visual and Literary Culture in the Harlem Renaissance* (New Brunswick, NJ: Rutgers University Press, 2007); Maxwell, *New Negro, Old Left*; Moses, "The Lost World of the Negro"; Martha Jane Nadell, *Enter the New Negroes: Images of Race in American Culture* (Cambridge, MA: Harvard University Press, 2005); Anna Pochmara, *The Making of the New Negro* (Amsterdam: Amsterdam University Press, 2011); Marlon B. Ross, *Manning the Race* (New York: New York University Press, 2004).

When Gates published his landmark essay on the New Negro twenty years ago, he defined 1895–1925 as the "crux of the period of black intellectual reconstruction" ("The Trope of a New Negro," 131). For literary critics, Gates argues, the years between Reconstruction and World War II are a logical place to investigate the trope of the New Negro in African American discourse because the seventy-five novels produced during that time far exceed the two produced by black people between the close of the Civil War and the Hayes-Tilden Compromise of 1877, which ended Reconstruction. Gates never makes clear, however, why, after demonstrating that the New Negro is a nineteenth-century figure, he starts his serious consideration of the New Negro in 1895, so many years after Reconstruction. Perhaps he was focusing on novels as the sole form of New Negro expression. Even so, the year 1895 was not tied to any significant literary publication, nor was it associated with any historical moment of great importance. Rather Gates, like many scholars discussing the New Negro, may have chosen 1895 as a starting point based on August Meier's *Negro Thought in America 1880–1915* (Ann Arbor: University of Michigan Press, 1968), which quotes a *Cleveland Gazette* article that discusses "a class of colored people, the 'New Negro,' who have risen since the war, with education, refinement, and money" and who refused to be marginalized by white society or refused their civil rights as American citizens (258). Gates's choice seems particularly limited because he points out that the six novels produced by African Americans between 1853 and 1865, during slavery, exceed their intellectual contributions during the years of Reconstruction, 1867–76, a period of freedom—creating what he terms the great paradox of African American intellectual history, a paradox he resolved to "explore at length elsewhere" (131).

61. Moses, "The Lost World of the Negro," 76.

62. Erin D. Chapman, *Prove It on Me: New Negroes, Sex, and Popular Culture in the 1920s* (Oxford: Oxford University Press, 2012), 9.

63. Sherrard-Johnson, *Portraits of the New Negro Woman*, xviii.

64. Steven C. Tracy, *Langston Hughes and the Blues* (Chicago: University of Illinois Press, 1988), 3, 75.

65. This quotation can be found in ibid., 72, and in its original form in Langston Hughes, "Songs Called the Blues," *Phylon* 2 (1941): 143.

66. Most scholars would agree that *modernism* is often a nebulous term and that the definition of *black modernism* can be equally vague. Even a recent MLA special panel required experts to examine this "elusive" and "enigmatic" term, questioning whether African American modernism is "a style, a study, or an approach" ("Call for Papers: African American Modernism," https://www.h-net.org/announce/show. cgi?ID=136290). My interpretation of *black modernism* is influenced by Houston Baker Jr., whose own efforts to revisit an earlier work, *Modernism and the Harlem Renaissance* (Chicago: University of Chicago Press, 1987), led him to redefine its meaning by what he terms "GOOD LIFE" (*Turning South Again* [Durham, NC: Duke University Press, 2001], 83). At its core this understanding of African American modernism is invested in one's ability to move freely and unencumbered across national and international borders; to be invested with and allowed to exercise full citizenship rights, including but not limited to suffrage, job opportunity, and equal compensation; to be protected from racially motivated violence; and to be allowed to move uninhibited toward economic or political viability (83). However, I do not differentiate between black modernisms for the New Negro of the South and do not find what Baker calls "mulatto modernism" or a proto-nationalism focused on "bourgeois, middle-class individualism, vestimentary and hygienic impeccability, oratorical and double conscious 'race pride'" to be exemplary of the New Negro of the post-Reconstruction South (33). On the contrary, I find that the New Negroes of the South exhibits a much greater degree of racial and class solidarity than those of the North and view their racial identity as an essential part of regional and national identity formation.

67. Baker, *Turning South Again*, 24.

68. For biographical information on Hayes and Tilden and an assessment of the 1877 Compromise, see Michael L Benedict, "Southern Democrats in the Crisis of 1876–1877: A Reconsideration of Reunion and Reaction," *Journal of Southern History* 46 (November 1980): 489–524; Vincent Press DeSantis, "Rutherford B. Hayes and the Removal of Troops and the End of Reconstruction," in *Region, Race, and Reconstruction,* ed. Morgan Kousser and James McPherson (New York: Oxford University Press, 1982), 417–50; Elbert William Robinson Ewing, *History and Law of the Hayes-Tilden Contest* (Washington, DC: Cobden, 1910); Paul Leland Haworth, *The Hayes-Tilden Disputed Presidential Election of 1876* (Cleveland, OH: Burrows Brothers, 1906); Michael F. Holt, *By One Vote* (Lawrence: University Press of Kansas, 2008); Ari Hoogenboom, *Rutherford B. Hayes: Warrior and President* (Lawrence: University Press of Kansas, 1995), 274–94; Roy Morris Jr., *Fraud of the Century: Rutherford B. Hayes, Samuel Tilden, and the Stolen Election of 1876* (New York: Simon & Schuster, 2003); Allan Peskin, "Was There a Compromise of 1877?," *Journal of American History* 60 (March 1973): 63–75; Keith Ian Polakoff, *The Politics of Inertia: The Election of 1876 and the End of Reconstruction* (Baton Rouge: Louisiana State University Press, 1973); William H Rehnquist, *The Centennial Crisis: The Disputed Election of 1876* (New York: Knopf, 2004); Mark Wahlgren Summers, *The Era of Good Stealings* (Oxford: Oxford University Press, 1993), 287–99; C. Vann Woodward, *Reunion and Reaction* (Boston:

Little, Brown, 1951); C. Vann Woodward, "Yes, There Was a Compromise of 1877," *Journal of American History*, June 1973, 215–23.

69. According to C. Vann Woodward, in the decades following the compromise "there were no serious infringements of the basic agreements of 1877—those regarding intervention by force, respect for state rights, and the renunciation of federal responsibility for the protection of the Negro" (*Reunion and Reaction*, 245). African American civil liberties were ignored not only by the federal government in the decades following the compromise but also by the courts, which nullified or infringed upon their rights in a number of rulings. Noted among these decisions was the 1883 Supreme Court ruling that found the 1875 Civil Rights Act unconstitutional and the 1896 *Plessy v. Ferguson* decision that provided constitutional sanction for "separate but equal."

70. Paul M. Gaston, *The New South Creed: A Study in Southern Mythmaking* (New York: Vintage Books, 1973).

71. W. J. Cash, *The Mind of the South* (New York: Vintage Books, 1991), 183–84.

72. The term *Lost Cause* was popularized by the journalist Edward A. Pollard's *Lost Cause: A Southern History of the War of the Confederates* (New York: E. B. Treat, 1890). With the Civil War ended, Pollard argued, "all that is left the South is the war of ideas," a vital struggle to maintain southern identity in the restored Union (750).

73. James C. Cobb, *Away Down South* (Oxford: Oxford University Press, 2005), 73, 84. On the Lost Cause, see David W. Blight, *Race and Reunion: The Civil War in American Memory* (Cambridge, MA: Belknap Press of Harvard University Press, 2001); William C. Davis, *The Cause Lost: Myths and Realities of the Confederacy* (Lawrence: University Press of Kansas, 1996), 175–90; Gaines M. Foster, *Ghosts of the Confederacy: Defeat, the Lost Cause, and the Emergence of the New South 1865–1913* (Oxford: Oxford University Press, 1987); Gary W. Gallagher and Alan T. Nolan, eds., *The Myth of the Lost Cause and Civil War History* (Bloomington: Indiana University Press, 2000); Rollin G. Osterweis, *The Myth of the Lost Cause, 1865–1900* (Hamden, CT: Archon Books, 1973); Charles Reagan Wilson, *Baptized in Blood: The Religion of the Lost Cause, 1865–1920* (Athens: University of Georgia Press, 1980).

74. Cobb, *Away Down South*, 90.

75. "Around the World," *Christian Advocate*, July 20 1893, in Wilson, *Baptized in Blood*, 106.

76. Gates, "The Trope of a New Negro," 150.

77. C. Vann Woodward, *The Strange Career of Jim Crow* (New York: Oxford University Press, 1966). 93.

78. Sterling Brown, *The Negro in American Fiction* (New York: Argosy-Antiquarian, 1969), 53, 54.

79. Joel Chandler Harris, *Uncle Remus, His Songs and His Sayings: The Folk-Lore of the Old Plantation* (New York: D. Appleton, 1881), 223.

80. Qtd. in Cobb, *Away Down South*, 73.

81. Thomas Nelson Page, *Novels, Stories, Sketches, and Poems of Thomas Nelson Page: The Old South Essays Social and Political* (New York: C. Scribner's Sons, 1906).

82. Thomas Nelson Page, *The Negro: The Southerner's Problem* (New York: C. Scribner's Sons, 1904), 166, 173, 164.

83. Cobb, *Away Down South*, 98.

84. Qtd. in Cash, *The Mind of the South*, 175.

85. Cobb, *Away Down South*, 80.

86. "More Rapes, More Lynchings," Memphis *Commercial*, May 17, 1892.

87. Du Bois, *The Souls of Black Folk*, 42.

88. Page, *Novels, Stories, Sketches, and Poems of Thomas Nelson Page*, 164.

89. Leon F. Litwack, *Trouble in Mind: Black Southerners in the Age of Jim Crow* (New York: Vintage Books, 1999).

90. Gates, "The Trope of a New Negro," 132.

91. Booker T. Washington, *Up from Slavery* (New York: Dover, 1995), 11, 17.

92. Frederick Douglass, *Narrative of the Life of Frederick Douglass, an American Slave* (Boston: Anti-Slavery Office, 1845).

93. Gates and Jarrett, *The New Negro*, 5; Sojourner Truth, *Narrative of Sojourner Truth* (Oxford: Oxford University Press 1991), 164.

94. Mia Bay, *The White Image in the Black Mind* (Oxford: Oxford University Press, 2000), 219.

95. Nathan Irvin Huggins, *Harlem Renaissance* (London: Oxford University Press, 1971), 65.

96. Du Bois, *The Souls of Black Folk*, 2.

97. Cobb, *Away Down South*, 81.

98. Qtd. in Cash, *The Mind of the South*, 183.

99. Gates, "The Trope of a New Negro," 132.

100. Charles Reagan Wilson argues, in fact, that "white supremacy was a key tenet of a Southern Way of Life" and that "the Klan represented the mystical wing of the Lost Cause" (*Baptized in Blood*, 100–118). See James Welch Patton, *Unionism and Reconstruction in Tennessee 1860–1869* (Chapel Hill: University of North Carolina Press, 1934), 170–200.

101. Litwack, *Trouble in Mind*, 482.

102. For a more detailed look at the experience of southern African Americans who migrated west during this period, see Robert G. Athearn, *In Search of Canaan: Black Migration to Kansas 1879–80* (Lawrence: Regents Press of Kansas, 1978); Frederick Douglass, "The Negro Exodus from the Gulf States," *Frank Leslies Popular Monthly* 9 (January 1880): 39–48, University of Virginia Electronic Text Center, University of Virginia Library, http://www.inmotionaame.org/texts/index.cfm;jsessionid=f8303142571275336596047?migration=6&topic=99&type=text&bhcp=1; Roy Garvin, "Benjamin, or 'Pap' Singleton and His Followers," *Journal of Negro History* 33 (January 1948): 7–23; Kenneth Marvin Hamilton, *Black Towns and Profit Promotion and Development in the Trans-Appalachian West, 1877–1915* (Urbana: University of Illinois Press, 1991), 5–42; Bryan M. Jack, *The St. Louis African American Community and the Exodusters* (Columbia: University of Missouri Press, 2007); Nell Irvin Painter, *Exodusters: Black Migration to Kansas after Reconstruction* (New York: Norton, 1992); Glen Schwendemann, "St. Louis and the 'Exodusters' of 1879," *Journal of Negro History* 46 (January 1961): 32–46; Arvarh E. Strickland, "Toward the Promised Land: The Exodus to Kansas and Afterward," *Missouri Historical Review* 69 (July 1975): 376–412; John G. Van Deusen, "The Exodus of 1879," *Journal of Negro History* 21 (April 1936): 111–29; Nudie E. Williams, "Black Newspapers and the Exodusters of 1879," *Kansas History* 8 (Winter 1985–86): 217–25.

103. Litwack, *Trouble in Mind*, 485.

104. Painter, *Exodusters*, 147–48, 222.

105. Edward L. Ayers, *The Promise of the New South* (New York: Oxford University Press, 1992), 24.

106. Don H. Doyle, *New Men, New Cities, New South* (Chapel Hill: University of North Carolina Press, 1990), 11.

107. Ayers, *The Promise of the New South*, 55, 156.

108. Ibid., 22.

109. Litwack, *Trouble in Mind*, 118.

110. Ibid., 483.

111. Baker, *Turning South Again*, 26.

112. Meier, *Negro Thought in America*, 276.

113. W. E. B. Du Bois, "The Social Evolution of the Black South," *American Negro Monographs* 1 (March 1911): 7.

2 / Nashville: A Southern Black Metropolis

1. For a discussion of Kentucky's political and military status in 1861–62, see E. Merton Coulter, *The Civil War and Readjustment in Kentucky* (Chapel Hill: University of North Carolina Press, 1926), 18–124; Sam Davis Elliott, *Confederate Governor and United States Senator Isham G. Harris of Tennessee* (Baton Rouge: Louisiana State University Press, 2010), 75; Nathaniel S. Shaler, *Kentucky: A Pioneer Commonwealth* (Boston: Houghton, Mifflin, 1885), 241–48; William H. Townsend, *Lincoln and the Bluegrass* (Lexington: University of Kentucky Press, 1955), 239–68.

2. Nashville, along with New Orleans, was the South's most significant commercial center. A vast array of goods traveled throughout the South via the Louisville and Nashville Railroad, the Nashville and Chattanooga Railroad, the Tennessee and Alabama Railroad, the Edgefield and Kentucky Railroad, and the Nashville and Northwestern Railroad.

3. Gen. Don Carlos Buell accepted the surrender of Nashville, the first Confederate capital to fall into Union hands, on February 25, 1862. For more on the surrender of Nashville to Union forces, see Walter T. Durham, *Nashville the Occupied City* (Nashville: Tennessee Historical Society, 1985); Elliott, *Confederate Governor*, 75; John Miller McKee, *The Great Panic: Being Incidents Connected with Two Weeks of the War in Tennessee* (Nashville: Johnson and Whiting, 1862), 29–30; Stephen D. Engle, *Struggle for the Heartland* (Lincoln: University of Nebraska Press, 2001), 88–99; Bromford L Ridley, *Battles and Sketches of the Army of Tennessee* (Mexico: Missouri Printing & Publishing, 1906), 71–73.

4. On Johnson's years as military governor of Tennessee and, in particular, his unsympathetic attitudes toward freedmen after the Civil War, see John Cimprich, "Military Governor Johnson and Tennessee Blacks, 1862–65," *Tennessee Historical Quarterly* 39 (Winter 1980): 459–70; Clifton R. Hall, *Andrew Johnson, Military Governor of Tennessee* (Princeton, NJ: Princeton University Press, 1916); Martin E. Mantell, *Johnson, Grant, and the Politics of Reconstruction* (New York: Columbia University Press, 1973), 14–15; James Welch Patton, *Unionism and Reconstruction in Tennessee 1860–1869* (Chapel Hill: University of North Carolina Press, 1934), 30–34; Hans L. Trefousse, *Impeachment of a President: Andrew Johnson, the Blacks, and Reconstruction* (Knoxville: University of Tennessee Press, 1975), 3–29; Eric L. McKitrick, *Andrew Johnson and Reconstruction* (Chicago: University of Chicago Press, 1960), 126–30.

5. Howard N. Rabinowitz, *Race Relations in the Urban South 1865–1890* (New York: Oxford University Press, 1978), 21. According to G. W. Hubbard, in 1863 "eight to ten thousand freedmen collected in the city" (*A History of the Colored Schools in*

Nashville, Tennessee [Nashville: Wheeler, Marshall & Bruce, 1874], 7). To read more about the influx of African Americans to Nashville during and after the war, see Bobby Lovett, "The Negro in Tennessee, 1861–1866: A Socio-Military History of the Civil War Era," PhD diss., University of Arkansas, 1978, 31–37; Patton, *Unionism and Reconstruction in Tennessee*, 131, 154; *Nashville Dispatch*, August 16, 1865; *Nashville Daily Press and Times*, January 29, April 28, 1866; *Nashville Union and American*, November 27, 1870. For a map of Nashville contraband camps in 1865, see Bobby Lovett, *The African-American History of Nashville, Tennessee 1780–1930* (Fayetteville: University of Arkansas Press, 1999), 81.

6. Rabinowitz, *Race Relations in the Urban South*, 23. According to the records of the Adjutant General's Office, 1780s–1917, the 12th U.S. Colored Infantry regiment was organized at Elk Bridge and Nashville in August 1863, and the 13th was organized at Camp Mussy (Nashville) in November 1863. The 12th mustered out in January 1866, and the 13th on January 10, 1866. The 15th and 17th U.S. Colored Infantry regiments and at least two of the thirteen numbered artillery regiments, the 2nd U.S. Colored Light Artillery Battery A and the 9th U.S. Heavy Artillery, and one of the numbered infantry regiments, the 101st, were also organized in and mustered out of Nashville. See Adjutant General's Office, *Compiled Military Records of Volunteer Union Soldiers Who Served with the United States Colored Troops: Infantry Organizations 12th United States Colored Infantry*, National Archives and Records Administration (1985), Roll 79, Microfilm Publication M1821, Record Group 94.

7. *Eighth Census of the United States in 1860* (Washington, DC: Government Printing Office, 1864), 466; *Ninth Census of the United States in 1870* (Washington, DC: Government Printing Office, 1872), 262.

8. *Tennessee Code Annotated*, vol. 1A, 2007, 879. See also Lewis Laska, *The Tennessee State Constitution* (New York: Greenwood Press, 1990), 11–14.

9. On April 2, 1866, President Johnson declared an end to the insurrection of Tennessee and the remaining Confederate states. *Statues at Large, Treaties, and Proclamations of the United States of America from December, 1865, to March, 1867* (Boston: Little, Brown, 1868), 813. On July 19, 1866, a joint resolution of Tennessee's congress adopted the proposed Fourteenth Amendment to the Constitution of the United States. *Acts and Resolutions of the State of Tennessee, Thirty-fourth General Assembly* (Nashville: C. Mercer, July 1866), 29. Following this adoption, a joint resolution of the 39th U.S. Congress on July 24, 1866, restored Tennessee "to her Relations to the Union" and allowed for Tennessee's senators and representatives to be seated as members of Congress (*Statues*, 364). See also *House Executive Documents First Session of the Thirty-ninth Congress*, 1866, No. 151, 1–3. In turn a joint resolution of Tennessee's congress thanked the U.S. Congress for admitting the senators and representatives from Tennessee to that body and it also pledged "the faith of the State to the Support of the Constitution of the United States" while "congratulating the People upon their admission into the Union" (*Acts*, 29). See also Laska, *Tennessee State Constitution*, 11–14; Patton, *Unionism and Reconstruction in Tennessee*, 208–25; *Nashville Daily Press and Times*, July 2, 1866.

10. Don H. Doyle, *New Men, New Cities, New South* (Chapel Hill: University of North Carolina Press, 1990), 27–28.

11. St. Clair Drake and Horace R. Cayton, *Black Metropolis* (New York: Harcourt, Brace, 1945), 12; Davarian L. Baldwin, *Chicago's New Negroes: Modernity, the Great*

Migration and Black Urban Life (Chapel Hill: University of North Carolina Press, 2007), 8.

12. Drake and Cayton, *Black Metropolis*, 12.

13. Lovett, *African-American History of Nashville, Tennessee*, 135. For information on the education of African Americans in Nashville prior to 1865, see Hubbard, *History of the Colored Schools in Nashville, Tennessee*.

14. Popularized in the nineteenth century, "Athens of the South" was a label that distinguished Nashville from other southern cities as a refined center of arts, education, and history. See Christine M. Kreyling, *Classical Nashville: Athens of the South* (Nashville: Vanderbilt University Press, 1996); Henry McRaven, *Nashville: Athens of the South* (Chapel Hill, NC: Scheer and Jervis, 1949).

15. Roger Williams University produced a steady stream of graduates who served as teachers and founders of other educational institutions in Nashville and throughout the country, including Dr. John Hope, Dr. Mordecai Johnson, and Dr. A. M. Townsend. For more on Nashville Normal and Theological Institute and its transformation to Roger Williams University in 1883, see Hubbard, *History of the Colored Schools in Nashville, Tennessee*, 25–27; Lovett, *African-American History of Nashville, Tennessee*, 147–54; Charles Edwin Robert, *Negro Civilization in the South* (Nashville: Wheeler Brothers, 1880), 141–43; Alrutheus Ambush Taylor, *The Negro in Tennessee 1865–1880* (Washington, DC: Associated Publishers, 1941), 189–91; Eugene TeSelle Jr., "The Nashville Institute and Roger Williams University: Benevolence, Paternalism, and Black Consciousness, 1867–1910," *Tennessee Historical Quarterly* 41 (Winter 1982): 360–79.

16. On the development of Tennessee Manual Labor University, see Lovett, *African-American History of Nashville, Tennessee*, 145–47; W. K. Pendleton, "Tennessee Manual Labor University," *Millennial Harbinger* 39 (1868): 227–28.

17. Central Tennessee College began in 1865 in Clark Chapel and moved the following year to an abandoned Confederate gun factory on South College Street that was owned by the federal government. After encountering opposition to "Nigger schools" in predominantly white Nashville areas, the trustees secured property on Maple Street known as the Nance Property. The school was renamed Walden University in 1900. For more on the evolution of this institution, see Hubbard, *History of the Colored Schools in Nashville, Tennessee*, 17–20; Lovett, *African-American History of Nashville, Tennessee*, 154–58; Robert, *Negro Civilization in the South*, 143–49; Taylor, *The Negro in Tennessee*, 191–96.

18. One graduate, Dr. Robert Fulton Boyd, perhaps Nashville's most prominent African American physician, was one of ten African American physicians in the country responsible for organizing the Society of Colored Physicians, a national fraternity that later became the National Medical Association. On the evolution of Meharry Medical College, see Lovett, *African-American History of Nashville, Tennessee*, 157–59; C. V. Roman, *Meharry Medical College, a History* (Nashville: Sunday School Publishing Board of the National Baptist Convention, 1934); James Summerville, *Educating Black Doctors: A History of Meharry Medical College* (Tuscaloosa: University of Alabama Press, 1983).

19. Joe Martin Richardson, *A History of Fisk University, 1865–1946* (Tuscaloosa: University of Alabama Press, 1980), 4. On the history of Fisk, see Rodney T. Cohen, *Fisk University* (Charleston, SC: Arcadia, 2001); Joe Martin Richardson, "Fisk University:

The Critical Years," *Tennessee Historical Quarterly* 29 (1970): 24–41; Robert, *Negro Civilization in the South*, 149–59; Taylor, *The Negro in Tennessee*, 198–204; Alrutheus Taylor, "Fisk University and the Nashville Community 1866–1900," *Journal of Negro History* 39 (April 1954): 111–26.

20. On the Jubilee Singers and their musical influence in America, see J. B. T. Marsh, *The Story of the Jubilee Singers: With Their Songs* (Boston: Houghton, Osgood, 1880); Gustavus D. Pike, *The Jubilee Singers, and Their Campaign for Twenty Thousand Dollars* (Boston: Lee and Shepard, 1873); *The Story of Music at Fisk University* (Nashville: Fisk University, n.d.), 5–27; Theodore F. Seward, *The Singing Campaign for 10,000 Pounds; or, The Jubilee Singers in Great Britain* (New York: American Missionary Association, 1875); Robert C. Tipton, "The Fisk Jubilee Singers," *Tennessee Historical Quarterly* 29 (1970): 42–48. There is also an interesting preface in *Jubilee Songs: As Sung by the Jubilee Singers of Fisk University* (New York: Biglow & Main, 1872).

21. On July 6, 1911, Tennessee's congress approved an act to appropriate funds for the creation of the Tennessee Agricultural and Industrial Normal School for Negroes. The university opened in 1912; there were 247 students from nine states attending. *Public Acts of the State of Tennessee Passed by the Fifty-seventh General Assembly*, 1911, 138–39. For additional university history, see Lester C. Lamon, "The Tennessee Agricultural and Industrial Normal School: Public Higher Education for Black Tennesseans," *Tennessee Historical Quarterly* 32 (Spring 1973): 42–58; R. Grann Lloyd, *Tennessee Agricultural and Industrial State University, 1912–1962* (Nashville: N.p., 1962); Herman B. Long, "The Negro Public College in Tennessee," *Journal of Negro Education* 31 (Summer 1962): 341–48; Lovett, *African-American History of Nashville, Tennessee*, 167–71. On the American Baptist Theological Seminary, see Lewis G. Jordan, *Negro Baptist History* (Nashville: Sunday School Publishing Board, 1930), 242–47; Ruth M. Powell, *Lights and Shadows: The Story of the American Baptist Theological Seminary, 1924–1964* (Nashville: American Baptist Theological Seminary, 1964).

22. To read more about Nashville's African American antebellum churches and their move toward independence from white institutions, see T. O. Fuller, *History of the Negro Baptists of Tennessee* (Nashville: Haskins, 1936), 41–42; John T. Jenifer, *Centennial Retrospect History of the African Methodist Episcopal Church* (Nashville: Sunday School Union Print, 1915), 83–84; Lynn E. May Jr., *The First Baptist Church of Nashville Tennessee* (Nashville: First Baptist Church, 1970); Herman Norton, *Religion in Tennessee 1777–1945* (Knoxville: University of Tennessee Press, 1981), 78–79; Herman Norton, *Tennessee Christians: A History of the Christian Church (Disciples of Christ) in Tennessee* (Nashville: Reed, 1971), 126–35; Mildred H. Sloan, "A Historical Survey of the Two Oldest Negro Baptist Churches in Nashville," thesis, Tennessee A. and I. State College, 1938, 1–15; Mechal Sobel, "'They Can Never Prosper Together': Black and White Baptists in Antebellum Nashville, Tennessee," *Tennessee Historical Quarterly* 38 (Fall 1979): 296–307.

23. Qtd. in Lester C. Lamon, *Black Tennesseans 1900–1930* (Knoxville: University of Tennessee Press, 1977), 45.

24. Donald Franklin Joyce, *Black Book Publishers in the United States* (Westport, CT: Greenwood Press, 1991), 20.

25. There are three other leading religious publishing houses outside of Nashville. The American Methodist Episcopal Zion Publishing House originated in New York City (1841), where it remained until 1894, when it moved to its present location in

Charlotte, North Carolina. The Colored Methodist Episcopal Publishing House was located in Jackson, Tennessee, from 1870 to 1972, before moving to its present location in Memphis. The country's oldest publisher of religious and secular works for African Americans is the African Methodist Episcopal Book Concern. Numerous cities have provided a home for the A.M.E. Book Concern since its inception: Philadelphia (1817–35 and 1852–1952), New York (1835–48), and Pittsburgh (1848–52)). See Daniel A. Payne, *History of the African Methodist Episcopal Church* (Nashville: Publishing House of the A.M.E. Sunday School Union); Donald Franklin Joyce, *Gatekeepers of Black Culture* (New York: Greenwood Press, 1983); Donald Franklin Joyce, *Black Book Publishers in the United States* (New York: Greenwood Press, 1991).

26. Lucretia H. Coleman, *Poor Ben: A Story of Real Life* (Nashville: A.M.E. Sunday-School Union, 1890); Charles S. Smith, *Glimpses of Africa, West and Southwest Coast* (Nashville: A.M.E. Church Sunday School Union, 1895).

27. Joyce, *Black Book Publishers*, 21.

28. R. H. Boyd, *A Story of the National Baptist Publishing Board: The Why, How, When, Where and by Whom It Was Established* (Nashville: National Baptist Publishing Board, 1915), 10. For more on R. H. Boyd and his leadership in the black separatist movement that established the National Baptist Publishing Board, see Wilson Fallin Jr., *Uplifting the Race* (Tuscaloosa: University of Alabama Press, 2007), 92–92, 99–101; Leroy Fitts, *A History of Black Baptists* (Nashville: Broadman Press, 1985), 82–83, 90–92; Paul Harvey, *Redeeming the South* (Chapel Hill: University of North Carolina Press, 1997), 69–72, 244–47; Jordan, *Negro Baptist History*, 247–55; Bobby Lovett, *A Black Man's Dream: The First 100 Years. Richard Henry Boyd and the National Baptist Publishing Board* (Nashville: Mega, 1993); Bobby Lovett, *How It Came to Be* (Nashville: Mega, 2007); Owen D. Pelt and Ralph Lee Smith, *The Story of the National Baptists* (New York: Vantage Press, 1960), 102–04.

29. Boyd, *A Story of the National Baptist Publishing Board*, 13.

30. Booker T. Washington, *The Negro in Business* (Boston: Hertel, Jenkins, 1907), 192.

31. W. E. B. Du Bois, ed., *Economic Co-operation among Negro Americans: Report of a Social Study Made by Atlanta University under the Patronage of the Carnegie Institution of Washington, D.C. Together with the Proceedings of the 12th Annual Conference for the Study of the Negro Problems, Held at Atlanta University, on Tuesday, Mar the 28th, 1907* (Atlanta, GA: Atlanta University Press, 1907), 68.

32. John H. Holman, *Methods of Histology and Bacteriology* (Nashville: National Baptist Publishing Board, 1903); R. H. Boyd, *The Separate or "Jim Crow" Car Laws; or, Legislative Enactments of Fourteen Southern States* (Nashville: National Baptist Publishing Board, 1909); John Wesley Grant, *Out of the Darkness; or, Diabolism and Destiny* (Nashville: National Baptist Publishing Board, 1909). Boyd even helped finance the African American novelist Sutton Griggs's first work, *Imperium in Imperio* (1899), a novel discussed in greater detail in chapter 4 of this book.

33. James M. Frost to R. H. Boyd, May 7, 1915, in Boyd, *A Story of the National Baptist Publishing Board*, 24.

34. Linda T. Wynn, "Sunday School Publishing Board of the National Baptist Convention, United States of America, Incorporated (1915–Present)," in *Profiles of African Americans in Tennessee*, ed. Bobby L. Lovett and Linda T. Wynn (Nashville: Tennessee State University, 1996), 117. On the Sunday School Publishing Board of the National

Baptist Convention see Fallin, *Uplifting the Race*, 191; Pelt and Smith, *The Story of the National Baptists*, 110–24. See also "Printing Houses Operated by Negroes in Nashville," *Nashville Globe*, November 5, 1909; "New Papers for Nashville," *Nashville Globe*, May 31, 1912; "National Baptist Publishing Board," *Nashville Globe*, September 4, 1908; "Leading the World," *Nashville Globe*, November 22, 1912; "Progress of the Church," *Nashville Banner*, January 21, 1889.

35. "Colored Men of Property," *Nashville Press and Times*, April 4, 1868.

36. For additional African American business enterprises in Nashville during the period, see "Death of a Good Colored Man," *Nashville Daily American*, April 24, 1886; "Notice," *Colored Tennessean*, July 18, 1866, for discussion of a "grand festival" of the Nashville Mechanics Association; "A Colored Real Estate Company," *Nashville Republican Banner*, March 16, 1872. See also W. E. B. Du Bois, *The Negro Artisan* (Atlanta, GA: Atlanta University Press, 1902), 142–43.

37. Lovett, *African-American History of Nashville, Tennessee*, 108.

38. For an overview of Nashville's chapter of the National Negro Business League, see Don H. Doyle, *Nashville in the New South 1880–1930* (Knoxville: University of Tennessee Press, 1985), 116–17, 119; David H. Jackson, *Booker T. Washington and the Struggle against White Supremacy* (New York: Palgrave Macmillan, 2008), 78 and appendix for a detailed roster of Business League members in Tennessee; Lamon, *Black Tennesseans*, 176–79; Lester Lamon, *Blacks in Tennessee, 1791–1970* (Knoxville: University of Tennessee Press, 1981), 61–62; Lovett, *African-American History of Nashville, Tennessee*, 114–15. On the Urban League, see Lamon, *Black Tennesseans*, 214–21; Lovett, *African-American History of Nashville, Tennessee*, 128, 163. On the Board of Trade, see Lamon, *Black Tennesseans*, 211–13; Lovett, *African-American History of Nashville, Tennessee*, 115–16.

39. *The Nashville and Edgefield Directory* (Nashville: Marshall & Bruce, 1878).

40. *Nashville City Directory* (Nashville: Marshall & Bruce, 1900).

41. For information on the Nashville branch of the Freedman's bank, see *Freedman's Savings and Trust Register, Signatures of Depositors, Nashville and Memphis, Tennessee, Norfolk, Richmond, Virginia 1871–74*, Tennessee State Library and Archives, Microfilm 1380; *Freedmen's Savings and Trust Company, Index to Deposit Ledgers, 1865–1874*, Tennessee State Library and Archives, Microfilm 1380; Walter L. Fleming, *The Freedmen's Savings Banks* (Chapel Hill: University of North Carolina Press, 1927), 50, 66; Carl R. Osthaus, *Freedmen, Philanthropy, and Fraud* (Urbana: University of Illinois Press, 1976), 38, 111, 113,131, 133, 171–72.

42. Lamon, *Blacks in Tennessee*, 73.

43. "The Junior," *Nashville Globe*, January 21, 1910. See also Lamon. *Black Tennesseans*, 184–87; Lovett, *African-American History of Nashville, Tennessee*, 117–20; "4,000,000," *Nashville Globe*, January 13, 1911; "One-Cent Savings Bank," *Nashville Globe*, September 4, 1908; "Third Annual Report of the One Cent Savings Bank," *Nashville Globe*, January 18, 1907; "Negro Banks and Banking Concerns," *Nashville Globe*, September 4, 1908.

44. "One-Cent Savings Bank."

45. "The Junior."

46. *The National Baptist Union*, January 23, 1909, 12.

47. See *Nashville City Directory* (1900); *Nashville City Directory* (Nashville: Marshall-Bruce-Polk, 1915).

48. "Social Uplift," *Crisis* 5 (January 1913): 112.

49. On the creation of Hadley Park, see Leland R. Johnson, *The Parks of Nashville* (Nashville: Metropolitan Nashville Board of Parks and Recreation, 1986).

Josephine Groves Holloway (1898–1988) became interested in the Girl Scouts while working at Bethlehem Center, a "social settlement in Nashville's African American community" in 1923 (Elisabeth Israels Perry, "The Very Best Influence: Josephine Holloway and Girl Scouting in Nashville's African-American Community," *Tennessee Historical Quarterly* 52 [Summer 1993]: 82). Undeterred by prejudice, and later, segregation, Holloway developed the country's first African American troop. She believed that the organization created "examples of black strength and pride," and she remained committed to it for the next forty years. See Perry, "The Very Best Influence," 73–85; Jessie Carney Smith, "Josephine Holloway," in *Notable Black American Women II*, ed. Jessie Carney Smith (Detroit: Gale Research, 1996).

50. Sampson W. Keeble (1833–87), a former slave, was the first African American elected to Tennessee's General Assembly (38th R). For biographical information on Keeble and his time in office, see Joseph H. Cartwright, "Black Legislators in Tennessee in the 1800s: A Case Study in Black Political Leadership," *Tennessee Historical Quarterly* 32 (Fall 1973): 265–84; Kathy Lauder, "Sampson W. Keeble, 1833–1887," http://www.tn.gov/tsla/exhibits/aale/keeble.htm; Robert M. McBride and Dan M. Robison, *Biographical Directory of the Tennessee General Assembly 1861–1901* (Nashville: Tennessee State Library and Archives and the Tennessee Historical Commission, 1979), 2: 484–85; "Our Representative Men," *Nashville Union and American*, December 6, 1872; "Our Representatives," *Nashville Union and American*, November 7, 1872. Also see *Nashville City Directories* (1866–90). Thomas A. Sykes (1835–1900) was the second African American to serve in Tennessee's legislature (R), where he represented Davidson County in the 42nd General Assembly (1881–83). While information on Sykes is scarce, see Tennessee State Library and Archives, http://www.tennessee.gov/tsla/history/blackhistory/bios/sykes.htm; McBride and Robison, *Biographical Directory of the Tennessee General Assembly*, 2:878; *Nashville City Directories* (1870–1913).

51. For more on Napier and his relationship with Booker T. Washington, see Jackson, *Booker T. Washington*, 77–97; Lamon, *Black Tennesseans*, 5–6, 47–48; Bobby Lovett, "James Carroll Napier (1845–1940): From Plantation to City," in *The Southern Elite and Social Change*, ed. Randy Finley and Thomas DeBlack (Fayetteville: University of Arkansas Press, 2002), 73–94; "James C. Napier," *Journal of Negro History* 25 (July 1940): 400–401. See also "J. C. Napier's Name to Go before Senate in a Few Days," *Nashville Globe*, February 10, 1911.

52. Lamon, *Black Tennesseans*, 48.

53. Herbert Clark, "James C. Napier," Tennessee Encyclopedia of History and Culture, February 23, 2011, http://tennesseeencyclopedia.net/entry.php?rec=961.

54. An extensive discussion of Du Bois and his years in Nashville can be found in chapter 3 of this book. See also David Levering Lewis, *W. E. B. Du Bois: Biography of a Race, 1868–1919* (New York: Henry Holt, 1993); David Levering Lewis, *W. E. B. Du Bois: The Fight for Equality and the American Century 1919–1963* (New York: Henry Holt, 2001); W. E. B. Du Bois, *The Autobiography of W. E. B. Du Bois* (New York: International, 1968); W. E. B. Du Bois, *Darkwater* (New York: Humanity Books, 2003); W. E. B. Du Bois, *Dusk of Dawn* (London: Transaction, 2002); W. E. B. Du Bois, *The Souls of Black Folk* (New York: A. C. McClurg, 1903).

55. A comprehensive discussion of Griggs's novels can be found in chapter 5 of this book. For an overview of his major works, see Bernard Bell, *The Afro-American Novel and Its Tradition* (Amherst: University of Massachusetts Press, 1987); Robert A. Bone, *The Negro Novel in America* (New Haven, CT: Yale University Press, 1966); Tess Chakkalakal and Kenneth Warren, eds., *Jim Crow, Literature, and the Legacy of Sutton E. Griggs* (Athens: University of Georgia Press, 2013); Finnie D. Coleman, *Sutton E. Griggs and the Struggle against White Supremacy* (Knoxville: University of Tennessee Press, 2007); Arthur P. Davis and Saunders Redding, eds., *Cavalcade: Negro American Writing from 1760 to the Present* (Boston: Houghton Mifflin, 1971); Robert E. Fleming, "Sutton E. Griggs: Militant Black Novelist," *Phylon* 34.1 (1973): 73–77; Hugh M. Gloster, "Sutton E. Griggs, Novelist of the New Negro," *Phylon* 4.4 (1943): 335–45; Hugh M. Gloster, *Negro Voices in American Fiction* (New York: Russell & Russell, 1976); Sutton E. Griggs, *The Story of My Struggles* (Memphis: National Public Welfare League, 1914); August Meier, *Negro Thought in America 1880–1915* (Ann Arbor: University of Michigan Press, 1968); Wilson J. Moses, "Literary Garveyism: The Novels of Reverend Sutton E. Griggs," *Phylon* 40.3 (1987): 203–16; Stephen Knadler, "Sensationalizing Patriotism: Sutton Griggs and the Sentimental Nationalism of Uncle Tom," *American Literature* 79.4 (2007): 673–99; David M. Tucker, *Black Pastors and Leaders* (Memphis: Memphis State University Press, 1975); Roger Whitlow, "The Revolutionary Black Novels of Martin R. Delany and Sutton Griggs," *MELUS* 5.3 (1978): 26–36.

56. Additional religious and secular publications in nineteenth-century Nashville include *Southern Christian Recorder* (1886–91), published and edited by Rev. C. L. Bradwell; *Emigration Herald* (1878–79); *Tennessee Baptist* (1890–98), edited by Rev. S. W. Duncan; *Christian Plea* (1892–1949), *Landmark Baptist* (1896–97), published and edited by Rev. T. J. Jones; *Cornerstone* (1881–92), published and edited by J. L. Brown and S. R. Walker; *Freelance* (1885–86); and the *Republican* (1891–92), edited by T. A. Thompson. Additional African American newspapers in early twentieth-century Nashville include the *Nashville Tribune* (1912–13), the *Nashville News* (1914–18), the *Nashville Independent* (1929–38), and the *Nashville World* (1932–38). For additional information on religious and secular newspapers in Nashville, see Karen Fitzgerald Brown, "The Black Press of Tennessee: 1865–1980," PhD diss., University of Tennessee, 1982; Barbara K. Henritze, *Bibliographic Checklist of African American Newspapers* (Baltimore: Genealogical Publishing, 1995); Samuel Shannon, "Tennessee," in *The Black Press in the South, 1865–1979*, ed. Henry Lewis Suggs (Westport, CT: Greenwood Press, 1983), 313–55; *N. W. Ayer & Son American Newspaper Annual and Directory 1880–1929*, 20 vols. (Philadelphia: N. W. Ayer and Son, 1880–1909); *Newspapers Published in Tennessee*, 3 vols., Tennessee State Library and Archives; *Rowell's American Newspaper Directory* (New York: G. P. Rowell, 1908).

57. *The National Baptist Union*, April 10, 1909, 11. Unfortunately, as Samuel Shannon has noted, there has been no systematic attempt to preserve early African American newspaper editions ("Tennessee," 313). As a result numerous issues of the *Globe* were destroyed by fire or have simply been lost. There are no known copies from 1906, 1914–16, and 1919–25. In the years between, specific issues are also not available. The abundance of available material reveals the *Globe*'s significance to African American communities throughout Tennessee and highlights its reputation as a resounding voice of black progressivism.

58. Rayford Logan, *The Negro in American Life and Thought: The Nadir, 1877–1901* (New York: Dial Press, 1954), 52.

3 / Soul Searching: W. E. B. Du Bois in the "South of Slavery"

1. W. E. B. Du Bois, The Suppression of the African Slave Trade to the United States of America, 1638–1870 (New York: Longmans, Green, 1896).

2. W. E. B. Du Bois, *Philadelphia Negro* (New York: Lippincott, 1899).

3. W. E. B. Du Bois, *The Souls of Black Folk* (New York: A. C. McClurg, 1903).

4. W. E. B. Du Bois, *Black Reconstruction in America, 1860–1880* (New York: Harcourt, Brace, 1935).

5. Herbert Aptheker, *Annotated Bibliography of the Published Writings of W. E. B. Du Bois* (Millwood, NY: Kraus-Thomson Organization, 1973).

6. Houston A. Baker Jr., *Long Black Song: Essays in Black American Literature and Culture* (Charlottesville: University of Virginia Press, 1990), 99–100.

7. W. E. B. Du Bois, *The Autobiography of W. E. B. Du Bois* (New York: International, 1968), 83, 84.

8. Ibid., 84, 82.

9. Ibid., 85.

10. Du Bois, *The Souls of Black Folk*, 2. Although David Levering Lewis suggests "sympathetic skepticism" when examining an autobiographical episode from Du Bois, who often used such a technique to advance a larger argument or express a moral truism, the impact of this moment was profound enough to find its way into more than one autobiographical account as the earliest moment of racial awareness for Du Bois. David Levering Lewis, *W. E. B. Du Bois: Biography of a Race 1868–1919* (New York: Henry Holt, 1993), 33. See Du Bois, *The Souls of Black Folk*, 2; Du Bois, *The Autobiography of W. E. B. Du Bois*, 94.

11. Du Bois, *The Souls of Black Folk*, 2.

12. Ibid.

13. Du Bois, *The Autobiography of W. E. B. Du Bois*, 105, 106, 101–2.

14. Du Bois, *The Souls of Black Folk*, 2.

15. Du Bois, *The Autobiography of W. E. B. Du Bois*, 101–2; W. E. B. Du Bois, *Darkwater* (New York: Humanity Books, 2003), 42.

16. Du Bois, *The Autobiography of W. E. B. Du Bois*, 103.

17. Ibid., 105, 106.

18. W. E. B. Du Bois, *Dusk of Dawn* (London: Transaction, 2002), 22–23.

19. Du Bois, *Darkwater*, 42.

20. Du Bois, *Dusk of Dawn*, 23, 24.

21. Ibid., 24; Du Bois, *The Autobiography of W. E. B. Du Bois*, 111.

22. Du Bois, *The Autobiography of W. E. B. Du Bois*, 111; Du Bois, *Dusk of Dawn*, 24.

23. Du Bois, *The Autobiography of W. E. B. Du Bois*, 108.

24. Ibid., 112.

25. Du Bois, *Dusk of Dawn*, 101.

26. Du Bois, *The Autobiography of W. E. B. Du Bois*, 112.

27. Ibid., 125. According to Aptheker, from April 14, 1883, until May 16, 1885, Du Bois contributed twenty-seven articles on various subjects to the *New York Globe*, an African American weekly newspaper published by Timothy Thomas Fortune (*Annotated Bibliography of the Published Writings of W. E. B. Du Bois*, 1).

28. W. E. B. Du Bois, editorial, *Fisk Herald*, September 1887; Du Bois, editorial, *Fisk Herald*, December 1887; Du Bois, "Editorial Toothpick," *Fisk Herald*, March 1888; Du Bois, editorial, *Fisk Herald*, December 1887.

29. Du Bois, editorial, *Fisk Herald*, November 1887.

30. Du Bois, *The Autobiography of W. E. B. Du Bois*, 123.

31. Du Bois, *Dusk of Dawn*, 23.

32. Du Bois, *The Autobiography of W. E. B. Du Bois*, 123.

33. Du Bois, *The Souls of Black Folk*, 155.

34. Du Bois, *The Autobiography of W. E. B. Du Bois*, 120.

35. Du Bois, *Dusk of Dawn*, 119.

36. Ibid.; Du Bois, *The Souls of Black Folk*, 41.

37. Du Bois, *The Souls of Black Folk*, 156.

38. Du Bois, *The Autobiography of W. E. B. Du Bois*, 121, 108, 109.

39. Du Bois, *Dusk of Dawn*, 30.

40. Du Bois, *The Autobiography of W. E. B. Du Bois*, 121, 125, 122.

41. W. E. B. Du Bois, "A Negro Schoolmaster in the South," *Atlantic Monthly*, January 1899, 99–105.

42. W. E. B. Du Bois, "The Hills of Tennessee," *Fisk Herald*, October 1886; Du Bois, "How I Taught School," *Fisk Herald*, November 1886.

43. Du Bois, *The Autobiography of W. E. B. Du Bois*, 114. Despite scholars such as Arnold Rampersad who view Du Bois's use of the term *folk* in *Souls* as political or "interchangeable with the more daring term nation" (qtd. in Bell 111), when using the term in this essay I am referring to Bernard Bell's definition. After years of studying Du Bois's use of the term, he believes it "racially and culturally connotes a distinctive group of persons bound together by common experiences, memories, and aspirations. See Bernard Bell, "W. E. B. Du Bois's Struggle to Reconcile Folk and High Art," in *Critical Essays on W. E. B. Du Bois*, ed. William L. Andrews (Boston: G. K. Hall, 1985), 111.

44. Peter Conn, "Narrative and the Making of History," Occasional Paper 10, American Council of Learned Societies, accessed September 25, 2008, http://archives. acls.org/op/op10conn.htm, 1.

45. Du Bois, *The Souls of Black Folk*, 37; Conn, "Narrative and the Making of History," 1.

46. Du Bois, *The Souls of Black Folk*, 6.

47. Friedrich Schiller, *Die Jungfrau von Orleans*, SMU Joan of Arc course site, accessed October 1, 2008, http://faculty.smu.edu/bwheeler/Joan_of_Arc/OLR/crschiller.pdf. The English translation of these lines is:

> Wilt thou have thy might proclaimed,
> Choose but those by sin unblamed,
> Standing in thy long-lived home.
> Thine own spirits send to roam,
> Those most pure, those undying,
> Those who know not feeling, crying!
> Do not choose the tender maiden,
> Shepherdess with soft heart laden (4.1).

48. Ibid., 1, 4.1.

49. Here are the complete lyrics:

Oh breth-er-en, my way,
My way's cloud-y, my way;
Go send them an-gels down.
Oh! Breth-er-en, my way,
my way's cloud-y, my way;
Go send them an-gels down.
There's fire in the East and fire in the West,
And fire among the Methodists;
Old Satan's mad and I am glad,
He missed the soul he thought he had
[to Refrain]
I'll tell you now as I told you before,
To the Promised Land I'm bound to go;
This is the year of Jubilee,
The Lord has come to set us free.
[to Refrain].

50. J. B. T. Marsh, *The Story of the Jubilee Singers: With Their Songs* (Boston: Hough-ton Mifflin, 1881), 167.

51. Du Bois, *The Souls of Black Folk*, 158, 159, 161.

52. Schiller, *Die Jungfrau von Orleans*, 2.7, 3.10, my emphasis.

53. Du Bois, *The Souls of Black Folk*, v.

54. Robert B. Stepto, *From behind the Veil: A Study of Afro-American Narrative* (Urbana: University of Illinois Press, 1979), 67, 66.

55. Du Bois, *The Autobiography of W. E. B. Du Bois*, 114.

56. Louis M. Kyriakoudes, *The Social Origins of the Urban South* (Chapel Hill: University of North Carolina Press, 2003), 41. According to Kyriakoudes, late nineteenth-century Tennessee farmers practiced "a diversified agriculture based primarily upon corn cultivation augmented by wheat, tobacco, hay, and livestock." (43).

57. Ibid., 45, 47.

58. Du Bois, *The Souls of Black Folk*, 39.

59. Ibid.

60. Du Bois, "How I Taught School."

61. Ibid.

62. Du Bois, "The Hills of Tennessee."

63. Du Bois, *The Souls of Black Folk*, 40.

64. Du Bois, "How I Taught School."

65. Du Bois, *The Autobiography of W. E. B. Du Bois*, 106.

66. Du Bois, *The Souls of Black Folk*, 40.

67. Ibid., 56, 38–39, 40.

68. E. Franklin Frazier, "The Du Bois Program in the Present Crisis," *Race*, Winter 1935–36, 11. Though his years at Harvard were significant in his development, Du Bois always claimed that he was "in Harvard not of it" (*Dusk of Dawn*, 37).

69. Frazier, "The Du Bois Program in the Present Crisis," 11.

70. Bell, "W. E. B. Du Bois's Struggle to Reconcile Folk and High Art," 110.

71. Baker, *Long Black Song*, 106.

72. Bell, "W. E. B. Du Bois's Struggle to Reconcile Folk and High Art," 111.

73. Du Bois, *The Souls of Black Folk*, 39.

74. Ibid., 41.

75. Stepto, *From behind the Veil*, 73.

76. Du Bois, *The Souls of Black Folk*, 42, 4.

77. Ibid., 42.

78. Ibid.

79. Ibid.

80. Ibid., 43, 2.

81. Ibid., 44.

82. Ibid., 40, 44.

83. Ibid., 38, 45.

84. Ibid., 42.

85. Ibid., 53.

86. My final line is an allusion to Du Bois's ideological position at the beginning of *The Souls of Black Folk* that "the problem of the Twentieth Century is the problem of the color-line" (v).

4 / "Mightier than the Sword": The New Negro Novels of Sutton E. Griggs

1. Sutton E. Griggs, *The Hindered Hand; or, The Reign of the Impressionist* (Nashville: Orion, 1905).

2. Ibid., 9–10. Though translations vary according to language, *alma* is the Latin feminine of *almus* and describes a kind, nourishing, life-giving force. Although it serves as a cover name for Nashville, Griggs likely employs the term to refer to the South, a region that has nourished African Americans and whites and where he seeks to establish his vision of community with members of both races.

3. Ibid., 10.

4. Sutton E. Griggs, *The One Great Question* (Nashville: Orion, 1907).

5. Sutton Elbert Griggs was born in Chatfield, Texas, on June 19, 1872, the second of eight children born to Allen R. Griggs and Emma Hodge. Griggs's father, Rev. Allen Griggs, was an exceptional man who rose from slavery to become one of the most influential African American Baptist ministers of his era. In addition to his work as a minister, the elder Griggs was an editor and educator who helped establish a number of African American educational institutions, including Bishop College in Marshall, Texas, and North Texas Baptist College in Denison. He is also credited with creating the first African American newspaper published in Texas. Sutton Griggs attended public school in Dallas before graduating from Bishop College in 1890 and Richmond Theological Seminary in Virginia in 1894. Following his ordination, he assumed a pastorate at the First Baptist Church in Berkeley, Virginia, for two years, during which time he married Emma J. Williams, who was working as a public school teacher. At the age of twenty-seven Griggs moved to Nashville, where he became pastor of the First Baptist Church of East Nashville. In addition to his work as a minister, publisher, and novelist, Griggs also served as the corresponding secretary of the National Baptist Convention (a merger between the American Baptists and the Southern Baptist Convention) and as the Tennessee state secretary for the Niagara Movement.

6. In 1913 Griggs relocated from Nashville to Memphis, where he became pastor of the Tabernacle Baptist Church. In addition to his role as a member of the city's Inter Racial League, Griggs recorded a series of sermons in Memphis and published regularly on issues of race through his second publishing venture, the National Public

Welfare League. Notable among his publications are his autobiography, *The Story of My Struggles* (1914), and his philosophical work, *Guide to Racial Greatness; or, The Science of Collective Efficiency* (1923). For a more detailed investigation of Griggs's recorded sermons, see Steven C Tracy, "Saving the Day: The Recordings of the Reverend Sutton E. Griggs," *Phylon* 47.2 (1986): 159–66. When financial instability forced the sale of the Tabernacle Baptist Church in 1930, Griggs returned to Texas, where he worked in various cities with civic and religious institutions until his death in Houston on January 2, 1933; he is buried in Dallas.

7. Sutton E. Griggs, *Imperium in Imperio* (Cincinnati, OH: Editor, 1899); Sutton E. Griggs, *Overshadowed* (Nashville: Orion, 1901); Sutton E. Griggs, *Unfettered* (Nashville: Orion, 1902); Sutton E. Griggs, *Pointing the Way* (Nashville: Orion, 1908); Sutton E. Griggs, *Wisdom's Call* (Nashville: Orion, 1911). Among the many influential relationships Griggs formed in Nashville was one with Dr. R. H. Boyd, founder and manager of the National Baptist Publishing Board. Boyd recognized Griggs's talents as a writer and orator, encouraged him to expand his creative and political interests, and even helped him secure a publisher for his first novel. In addition to Boyd, Griggs formed important relationships with other influential African Americans in Nashville, including James Bond, S. W. Crosthwaite, E. W. D. Isaac, and A. Crosthwaite, all of whom contributed with Griggs to the $10,000 capital stock as incorporators of the Orion Publishing Company (*State of Tennessee Charters of Incorporation*, February 4, 1905).

8. Griggs, *The One Great Question*, 11, 12.

9. Ibid., 12.

10. Ibid., 32, 30–31.

11. While it is likely that Roger Williams University, based on its footprint and ideology, was Griggs's inspiration for Stowe University, he may also have patterned Stowe after Fisk University, Walden University, or Tennessee Manual Labor University, all of which were established in Nashville to educate freedmen following the Civil War.

12. Griggs, *Imperium in Imperio*, 46.

13. James Weldon Johnson, *Along This Way* (New York: Viking Press, 1933), 411.

14. After beginning his work at Fisk, Johnson reflected, "It was a grateful relief from the stress and strain that had entered into so considerable a part of my life; and I wondered how I had been able, in such degree as I had, to make of myself a man of action, when I was always dreaming of the contemplative life" (ibid., 408). Johnson continued to write and lecture during his years at Fisk. In addition to his autobiography, Johnson published *Black Manhattan* (New York: Knopf, 1930) and *Saint Peter Relates an Incident* (New York: Viking, 1935). He also taught as a visiting professor at New York University. Johnson was killed in an automobile accident while vacationing in Maine.

15. Among those responsible for Griggs's marginalization were early critics such as Hugh Gloster, who emphasized Griggs's artistic failings; Robert Bone, who labeled Griggs's writing "badly written and tractarian in the extreme"; and Sterling Brown, who found Griggs's novels "trite and pompous" and believed that they lacked the "mettle" of J. W. Grant and the "force" of J. A. Rogers, contemporaries of Griggs whose radical sensibilities Brown identified with New Negroes such as Du Bois. See Hugh M. Gloster, "Sutton E. Griggs, Novelist of the New Negro," *Phylon* 4 (1943): 335–45; Hugh M. Gloster, *Negro Voices in American Fiction* (Chapel Hill: University

of North Carolina Press, 1948); Robert A. Bone, *The Negro Novel in America* (New Haven, CT: Yale University Press, 1966), 32; Sterling Brown, *The Negro in American Fiction* (New York: Argosy-Antiquarian, 1969), 102–3. The titles referenced by Brown are J. W. Grant, *Out of the Darkness or Diabolism and Destiny* (Nashville: National Baptist Publishing Board, 1909) and J. A. Rogers, *From Superman to Man* (Chicago: M. A. Donahoe, 1917). John Wesley Grant was an attorney and author who also lived and worked in Nashville. Critical investigation of Griggs's work all but disappeared in the wake of these early assessments. However, its volume increased significantly with the rise of the black studies movement and a renewed emphasis on black culture. From this period see Wilson J. Moses, "Literary Garveyism: The Novels of Reverend Sutton E. Griggs," *Phylon* 3 (1979): 203–16; Wilson J. Moses, *The Golden Age of Black Nationalism, 1850–1925* (Hamden, CT: Shoe String, 1978); Roger Whitlow, "The Revolutionary Black Novels of Martin R. Delany and Sutton Griggs," *MELUS* 5 (1978): 26–36; Bernard Bell, *The Afro-American Novel and Its Tradition* (Amherst: University of Massachusetts Press, 1987). For contemporary critical sources on Griggs see chapter 2, note 55.

16. Finnie D. Coleman, *Sutton E. Griggs and the Struggle against White Supremacy* (Knoxville: University of Tennessee Press, 2007), 39.

17. Griggs, *Overshadowed*, 5.

18. The reference to Washington alludes to the claim in his Atlanta Exposition address, "It is at the bottom of life [African Americans] must begin, and not at the top." See Booker T. Washington, *Up from Slavery* (New York: Doubleday, Page, 1901).

19. Griggs, *Unfettered*, 49.

20. Ibid., 51, 53.

21. Griggs, *Overshadowed*, 5.

22. Griggs, *The Hindered Hand*, 132, 130, 131.

23. Ibid., 133, 134.

24. Ibid., 134, 136.

25. *Thirty Years of Lynching in the United States, 1889–1918* (New York: NAACP, 1919). While the total number of lynching victims in America is unknown, statistics are available from 1892, when the *Chicago Tribune* and later the Tuskegee Institute began collecting and publishing data. The NAACP adopted a similar analysis in 1912. Though numbers among these sources vary, they provide the most comprehensive figures available. According to the NAACP, between 1889 and 1918 there were 3,224 lynching victims in America; 702 of these men and women were white, and 2,522 were African American. Though conservative, these figures provide statistical evidence that African Americans were lynched with much greater frequency than whites.

26. Ida B. Wells, *A Red Record* (Chicago: Donohue & Henneberry, 1895), 103.

27. Griggs, *The Hindered Hand*, 5.

28. Ibid., 133.

29. Ernest Hemingway, *In Our Time* (New York: Boni & Liveright, 1925), 51.

30. Griggs, *Overshadowed*, 133.

31. Ibid., 132, 134.

32. Ibid., 156, 162, 165, 166.

33. Griggs, *Imperio in Imperio*, 100.

34. Ibid., 104, 107.

35. Griggs, *Overshadowed*, 100, 101, 104–5.

36. Griggs, *The Hindered Hand*, 37–38.

37. Ibid., 185, 190.

38. Ibid., 192.

39. Claude McKay, "If We Must Die," *Liberator* 2 (July 1919): 21.

40. Although neither was able to carry out the revolt they planned, Gabriel (1776–1800) and Denmark Vesey (1767–1822) were revolutionaries who fought for the emancipation of blacks held by American slavers. Each was killed for their plot, but their names lived on as symbols of rebellion. Their actions are responsible for inspiring tremendous fear in white communities and stood as proof of the threat posed by large numbers of black slaves in southern territory.

41. "American Ethnology," *American Whig Review*, April 1849, 385, 386.

42. Bruce Dain, *A Hideous Monster of the Mind* (Cambridge, MA: Harvard University Press, 2002), 206.

43. Michael Omi and Howard Winant, *Racial Formation in the United States* (New York: Routledge, 1994), 66.

44. Jennifer L. Hochschild and Brenna M. Powell, "Racial Reorganization and the United States Census 1850–1930: Mulattoes, Half-Breeds, Mixed Parentage, Hindoos, and the Mexican Race," *Studies in American Political Development* 22.1 (2008): 67.

45. *Negro Population in the United States 1790–1915* (New York: Arno Press and New York Times, 1968), 207.

46. Hochschild and Powell, "Racial Reorganization and the United States Census," 69.

47. *Negro Population in the United States 1790–1915*, 209.

48. Ibid. According to the 1850 census, the highest proportion of mulattoes was found in the North, where they totaled 24.8 percent of the African American population. While these numbers reflect the out-migration of African Americans during the era, they also provide evidence that racist attitudes toward people of mixed parentage were an American and not a southern dilemma.

49. *Plessy v. Ferguson*, 163 U. S. 537 (1896).

50. Griggs, *Imperium in Imperio*, 14.

51. Ibid., 63.

52. Griggs, *The Hindered Hand*, 71.

53. Frederick L. Hoffman, "Race Amalgamation," in *Plessy v. Ferguson*, ed. Brook Thomas (Boston: Bedford Books, 1997), 99.

54. The historical allusion in this paragraph refers to a portion of the majority opinion from the 1857 *Dred Scott v. Sanford* decision in which Chief Justice Roger B. Taney refers to the status of blacks on American soil: "They had for more than a century before been regarded as beings of an inferior order and altogether unfit to associate with the white race, either in social or political relations; and so far inferior that they had no rights which the white man was bound to respect; and that the Negro might justly and lawfully be reduced to slavery for his benefit." Judgment in the U.S. Supreme Court Case *Dred Scott v. John F. A. Sanford*, March 6, 1857, Case Files 1792–1995; Record Group 267, Records of the Supreme Court of the United States, National Archives.

55. Griggs, *Wisdom's Call*, 51.

56. Ibid., 130, 139, 129.

57. Griggs, *The Hindered Hand*, 71.

58. Book of Esther 3–7.

59. Caroline Levander, "Sutton Griggs and the Borderlands of Empire," *American Literary History* 22.1 (2010): 62.

60. An Act to Provide for the Allotment of Lands in Severalty to Indians on the Various Reservations (General Allotment Act or Dawes Act), Statutes at Large 24, 388, NADP Document A1887.

61. Howard Zinn and Anthony Arnove, eds., *Voices of a People's History of the United States* (New York: Seven Stories Press, 2004), 149–52.

62. Griggs, *Imperium in Imperio*, 153–54, 168, 163.

63. Ibid., 173.

64. Griggs, *Overshadowed*, 216.

65. Ibid., 217.

66. Ibid., 216.

67. Despite his dismissal of Africa as a final point of destination, Astral's reference to an era when "the shadows which now envelope the darker races in all lands shall have passed away" suggests that at some time in the future, emigration to Africa is possible. The quotation also indicates a past, present, and future kinship between Astral and other black people that evokes fundamental ideas from the pan-African movement and provides a link between Griggs and leaders such as Marcus Garvey, whose own "Declaration of Rights of the Negro Peoples of the World" demanded "complete control of our social institutions without interference by any alien race or races" (in *Philosophy and Opinions of Marcus Garvey*, ed. Amy Jacques-Garvey [New York: Atheneum, 1969], 2: 140). In *The Hindered Hand*, published three years later, Griggs's protagonist Ensal Ellwood travels to Africa and considers the possibility of life abroad should America fail to provide African Americans with civil and political rights. At the end of the novel, Griggs comments on this scenario in "Notes for the Serious": "The overwhelmingly predominant sentiment of the American Negroes is to fight out their battle on these shores. The assigning of the thoughts of the race to the uplift of Africa, as affecting the situation in America, must be taken more as the dream of the author rather than as representing any considerable responsible sentiment within the race, which, as has been stated, seems at present thoroughly and unqualifiedly American" (297).

68. Bone, *The Negro Novel in America*, 33; Griggs, *Pointing the Way*, 99.

69. Griggs, *Pointing the Way*, 64.

70. Ibid., 101.

71. Ibid., 145.

72. Ibid., 216.

73. Ibid., 207.

74. For a more detailed discussion of what Griggs terms "social epilepsy," see Griggs, *Guide to Racial Greatness*, 3–10.

75. Griggs, *Imperium in Imperio*, 133.

76. Griggs, *The Hindered Hand*, 277.

77. Ibid., 284.

5 / "Tried by Fire": The African American Boycott of Jim Crow Streetcars in Nashville, 1905–1907

1. Included among the sixteen incorporators were J. C. Napier, George N. Washington, Preston Taylor, W. T. Hightower, Evans Tyree, T. G. Ewing, R. H. Boyd,

W. D. Chappelle, Luke Mason, J. W. Grant, C. V. Roman, H. T. Noel, A. T. Landers, S. G. Merrill, Robert Robertson, and Wm. Beckham. According to the charter, the Union Transportation Company was entitled to provide "convenient transportation of passengers, merchandise traffic and freight throughout the cities and towns of Tennessee, and the United States of America, with an authorized capital stock of twenty five thousand dollars ($25.000) divided into shares of ten dollars ($10.00) each." State of Tennessee Charters of Incorporation, 1905, U7, 212, 213.

2. Acts of the State of Tennessee Passed by the Fifty-fourth General Assembly, 1905, 321. House Bill 87 was introduced by Representative Fahey on January 10, 1905. During the bill's third reading, four amendments were adopted. The first required that "no conductor shall assign a person or passenger to a seat except those designated or set apart for the race to which said passenger belongs" (133). The second amendment modified the language set forth in the 1903 Senate Bill 37 by adding "in counties of not over 140,000 population by the census of 1900 and any subsequent census" (132). These amendments were accepted by a vote of 71-14. A third amendment requested, "Signs shall be placed in the car designating place for the respective races" (134); a fourth amendment provided that "the race occupying the front shall enter from the front of the car and those occupying the rear shall enter through the rear" (134). The final two amendments passed by a vote of 58-28. House Bill 87 passed in the House of Representatives on January 20, 1905, in the senate on March 14, 1905, and was enacted on April 4, 1905.

3. In 1891 Georgia became the first state to pass legislation allowing for the segregation of streetcar passengers in its cities (Acts and Resolutions of the General Assembly of the State of Georgia, 1891, 157-58). In the following years Mississippi, Louisiana, Florida, Virginia, North Carolina, and Tennessee legislatures passed requirements similar to those in Georgia, enacting streetcar segregation laws throughout each state. The practice of streetcar segregation also existed in the remaining southern states.

4. Qtd. in "Negro Celebration," Nashville American, September 5, 1905.

5. August Meier and Elliott Rudwick, "Negro Boycotts of Jim Crow Streetcars in Tennessee," American Quarterly 4 (1969): 763.

6. Introduced by Representative Coston on January 23, 1899, House Bill 278 sought "to amend separate coach law so as to apply to street cars." "To Make Separate Coach Law Apply to Street Cars," Journal of the House of Representatives of the Fifty-first General Assembly of the State of Tennessee (1899): 210, 225. After passing the two initial considerations, the bill died in the Judiciary Committee on January 24.

7. "Fixing Street Car Accommodations for White and Colored," House Journal of the Fifty-second General Assembly of the State of Tennessee (1901): 403. Representative Mitchell of Warren County introduced House Bill 389 on January 30, 1901. The bill passed its second consideration on January 31 and was sent to the Railroad Committee, where it was recommended for rejection on February 5. After a motion to table, the House of Representatives rejected the bill by a 48-30 vote.

8. "The Car Service," Memphis Commercial-Appeal, February 8, 1903.

9. Acts of the State of Tennessee Passed by the Fifty-third General Assembly, 1903, 75. The bill passed unanimously (31-0) in the Senate on January 16, 1903, passed the House of Representatives on February 5, and was enacted on February 11.

10. Memphis Street Railway Company v. State, 110 TN 602, 603-19 (1903); U.S. Constitution, Amendment 14, http://www.loc.gov/rr/program/bib/ourdocs/14thamendment. html (accessed June 6, 2009).

11. "The Negro on the Streetcars," Nashville American, March 2, 1904.

12. Indianapolis Freeman, January 21, 1905, qtd. in Meier and Rudwick, "Negro Boycotts of Jim Crow Streetcars in Tennessee," 757.

13. Don H. Doyle, New Men, New Cities, New South (Chapel Hill: University of North Carolina Press, 1990), 280.

14. Ibid., 283.

15. Kenneth B. Clark, Dark Ghetto (Hanover, NH: Wesleyan University Press, 1989), 22.

16. John Kellogg, "Negro Urban Clusters in the Post Bellum South," Geographical Review 67 (July 1977): 313, 312.

17. Statistics of the Population of the United States at the Tenth Census (Washington, DC: Government Printing Office, 1883), 407; Thirteenth Census of the United States Taken in the Year 1910 (Washington, DC: Government Printing Office, 1913), 243.

18. For a detailed account of Nashville's residential expansion during this era, see Doyle, New Men, New Cities, New South, 280; John M. Marshall, "Residential Expansion and Central-City Change," in Growing Metropolis: Aspects of Development in Nashville, ed. James F. Blumstein and Benjamin Walter (Nashville: Vanderbilt University Press, 1975), 10, 12, 24; Benjamin Walter, "Ethnicity and Residential Succession: Nashville, 1850–1920," in Blumstein and Walter, Growing Metropolis, 48–9, 57–60; William Waller, ed., Nashville 1900 to 1910 (Nashville: Vanderbilt University Press, 1972).

19. See Lena R. Marbury, "Nashville's 1905 Streetcar Boycott," MA thesis, Tennessee State University, 1985, 14–15.

20. Doyle, New Men, New Cities, New South, 202.

21. "Black Bottom," Nashville American, June 30, 1905.

22. "Civic Improvement Committee Bulletin," Nashville Banner, May 11, 1910.

23. Doyle, New Men, New Cities, New South, 285.

24. "Civic Improvement Committee Bulletin."

25. Acts of the State of Tennessee Passed by the Fifty-fourth General Assembly, 1905, 321.

26. Cleveland Gazette, July 29, 1905, qtd. in Meier and Rudwick, "Negro Boycotts of Jim Crow Streetcars in Tennessee," 757.

27. Qtd. in August Meier and Elliott Rudwick, "Negro Boycotts of Segregated Streetcars in Florida, 1901–1905," South Atlantic Quarterly 4 (1970): 526.

28. Qtd. in L. M. Blair Kelley, Right to Ride: Streetcar Boycotts and African American Citizenship in the Era of Plessy v. Ferguson (Chapel Hill: University of North Carolina Press, 2010), 125; August Meier and Elliott Rudwick, "Negro Boycotts of Segregated Streetcars in Virginia, 1904–1907," Virginia Magazine of History and Biography 81 (1973): 481.

29. "What One Woman Learned," Nashville American, March 2, 1900, qtd. in Lester Lamon, Black Tennesseans 1900–1930 (Knoxville: University of Tennessee Press, 1977).

30. "Jim Crow Law in Operation," Nashville Banner, July 5, 1905.

31. "Sit Separate Today," Nashville American, July 5, 1905.

32. John William Graves, Town and Country: Race Relations in an Urban-Rural Context, Arkansas, 1865–1905 (Fayetteville: University of Arkansas Press, 1990), 224.

33. Edward L. Ayers, The Promise of the New South (New York: Oxford University Press, 1992), 433.

34. "Race Identity in New Orleans," Southwestern Christian Advocate, July 19, 1900, 8, qtd. in Kelley, Right to Ride, 95.

35. Ayers, The Promise of the New South, 434.

36. "Sit Separate Today."

37. "Jim Crow Law in Operation."

38. "More Jim Crow Signs Placed," Nashville Banner, June 6, 1907.

39. "Separate Car Law," Nashville American, July 6, 1905; "Some Negroes Say Will Walk," Nashville Banner, July 7, 1905.

40. "Some Negroes Say Will Walk."

41. "Sit Separate Today."

42. "The Negro on the Streetcars."

43. Mobile Daily Register, May 17, 1905, qtd. in David E. Alsobrook, "The Mobile Streetcar Boycott of 1902: African American Protest or Capitulation?," Alabama Review 56 (2003): 91. The boycott of segregated streetcars in Mobile, which began on November 1, 1902, was over by the end of December. African Americans represented nearly half of Mobile's forty thousand residents; however, their boycott was halted by ineffective organization and a lack of leadership among protestors.

44. Nashville American, March 2 and 5, 1903, qtd. in Marbury, "Nashville's 1905 Streetcar Boycott," 29.

45. Kansas City American Citizen, March 3, 1905, qtd. in Meier and Rudwick, "Negro Boycotts of Jim Crow Streetcars in Tennessee," 760.

46. "Some Negroes Say Will Walk."

47. "The Dispensary," Nashville American, February 2, 1903.

48. Preston Taylor began his life in Nashville as minister of the Gay Street Christian Church. Like so many other religious leaders in Nashville, he had an entrepreneurial spirit that helped him establish a lucrative funeral company and a cemetery for African Americans. Taylor certainly became wealthy through such ventures, reinvesting much of his profit in such community operations as the One-Cent Savings and Trust Company Bank and the Tennessee State Agricultural and Industrial State Normal College. Perhaps his most popular venture was the creation of Greenwood Park (1905) for Nashville's African American community. Taylor's commitment to the inclusion of African Americans in the participation of civic and economic affairs and his dedication to the African American community are representative of the vital role played by New Negroes in Nashville. Richard Henry Boyd rose from slavery to create the National Baptist Publishing Board (1896), a visionary publishing facility owned and operated by African Americans. In addition to his work with the Publishing Board, he was affiliated with many civic and professional organizations in Nashville, through which, like so many of Nashville's New Negroes, he continued to agitate for social and economic independence among African Americans.

49. "Money to Fight Jim Crow Law," Nashville Banner, August 1, 1905.

50. Ibid.

51. "Did Jim Crow Law Cause This?," Nashville Banner, August 28, 1905.

52. See Lamon, Black Tennesseans, 27.

53. "Did Jim Crow Law Cause This?"

54. Qtd. in Kelley, Right to Ride, 159.

55. "Did Jim Crow Law Cause This?"

56. "Boycott Don't Hurt St. Railway," Nashville Banner, September 22, 1905.

57. "Automobile Routes Chosen," Nashville Banner, September 22, 1905.

58. See Alsobrook, "The Mobile Streetcar Boycott of 1902," 83–97; Jennifer Roback, "The Political Economy of Segregation: The Case of Segregated Streetcars," Journal of Economic History 46 (1986): 913–14; Fon Louise Gordon, Caste and Class: The Black Experience in Arkansas, 1880–1920 (Athens: University of Georgia Press, 1995), 58–59, 110–12; Graves, Town and Country, 218–25.

59. "Automobile Routes Chosen."

60. "Nashville's Revolt against Jimcrowism," Voice of the Negro 2 (1905): 828–30.

61. "Boycott Don't Hurt St. Railway."

62. Linda T. Wynn, "Nashville's Streetcar Boycott (1905–1907)," Tennessee State University Library, http://ww2.tnstate.edu/library/digital/nashv.htm. (accessed November 1, 2006).

63. "Automobiles Have Arrived," Nashville Banner, September 29, 1905.

64. "Cars Utterly Inefficient," Nashville Banner, October 16, 1905.

65. "J. O. Battle," Nashville Globe, September 4, 1908.

66. Christopher MacGregor Scribner, "Nashville Globe," Tennessee Encyclopedia of History and Culture, http://tennesseeencyclopedia.net/author.php?rec=104 :(accessed January 11, 2007).

67. "Nine Machines to Be Bought," Nashville Banner, October 21, 1905.

68. "Nashville's Revolt against Jimcrowism," 830; W. E. B. Du Bois, ed., "Economic Co-operation among Negro Americans," Atlanta University Publications 12 (1907): 164.

69. "Nashville's Revolt against Jimcrowism," 830.

70. Linda T. Wynn, "Union Transportation Company (1905–1907)," Tennessee State University Library, http://ww2.tnstate.edu/library/digital/union.htm (accessed November 1, 2006).

71. Lamon, Black Tennesseans, 249.

72. "Notice to Stockholders of Union Transportation Company," Nashville Globe, March 29, 1907.

73. "Union Transportation Co. Sold Eight of Its Large Electric Automobiles," Nashville Globe, May 3, 1907.

74. "Union Transportation Co.'s Interesting Meeting Monday Night at National Baptist Chapel," Nashville Globe, April 12, 1907.

75. "Union Transportation Co. Sold Eight of Its Large Electric Automobiles."

76. Nashville Globe, February 1, 1907, qtd. in Lamon, Black Tennesseans, 35.

77. Nashville Globe, March 15, October 18, 1907, October 14, 1910, qtd. in Lamon, Black Tennesseans, 35.

78. Two Florida cities, Jacksonville (1901, 1905) and Pensacola (1905), passed ordinances that provided for separation of the races on streetcars. Despite initial successes by African American protesters in Jacksonville, who provided test cases challenging the constitutionality of streetcar segregation laws, new ordinances mandating segregation, repeated defeats in the legal system, and aggressive opposition from whites caused African Americans in Jacksonville and Pensacola to become disheartened, and they eventually succumbed to Jim Crow segregation. When a new law requiring streetcar segregation appeared in 1909, there was no public response from the

African American community. See Meier and Rudwick, "Negro Boycotts of Segregated Streetcars in Florida," 525–33; Paul Ortiz, Emancipation Betrayed: The Hidden History of Black Organizing and White Violence in Florida from Reconstruction to the Bloody Election of 1920 (Berkeley: University of California Press, 2005) 46, 71, 91; Roback, "The Political Economy of Segregation," 909–12; Shira Levine, "'To Maintain Our Self-Respect': The Jacksonville Challenge to Segregated Street Cars and the Meaning of Equality, 1900–1906," Michigan Journal of History, Winter 2005, 1–36. Also see Kelley, Right to Ride, 106, regarding additional court challenges in Virginia and Alabama.

79. See August Meier, "Boycotts of Segregated Street Cars, 1894–1906," Phylon 3 (1957): 297.

6 / "Before I'd Be a Slave": The Fisk University Protests, 1924–1925

1. W. E. B. Du Bois, "Address," Fisk Herald (New York), 33 (1924): 2.

2. James McPherson, "White Liberals and Black Power in Negro Education, 1865–1915," American Historical Review 75.5 (1970): 1357.

3. Francis Grimke, "Colored Men as Professors in Colored Institutions," A.M.E. Church Review, 1885, 146, 148.

4. Augmenting the creation of elementary and secondary schools, the AME established Brown Theological Institute (Edward Waters College), Jacksonville, Florida (1866–); Daniel Payne College, Birmingham, Alabama (1889–1979); Kittrell College, Kittrell, North Carolina (1886–1975); Morris Brown College, Atlanta, Georgia (1881–); Paul Quinn College, Austin, Texas (1872–); Payne Institute (Allen University), Columbia, South Carolina (1870–); Western University, Quindaro, Kansas (1865–1943); and Wilberforce University, Wilberforce, Ohio (1856–). The AME Zion colleges included the Clinton Institute (Clinton Junior College), Rock Hill, South Carolina (1894–) and the Zion Wesley Institute (Livingstone College), Salisbury, North Carolina (1879–). Enacted July 2, 1862, the Morrill Act provided "public lands to the several States and [Territories] which may provide colleges for the benefit of agriculture and the Mechanic arts," establishing the foundation for the nation's public university system. To ensure the equitable growth and development of these state colleges, Congress passed a second Morrill Act on August 30, 1890. Notable among its provisions was the second, which stated, "No money shall be paid out under this act to any State or Territory for the support and maintenance of a college where a distinction of race or color is made in the admission of students, but to the establishment and maintenance of such colleges separately for white and colored students shall be held in compliance with the provisions of this act if the funds received in such State or Territory be equitably divided as hereinafter set forth." Passage of this legislation resulted in the creation of eighteen black land grant colleges.

5. Notable among these moments of crisis was the effort of Howard University's board of trustees to find a replacement for departing president Gen. Oliver O. Howard in 1874–75. See Walter Dyson, Howard University: A History, 1867–1940 (Washington, DC: Graduate School, Howard University, 1941), 56–57; Rayford W. Logan, Howard University: The First Hundred Years 1867–1967 (New York: New York University Press, 1968), 74; McPherson, "White Liberals and Black Power in Negro Education." Another incident that garnered national attention occurred at Nashville's Roger Williams University in 1887, when 117 of 150 full-time students appealed directly to the American

Baptist Home Mission Society to request the removal of university president Dr. William H. Stifler and its treasurer, Theodore. E. Balch. Drawing from a litany of charges primarily aimed at Balch and ranging from "strict business practices" and "being unfair in his dealings with students" to moral lapses that included "improper proposals" to one white teacher and a black student, students (of whom one-third were women) collectively requested an honorable dismissal until their interests were attended to because they "refused to remain under men in whom they have no confidence" ("Trouble in a Colored University," *Chicago Daily Tribune*, March 8, 1887). Rather than acknowledge any administrative failures, Stifler affirmed his status as university president and stated his plans to "continue the regular work of the college whether the students come in or not. It is simply a war of races, as there will always be when the negroes have the chance, but I tell you they have to submit this time" ("War in a University," *New York Times*, March 2, 1887). The standoff between the two sides lasted a week, while the Home Mission Society's Education Board conducted a thorough investigation of charges on both sides. Rather than attend classes, students remained in their rooms or boarded in neighboring homes with supportive community members. Though future resolutions were left to the Nashville Board of Management, the Mission Society's home office in New York decided to suspend President Stifler, a move that apparently pacified the students and ended the demonstrations. For more on this protest, see "War in a University"; "No War of Races," *New York Times*, March 3, 1887; "An Empty Study Hall," *New York Times*, March 4, 1887; "The Rebellious Students," *New York Times*, March 4, 1887; "Students in Revolt," *New York Times*, March 5, 1887; "Trouble in a Colored University"; "College Troubles Ended," *New York Times*, March 10, 1887; "The Race Is Rising," *Nashville Freelance*, March 13, 1887; "Roger Williams University," *Southwestern Christian Advocate*, April 14, 1887, 4.

6. "Trouble in a Colored University."

7. "The Race Is Rising," qtd. in "Roger Williams University," 4.

8. Alain Locke, "Negro Education Bids for Par," *Survey*, September 1925, 569.

9. For evolving definitions of manhood, a gendered and highly politicized term, see Steve Estes, *I Am a Man! Race, Manhood, and the Civil Rights Movement* (Chapel Hill: University of North Carolina Press, 2005); Martin Summers, *Manliness and Its Discontents: The Black Middle Class and the Transformation of Masculinity, 1900–1930* (Chapel Hill : University of North Carolina Press, 2004).

10. Alain Locke, Enter the New Negro," *Survey Graphic* 6 (1925): 631–34.

11. John Davis, "Unrest in the Negro Colleges," *New Student* 8 (1929): 13.

12. Ibid.

13. Charles S. Johnson, *The Negro College Graduate* (Chapel Hill: University of North Carolina Press, 1938), 9, 10.

14. V. P. Franklin, "Introduction: African American Student Activism in the 20th Century," *Journal of African American History* 88.2 (2003): 105.

15. Paula S. Fass, *The Damned and the Beautiful* (Oxford: Oxford University Press, 1977), 5, 45.

16. Herbert Aptheker, "The Negro College Student in the 1920s—Years of Preparation and Protest: An Introduction," *Science and Society* 33 (1969): 153.

17. The jurisdiction of educators in America over students can be traced to *in loco parentis*, an idea adopted form English Common Law that established their legal authority. *In loco parentis* translates to "in the place of a parent." Additionally

"faculties were concerned not only with intellectual advancement but also with the development of sound moral character, classical virtue, and conventional religious sensibility" (Brian Jackson, "The Lingering Legacy of In Loco Parentis: An Historical Survey and Proposal for Reform," *Vanderbilt Law Review* 44 [1991]: 1136). In the nineteenth century *State v. Pendergrass* (1837) established *in loco parentis* as legal doctrine, a ruling that continued to define the relationship among college personnel, students, and parents into the twentieth century, when *Gott v. Berea* (1913) entrenched *in loco parentis* as "the backdrop for policy and program development and provided the perspective that influenced individual interactions with students" (Gavin Henning, "Is In Consortio Cum Parentibus the New In Loco Parentis?," *NASPA Journal* 44 [2007]: 540).

18. Franklin, "Introduction," 105.

19. Grimke, "Colored Men as Professors in Colored Institutions," 142.

20. In addition to Fisk, 1920s campus revolts have been identified at the following historically black colleges and universities: Florida A&M University, Hampton Institute, Howard University, Johnson C. Smith University, Kittrell College, Knoxville College, Lincoln University (Missouri and Pennsylvania), Livingstone College, Morehouse College, Shaw University, Storer College, Saint Augustine's College, Tuskegee University, and Wilberforce University. See James E. Alford Jr., "For Alma Mater: Fighting for Change at Historically Black Colleges and Universities," PhD diss., Columbia University, 2013; Aptheker, "The Negro College Student in the 1920s," 150–67; Juan Williams and Dwayne Ashley, *I'll Find a Way or Make One* (New York: Amistad, 2004); Raymond Wolters, *The New Negro on Campus* (Princeton, NJ: Princeton University Press, 1975).

21. The Society of American Indians was "the first national American Indian rights organization developed and run by American Indians themselves, rather than by so-called 'Friends of the Indians.'" "SAI Centennial Symposium," American Indian Studies, https://americanindianstudies.osu.edu/symposium (accessed June 11, 2013).

22. During McKenzie's tenure, only three of eighteen trustees were African Americans: Robert R. Moton, William N. DeBerry, and James. C. Napier.

23. "Ideals of Fisk," Inaugural Address, Fisk University, Nashville, November 9, 1915, 1–10, Papers of Fayette McKenzie, Tennessee State Archives, Nashville.

24. "Fisk," *Crisis* 28 (1924): 251.

25. "Ideals of Fisk," 10.

26. Ibid., 8.

27. The *Fisk Herald* was founded in June 1883. The first student editor was Tolbert F. Sublett, who later earned a law degree from Harvard (1890). Within four years of Sublett's graduation, nineteen-year-old W. E. B. Du Bois assumed the position.

28. Wolters, *The New Negro on Campus*, 34; Du Bois, "Address," 6.

29. "Ideals of Fisk," 8.

30. "Jim Crow," *Fisk Herald* (New York), 33 (1924): 10; "Truth Is Mighty and Will Prevail," November 3, 1924, Papers of Fayette McKenzie, Tennessee State Archives, Nashville, 1. News of Du Bois's racist accusations elicited angry responses from local whites. Members of the Al Menah Temple Ancient and Accepted Order, Nobles of the Mystic Shrine responded with a public statement chastising him for his quick words. Outraged by Du Bois's suggestion of impropriety, Shrine members argued, "No man has the right to doubt the motives of such a body of men, conjure up suspicions and

broadcast them." They declared that if Du Bois had researched their organization he would have seen that the Shrine Club had been entertaining weekly luncheons since January 1923 dedicated to the "better understanding of Nashville's educational institutions." In a published statement members also argued that while their building, located at the time on Seventh Street and Broadway, may have been used as a tavern before their organization assumed possession in 1913, it had since been used for the "advancement of civic and societal conditions of the community." Undeterred by the Shriners' response, Du Bois continued to portray McKenzie as a racist who was unfit for his position at Fisk. See "Truth Is Mighty and Will Prevail," 1.

31. Truth Is Mighty and Will Prevail," 1. After mustering out of the Union Army following the Civil War, Erastus Milo Cravath was an agent of the American Missionary Association responsible for establishing schools for African Americans and impoverished whites. Among the schools he helped to establish, in conjunction with John Ogden and Edward Parmalee Smith, was Fisk University, where he served as president from 1875 to 1900. "Editorial: Personal Sketches: Rev. Erastus Milo Cravath, D.D.," *American Missionary*, February 1894, 76.

32. L. M. Collins, *One Hundred Years of Fisk University Presidents, 1875–1975* (Nashville: Hemphill's Creative Printing, 1989), 66.

33. This, of course, was not the first time Du Bois had suggested that the objectives of college administrators had been altered or compromised in order to secure the financial interests of outsiders or bolster self-advancement. He had cast similar aspersions in his groundbreaking compilation of essays, *The Souls of Black Folk* (1903), challenging the leadership of Booker T. Washington and polarizing the community over the issue of racial agitation among generations of men and women. Among the significant contributors to education in the late nineteenth and early twentieth centuries are George Peabody, Peabody Fund (1867); John F. Salter, Slater Fund (1882); John D. Rockefeller and his wife, Laura Spelman Rockefeller, General Education Fund Foundation (1904); Laura Spelman Memorial Fund (1918); Olivia Egleston Phelps and Caroline Phelps Stokes, Phelps-Stokes Fund (1911); and Julius Rosenwald, Rosenwald Fund (1917).

34. Du Bois, "Address," 6, 10.

35. Paul Cravath was the son of Fisk's first president, Erastus Milo Cravath.

36. "Negro Problem Solution Seen in Segregation," *Cleveland Times Commercial*, June 2, 1924.

37. "The Disturbances at Fisk," *Gazette Times* (Pittsburgh, PA), February 14, 1925.

38. "Flay Du Bois for Speech That Created Near Riot at Fisk," *Chicago Whip*, August 2, 1924.

39. "Trouble at Fisk University," *Springfield Massachusetts News*, January 31, 1925; "Flay Du Bois for Speech That Created Near Riot at Fisk."

40. "Fisk Successful," *Nashville Banner*, July 20, 1924.

41. "$50,000 Gift to Fisk Announced at Commencement," *Nashville Tennessean*, June 4, 1924, emphasis added. Not disclosed in these articles were the financial contributions totaling approximately seventy-five thousand dollars each year, which allowed several hundred students to attend Fisk University, or the monetary investment of those students in the Nashville economy through the purchase of goods and services supplied by merchants and industries owned by African Americans and whites. See "Fisk," *Crisis* 28 (1924).

42. "Brief History Is Given of Recent Trouble at Fisk University," clipping from unknown source, Fisk University Special Collections, Nashville.

43. "Jeers Greet Hostile Faculty Representative," *East Tennessee News* (Knoxville), November 12, 1924.

44. Ibid.

45. W. E. B. Du Bois to John Work, June 26, 1924, Papers of W. E. B. Du Bois, University of Massachusetts Library, Amherst.

46. W. E. B. Du Bois to Miss C. E. Wright, October 10, 1924, Papers of W. E. B. Du Bois, University of Massachusetts Library, Amherst.

47. "Editorial," *Fisk Herald* (New York) 33 (1924): 1.

48. Du Bois, "Address," 12.

49. J. W. Fowler Jr. to W. E. B. Du Bois, October 15, 1924, Papers of W. E. B. Du Bois, University of Massachusetts Library, Amherst.

50. "Statement by Edward Taylor," n.d., Fisk University Special Collections, Nashville, 3.

51. "Maxwell House Letter," January 1, 1925, Fisk University Special Collections, Nashville, 1.

52. "Bouttes Pharmacy Letter," May 14, 1925, Fisk University Special Collections, Nashville, 3.

53. "Statement by Edward Taylor," 1.

54. Ibid., 1–2; E. G. von Tobel to W. E. B. Du Bois, December 13, 1924, Papers of W. E. B. Du Bois, University of Massachusetts Library, Amherst.

55. "Statement by Edward Taylor," 3; "A Statement of Grievances against Fayette Avery McKenzie as President of Fisk University," n.d., Fisk University Special Collections, Nashville.

56. "Statement by Edward Taylor," 3–4.

57. "A Statement of Grievances against Fayette Avery McKenzie as President of Fisk University," 2; "Statement by Edward Taylor," 2.

58. "'Oust Dr. M'Kenzie' Fisk U. Students Insist," *Chicago Defender*, February 14, 1925.

59. "Bouttes Pharmacy Letter," 2. John Wesley Work II spent nearly twenty years at Fisk teaching Latin and history, while also directing and touring with the university's Jubilee Singers. He also contributed to the publication of *New Jubilee Songs as Sung by the Fisk Jubilee Singers* (Nashville: Work Brothers, 1901) and *Folk Songs of the American Negro* (Nashville: Work Brothers and Hart, 1907), vital repositories that are among the first collections of slave songs and spirituals to be published in the United States. Despite his connections to Fisk, Work left the university in 1923, under mysterious circumstances, to accept the position of president of Roger Williams University in Nashville. While no definitive evidence can be found to explain Work's departure from the university, correspondence between Work and his friends and colleagues suggests a contentious relationship between him and McKenzie. According to one friend and fellow alumnus, Work stated that "no colored with any manhood could stay on at Fisk" under McKenzie's tenure.

60. "Statement by Edward Taylor," 2.

61. Ibid.

62. "Bouttes Pharmacy Letter," 1, 2.

63. J. W. Fowler Jr. to W. E. B. Du Bois October 15, 1924.

64. Du Bois, "Address," 11; J. W. Fowler Jr. to W. E. B. Du Bois, October 15, 1924.

65. "Statement by Edward Taylor," 1.

66. J. W. Fowler Jr. Letter to W. E. B. Du Bois, October 15, 1924.

67. G. M. McClellan to W. E. B. Du Bois, March 10, 1925, Papers of W. E. B. Du Bois, University of Massachusetts Library, Amherst.

68. J. W. Fowler Jr. Letter to W. E. B. Du Bois, October 15, 1924.

69. "Statement by Edward Taylor," 1.

70. John Hope to W. E. B. Du Bois, November 15, 1924, Papers of W. E. B. Du Bois, University of Massachusetts, Amherst. Hope was a tireless race leader who helped Du Bois found the Niagara Movement, the forerunner of the NAACP, and served as the first president of Morehouse College. Hope's first faculty position following his graduation from Brown was in Nashville at Roger Williams University, where he taught from 1894 to 1898. Like Du Bois, Hope championed a liberal arts curriculum, which included four areas of study—classical, scientific, normal, and theological—rather than the Washington model that emphasized labor and industrial training. In an 1896 speech to his colleagues in Nashville, he lashed out at the accommodationist sentiments expressed by Washington's Atlanta Exposition speech, emphasizing instead the need to challenge openly discriminatory laws and racial attitudes that sought to subjugate or intimidate African Americans.

71. R. C. Bailey to W. E. B. Du Bois, February 18, 1925, Papers of W. E. B. Du Bois, University of Massachusetts Library, Amherst.

72. "Fisk President's Offer Accepted with Amendment," *Nashville Tennessean*, February 10, 1925.

73. Charles H. Wesley Letter to W. E. B. Du Bois, December 17, 1924, Papers of W. E. B. Du Bois, University of Massachusetts Library, Amherst.

74. "Bouttes Pharmacy Letter." An educator and fundraiser who earned a PhD from Columbia University, Jones is best known for his years as educational director of the Phelps Stokes Fund (1913–46). His questionable reputation among New Negroes is perhaps best expressed by Carter G. Woodson, who considered Jones's career "a fair warning to others of the white race to employ different methods in dealing with the self-asserting Negro." See Carter G. Woodson, "Thomas Jesse Jones," Journal of Negro History 35.1 (1950): 107–9.

75. John Wesley Work to W. E. B. Du Bois, November 15, 1924.

76. "Minutes of the Meeting," *Fisk Herald* (New York) 33 (1925): 14.

77. W. E. B. Du Bois to N. B. Brascher, November 17, 1924, Papers of W. E. B. Du Bois, University of Massachusetts Library, Amherst.

78. "Impressions," *Fisk Herald* (New York) 33 (1925): 26.

79. "The Emerging," *Nashville Tennessean*, January 31 1925.

80. "Statement by Edward Taylor," 2.

81. Ibid. These lyrics come from "Oh Freedom," a post-Emancipation spiritual that evokes a defiant, determined sensibility.

82. "Jeers Greet Hostile Faculty Representative."

83. "Statement by Edward Taylor," 2.

84. "Fisk," *Crisis* 29 (1925): 249.

85. "Fisk President Not to Prosecute Unruly Students," 2, Fisk University Special Collections, Nashville; "Police Smash Riot at Fisk," *Nashville Banner*, February 14, 1925.

86. "Statement by Edward Taylor," 3.

87. "Police Smash Riot at Fisk"; "Statement by Edward Taylor," 3.

88. "Negroes to Hold Mass Meeting on Trouble at Fisk," *Nashville Tennessean*, February 6, 1925; "Fisk President Not to Prosecute Unruly Students"; "50 Police Quell Demonstration of Fisk Students," 1, Fisk University Special Collections; "Scene of Riot by Students at Fisk University," *Nashville Banner*, February 5, 1925.

89. "50 Police Quell Demonstration of Fisk Students."

90. "Poor Judgment," *Chicago Defender*, February 21, 1925.

91. "The Situation at Fisk," *Florida Sentinel*, April 11, 1925.

92. "McKenzie, You're Through," *Chicago Defender*, February 14, 1925.

93. Due to racial discrimination, many soldiers were relegated to support positions. However, a number of regiments, including the 92nd, 93rd, and the 369th "Harlem Hellfighters," which was awarded France's Croix de Guerre in 1919, fought with valor and distinction. For a more nuanced discussion of the experience of soldiers during World War I, see Robert J. Dalessandro and Gerald Torrence, *Willing Patriots: Men of Color in the First World War* (Atglen, PA: Schiffer, 2009).

94. Woodrow Wilson, "Address of the President of the United States Delivered at a Joint Session of the Two Houses of Congress," Washington, DC, April 2, 1917, http://www.heritage.org/initiatives/first-principles/primary-sources/woodrow-wilsons-war-message-to-congress (accessed May 19, 2013).

95. "Fisk," *Crisis* 28 (1924): 249.

96. "McKenzie, You're Through."

97. "Fisk President Not to Prosecute Unruly Students," 1. Unknown to the public, Goodwin, Crossley, Anderson, Streator, Lewis, Perry, Taylor, and McKenzie agreed to terms established for their "mutual protection." As part of this agreement Fisk University gave the students their earned college credits "so as to enable them to matriculate to any other standard university." Further, McKenzie agreed not to "throw any objection or impediment" that might prohibit such movement by any student. In turn McKenzie asked the court to dismiss the charges without cost to the students. However, he required each of them to state that they would "protect the University and its president against any attack or criticism directly or indirectly connected with this incident." The document, signed by all parties in the presence of witnesses, was notarized on February 9, 1925. See "Agreement," February 9, 1925, Fisk University Special Collections, Nashville.

98. "Fisk," *Crisis* 29 (1925): 249; "Statement by Edward Taylor," 4.

99. "Fisk," *Crisis* 29 (1925): 249.

100. "Mass Meeting All 'One Sided,'" *Nashville Banner*, February 10, 1925.

101. "Fisk President's Offer Accepted with Amendment"; "Negroes to Hold Mass Meeting on Trouble at Fisk."

102. Residents from the neighboring streets included those on Harding Street, Sixteenth and Seventeenth avenues North, Phillips Street, and Jefferson Street. See "Whereas," letter signed by neighbors, March 25, 1925, Fisk University Special Collections.

103. Lester Lamon, "The Black Community in Nashville and the Fisk University Strike of 1924–1925," *Journal of Southern History* 40.2 (1974): 241.

104. "Few Leave Fisk University, Says Dr. F. A. McKenzie," *Nashville Tennessean*, February 7, 1925; "Statement by Edward Taylor," 5.

105. Interview with Meredith Ferguson, November 10, 1970, qtd. in Lamon, "The Black Community in Nashville and the Fisk University Strike of 1924–1925," 241.

106. "Mass Meeting All 'One Sided.'"

107. Ibid.

108. Ibid.; "Fisk President's Offer Accepted with Amendment." While Lewis's claim that Fisk was the leading educational institution at the time is debatable, schools such as Howard, which had been created as a seminary for preachers, and Hampton Normal and Agricultural Institute, which focused on industrial training, did not share Fisk's long commitment to the idea of a liberal arts curriculum that matched white universities operating in the same era.

109. Mass Meeting All 'One Sided'"; "Fisk President's Offer Accepted with Amendment."

110. James A. Jones, letter, *Nashville Globe*, November 22, 1912.

111. "Mass Meeting All 'One Sided'"; "Fisk President's Offer Accepted with Amendment."

112. "Mass Meeting All 'One Sided.'"

113. "Negroes to Hold Mass Meeting on Trouble at Fisk."

114. "Fisk President's Offer Accepted with Amendment."

115. Fayette McKenzie to Thomas Jesse Jones, February 19, 1925, Papers of Fayette McKenzie, Tennessee State Archives, Nashville.

116. "'Oust Dr. M'Kenzie' Fisk U. Students Insist."

117. Fayette McKenzie to Thomas Jesse Jones.

118. "Fisk President States Policy," *Nashville Banner*, February 8, 1925; "Striking Fisk Students Seek Removal of M'Kenzie," *Nashville Banner*, February 7, 1925.

119. "Arbitration Is Sought by Fisk," *Nashville Banner*, February 9, 1925.

120. "Striking Fisk Students Seek Removal of M'Kenzie"; "Arbitration Is Sought by Fisk."

121. "Arbitration Is Sought by Fisk."

122. "Fisk Trustees Stand Behind Dr. M'Kenzie," *Nashville Banner*, February 12, 1925; Fayette McKenzie to Thomas Jesse Jones

123. Fayette McKenzie to Thomas Jesse Jones; Unknown author to Thomas Jesse Jones, October 19, 1924, Papers of W. E. B. Du Bois; Joe Martin Richardson, *A History of Fisk University, 1865–1946* (Tuscaloosa: University of Alabama Press, 1980), 93.

124. Unknown author to Thomas Jesse Jones.

125. See "Letters and Telegrams from Parents of Fisk Students, Alumni, Students and Friends-at-Large together with Certain Statements relative to the Recent Disturbance at Fisk University February 4, 1925," Papers of Fayette Avery McKenzie, Tennessee State Library and Archives, Nashville.

126. Fayette McKenzie to Paul D. Cravath, April 15, 1925, Papers of Fayette McKenzie, Tennessee State Archives, Nashville.

127. "Flay Du Bois for Speech That Created Near Riot at Fisk." The "Diuturni Silenti" address was delivered by Du Bois to the alumni of Fisk University at Fisk Memorial Chapel on June 2, 1924.

128. "Fisk University Cries for a New Administration," *National Baptist Voice*, April 4, 1925, 1.

129. "Fisk," *Crisis* 29 (1925): 249.

130. Fayette McKenzie to Everett O. Fisk, May 11, 1925, Papers of Fayette McKenzie, Tennessee State Archives, Nashville.

131. Fayette McKenzie to Thomas Jesse Jones.

132. Isaac Fisher, "University Editor at Fisk during Nine Years of This President's Service to the University," Papers of Fayette Avery McKenzie, Tennessee State Library and Archives, Nashville.

133. McPherson, "White Liberals and Black Power in Negro Education," 1360.

134. "Arbitration Is Sought by Fisk."

135. Consider a speech delivered by U.S. President Warren Harding in Birmingham, Alabama, November 29, 1921, in which he referred to the "fundamental, inescapable, and eternal differences of race" between blacks and whites (qtd. in Kelly Miller, "Is Race Difference Fundamental, Eternal and Inescapable? An Open Letter to President Warren G. Harding," Howard University, Washington, DC, 1921, 7). For an excellent response to Harding's statement and to what he calls the "doctrine of eternal difference" that exists "contrary to the scientific, ethical and social tendencies of the age," see Kelly Miller, "Is Race Difference Fundamental, Eternal and Inescapable? An Open Letter to President Warren G. Harding" (Washington, DC: Howard University, 1921), 1–24.

136. Richardson, A History of Fisk University, 99, 110.

137. W. E. B. Du Bois to G. Victor Cools, April 28, 1925, Papers of W. E. B. Du Bois, University of Massachusetts Library, Amherst; Du Bois, "Address."

138. Fayette McKenzie to Thomas Jesse Jones, 2.

139. "Fisk University President to Quit," New York World, April 24, 1925.

140. "Fisk Adheres to White President," New York Times, February 25, 1926.

141. The committee members were Board of Trustees chairman L. Hollingsworth Wood, Dean Augustus F. Shaw, Professors Herbert A. Miller and Thomas M. Brumfield, Dean L. Elizabeth Collinge, and Registrar Minnie Lou Crosthwaite.

142. Richardson, A History of Fisk University, 102. Though it is ironic, considering the criticism directed at the publication by Du Bois and other alumni, the Fisk News was revived in 1927 as an alumni publication.

143. Jones earned an AB from Earlham College (1912), a BD (1915) and an AM (1917) from Hartford Theological Seminary, and completed his PhD at Columbia University (1926); see Richardson, A History of Fisk University; "Dr. Thomas E. Jones," New York Times, August 6, 1973.

144. Alphonse D. Phillipse, typescript, 1924, 3, Papers of W. E. B. Du Bois, University of Massachusetts Library, Amherst.

145. Richardson, A History of Fisk University, 107.

146. Qtd. in ibid., 106.

147. The initial appointees were Dr. Henry Hugh Proctor, Dr. Ferdinand Augustus Stewart, and Miss Minnie Lou Crosthwaite. When added to existing board members Dr. William N. DeBerry, James C. Napier, and Robert R. Moton, the number of African Americans on the board totaled six.

148. Richardson, A History of Fisk University, 116, 119.

149. Ibid., 114.

150. "Biographical Note," 2, Papers of Thomas Elsa Jones, Fisk University Archives, Nashville.

151. Various alumni and student associations from schools and colleges across the country issued press releases and wired support to Fisk students supporting their

opposition to McKenzie. For examples, see "Students at Fisk Stage Rebellion" and "Howard's Student Council Upholds Students of Fisk," *Chicago Defender*, February 28, 1925; "What Do They Want at Fisk?," *Vanderbilt Hustler*, February 29, 1925.

152. For a thorough assessment of student unrest at Howard see Alford, "For Alma Mater"; Wolters, *The New Negro on Campus*; Logan, *Howard University*.

153. "New Head for Hampton," *New York Times*, December 24, 1917.

154. W. E. B. Du Bois, "The Hampton Strike," *Nation*, November 2, 1927, 471–72.

155. Ibid., 472.

156. The year 1927 did not mark the end of student demonstrations at Hampton. Additional unrest continued into the 1930s and 1940s, contributing to the appointment of the university's first black president, Alonzo G. Moron, in 1949.

157. August Meier, review of *The New Negro on Campus: Black College Rebellions of the 1920s, Journal of Southern History* 41.4 (1975): 570.

158. W. E. B. Du Bois, *The Souls of Black Folk* (New York: A. C. McClurg, 1903), 2.

159. Davis, "Unrest in the Negro Colleges," 13.

160. Aptheker, "The Negro College Student in the 1920s," 156.

Epilogue

1. Charles S. Johnson, *The Negro in American Civilization; A Study of Negro Life and Race Relations in the Light of Social Research* (New York: Henry Holt, 1930); Charles S. Johnson, *The Collapse of Cotton Tenancy: Summary of Field Studies and Statistical Surveys, 1933–35* (Chapel Hill: University of North Carolina Press, 1935). Also see Patrick J. Gilpin and Marybeth Gasman, *Charles S. Johnson: Leadership beyond the Veil in the Age of Jim Crow* (Albany: State University of New York Press, 2003); Richard Robbins, *Sideline Activist: Charles S. Johnson and the Struggle for Civil Rights* (Oxford: University Press of Mississippi, 1996).

2. James Weldon Johnson, *Along This Way* (New York: Da Capo Press, 2000), 408, 409; James Weldon Johnson, *Negro Americans, What Now?* (New York: Da Capo Press, 1973).

3. On Douglas, see Susan Earle, ed., *Aaron Douglas: African American Modernist* (New Haven, CT: Yale University Press, 2007); Amy Helene Kirschke, *Aaron Douglas: Art, Race, and the Harlem Renaissance* (Oxford: University Press of Mississippi, 1995). On Bontemps, see Kirkland C. Jones, *Renaissance Man from Louisiana: A Biography of Arna Wendell Bontemps* (Westport, CT: Greenwood Press, 1992); "Arna Bontemps Remembered," printed eulogy, Fisk University, 1973, Fisk University Special Collections and Archives. Bontemps died on June 4, 1973, and was interred in Nashville's Greenwood Cemetery.

INDEX

Page numbers in *italics* indicate illustrations or photographs.

About the Author

Gabriel A. Briggs is a senior lecturer in the Department of English at Vanderbilt University, where he teaches courses in nineteenth- and early twentieth-century American and African American literature and culture. His publications include writing on the New Negro and Sutton Griggs and have appeared in journals such as *Southern Quarterly* and *Callaloo*.

CPSIA information can be obtained at www.ICGtesting.com
Printed in the USA
LVOW11s1630190416

484355LV00004B/203/P